# LORD OF THE ISLES

Lord Leverhulme in 1919

# LORD OF THE ISLES

## Nigel Nicolson

First printed in Great Britain

Set in 11 point Imprint
by C. Tinling & Co Ltd.
Liverpool, London and Prescot
17/6598

This book was first published in 1960
by Weidenfeld and Nicolson
20 New Bond Street, London W1.

This edition republished by Acair Ltd.,
7 James Street, Stornoway, Isle of Lewis,
in February 2000 and republished again in 2005,
by permission of the Orion Publishing Group Ltd.,
Orion House, 5 Upper St Martin's Lane,
London, WC2H 9EA.

A CIP catalogue record for this title
is available from the British Library

The publishers are grateful to
*The Stornoway Trust*
for their generous financial contribution
to the first republishing of this volume.

Cover artwork by Robbie Neish.
Cover designed by Windfall Press.
Printed in China by
Nordica Printing (Panyu) Co. Ltd.

ISBN 0 86152 215 X

Dedicated to the memory of

MALCOLM MACSWEEN

(1880—1947)

tenant of the Shiant Islands, Outer Hebrides,
during the ownership of

*Viscount Leverhulme*
from 1918 to 1925

*Sir Compton Mackenzie*
from 1925 to 1936
and

*the author of this book*
from 1937 until the present day

xii ACKNOWLEDGEMENTS

District of the Hydro-Electric Board; Mr D. Swanney; Mr F. S. Walker (formerly Chairman of Lever Brothers, Port Sunlight); Sir Angus Watson; Dr Harley Williams; and Mr Charles Wilson, historian of Unilever.

I am also indebted to the authors or publishers of the following works for permission to quote from them:

*Viscount Leverhulme* by his son (Allen & Unwin); *The Isle of Lewis and Harris* by Arthur Geddes (University Press, Edinburgh); *The History of Unilever* by Charles Wilson (Cassell); *Highland Journey* by Colin Macdonald (W &. R. Chambers); *Chiaroscuro* by Augustus John (Cape); *House of Commons Debates* (HM Stationery Office); *Arches of the Years* by Halliday Sutherland (Geoffrey Bles); *The Six-hour Day* by the first Lord Leverhulme (Allen & Unwin).

N. N.

# CONTENTS

# Chapter One

# WILLIAM LEVER

I DROVE TO the end of the road. For the last three miles north of Tolsta, the pot-holes had shaken the hired car like a dice-box. Few of the Lewis crofters use this road any more. It leads nowhere except to peat-banks, and the great bridge over the gorge of the Garry seems incongruously Roman for so un-Appian a way. Round two further bends, at a half-finished culvert, it disappears. The moor slides unbroken across the route that was surveyed for it forty years ago.

'Why,' I asked the postman on my way back through Tolsta, pretending ignorance of the answer, 'why was the road never finished?' 'It was started by Lord Leverhulme,' he answered, 'and the people wouldn't do what he wanted. So he left us, and went to Harris.' As an explanation of what occurred in the two northern islands of the Outer Hebrides between 1918 and 1925, his summary was not wholly unfair.

It raises two questions.

William Hesketh Lever, first Viscount Leverhulme, was unconnected by any ties of blood, business or obligation to these remotest of the British Isles. Having made a fortune by manufacturing and selling soap on a scale unequalled by any man before him, and still in supreme control of an expanding industrial empire, he decided at the age of sixty-six to purchase the islands and arrest their decline. *Why did he do it*?

He diverted a large part of his energy and personal fortune to the venture. He achieved popularity in the Hebrides, and his schemes appeared soundly based. Yet when he died, almost nothing of permanent value to the inhabitants remained. He had spent well over a million pounds, but the social evils that he had determined to remedy were only aggravated by his intervention. *Why did he fail*?

I

The answers lie deep in Leverhulme's personality and in the history of the islands.

William Lever, then a partner in his father's wholesale grocery business at Bolton and manager of its Wigan branch, first saw the Hebrides as a tourist in 1884, when he was barely thirty-three. The shipping firm of Langland's ran summer cruises from Liverpool round the north coast of Britain, calling at Oban, Stornoway in the Isle of Lewis, Stromness in Orkney, Aberdeen, and Newcastle. Mr and Mrs Lever, taking one of the few holidays that he ever allowed himself (there were none after 1904), were among the thirty or forty passengers. They reached Stornoway on an August afternoon of exceptional brilliance, and were joined there by the architect Jonathan Simpson, Lever's oldest and closest friend. Lever himself never recorded any details of the cruise, but it is unlikely, judging by Langland's normal schedule, that they had more than five or six hours ashore. There cannot have been time, even if there had been transport, for them to see much of Lewis outside the immediate neighbourhood of its only town. Stornoway was then a small place of only 2,600 inhabitants, and the summer fishing season had passed its peak. The island was going through a period of acute economic distress. Though there was little for them to see or do, in later years Lever was fond of recalling this sunlit visit as the origin of his deep affection for the island. 'I was greatly delighted by its natural beauty and variety of scenery,' he said in a public speech on his return to Stornoway thirty-four years later, 'by its wonderful healthiness of climate and the charm and attraction of its people.' There is no reason to doubt it. But at the time his mind was also on other things.

He was toying with the idea of retirement, and spoke to Simpson of buying a small island which was then for sale in the Orkneys.[1] As quickly as this extraordinary plan occurred to him, it was replaced by another. He would not retire: he would specialise in selling soap under his own trade-mark. He acted on the impulse. Within a few days of his return from the cruise, he registered his soap as 'Sunlight', a name suggested to him by a patent-agent in Liverpool. A year later he was not only selling the soap: he was manufacturing it at a ramshackle soap-factory which he rented at Warrington.

[1] The numbers in the text refer to notes which will be found at the end of the book.

1. Leverhulme at The Hill, Hampstead, in 1920

2. Port Sunlight

3. White house and black house, with a prehistoric monolith, at Callanish, Lewis, 1960

His threat of retirement need not be taken very seriously. The northern cruise had not induced in him anything more than a passing mood of lassitude or romanticism. His rapid changes of plan on the voyage between Stornoway and Newcastle suggest that he felt his energies to be confined by his father's business conservatism, and that he was determined, somehow, to shake himself free of it. To retire to an Orcadian islet at the age of thirty-three, with little accomplished except the reform of his father's primitive system of accountancy and the establishment of the Wigan branch, would be one way of asserting his independence; but it would be a confession of failure, even a gesture of spite against a parent whom he greatly revered. But to carry his father with him into new enterprises, to make him a share-holder and director in a company that manufactured a commodity in which old James Lever had dealt all his life, to make soap of a new kind, wrap it in a new way, support it by an advertising campaign of unprecedented skill and magnitude, this was the better plan that gradually took root in his mind during the year that followed his return from the Hebrides. It was the plan that made his fortune.

The Levers had never been poor. In later years Leverhulme would occasionally flatter himself by the pretence that he had risen from nothing. A story is still current in Harris that he once gave a boatman a tip of 6d, and when the man protested that a few weeks earlier his son had tipped him a sovereign for exactly the same service, Leverhulme replied, 'That may be: but he was born the son of a rich man; and I was the son of a poor man.' In fact, his father, James Lever, by hard work, hard bargaining and an abhorrence of waste, had amassed a considerable fortune. It is true that during the years of his apprenticeship William Lever received from him no more than a shilling a week as pocket-money, later increased to two, but in 1872, when he reached the age of twenty-one, he was taken into partnership at the then handsome salary of £800. Before the end of the same year he could afford to marry a school friend, Elizabeth Ellen Hulme, whose maiden name, to the consternation of the College of Heralds, he joined with his own when he was raised to the peerage. This early marriage, these well-endowed opportunities, the very notion of retirement at so young an age, and James Lever's large Jacobean house two miles from Bolton, do not indicate a background of struggle against penury.

The struggle was against the inertia of a father apprehensive of his son's ambition. When William Lever, and his younger brother James Darcy Lever, first mooted their scheme for leasing the moribund soap factory at Warrington,

to begin with, James Lever strongly opposed the idea and declared that, with seven daughters to provide for, he would never dream of lending his son any money for such a wild adventure. 'A cobbler should stick to his last,' he said. In the end, however, no doubt secretly admiring his son's pluck, even if he was staggered at his rashness, he agreed to make him a loan, and this sum, added to what he felt justified in withdrawing from the grocery business, furnished Lever with a starting capital of £4,000.[2]

From other sources within the family and the grocery business, the initial capital of Lever Brothers was raised to £27,000, and the venture was an immediate success. Within a year, Sunlight soap was being sold throughout the country, and in 1887 Lever was able to establish agencies on the continent of Europe, in Australia, South Africa and Canada. The demand was fast out-growing the capacity of the Warrington factory. The site and the factory buildings were not ideal, and Lever held them at the whim of a landlord. He looked around for a new site where he could build his own factory, and he found it on a neglected stretch of the River Mersey opposite Liverpool. Mrs Lever, on 3 March 1888, cut the first ceremonial sod in an oozing field, and there, in the course of the next thirty-five years, arose the four immense soap-factories and the 1,400 houses of Port Sunlight.

This is not a history of Lever Brothers, nor a biography of its founder. It is a portrait of the man in the last years of his life, when convinced by almost uninterrupted success that no achievement was beyond his powers, he at last found himself confronted by a major failure. The growth of his world-wide enterprises between the foundation of Port Sunlight and his purchase of the northern Hebrides can be briefly summarised.

Lever never had reason to regret his choice of Sunlight soap, except, as he later said, its name: the eight letters formed too long a word to strike the eye in a newspaper advertisement or on a hoarding, compared to the names of his later products, Vim and Lux, which though relatively inexpressive, stand out hugely even in a confined space. In every other respect Sunlight was a remarkable soap. Lever did not himself invent the formula for the most successful of the soaps sold under that name, being, as he told Angus Watson, 'as ignorant of soap-making as a baby in arms,' and the historian of Unilever was unable to discover where he obtained it.[3] Its particular virtue lay in its lathering qualities and the pleasant smell produced by mixing citronella with vegetable oils and tallow. Lever's second innovation was to sell his soap in ready-made tablets, instead of in chunks cut by the grocer from long bars, and to wrap each tablet in imitation parchment and enclose it in a carton. He began to advertise it by methods which at first shocked, but soon amused, his public. He bought from America the brilliant slogan, 'Why does a woman look old sooner than a man?', and from W. P. Frith his Academy picture *The New Frock*, which Lever worked into his advertisements above the caption 'So clean'. He offered prizes to his dealers and customers—25,000 Sunlight wrappers won a £250 motor car, worth more than the cost of the soap—and distributed copies of his *Sunlight Year Book* free to elementary schools.

By such original methods, combined with a huge sales staff which he personally supervised, and modern methods of manufacture which he inspired, he built up the original £27,000 Company within eight years into a public company with a capital of £1,500,000. All this he achieved with the single product, Sunlight soap. In 1894, he added Lifebuoy, in 1899 Monkey Brand, and in the same year, Lux, originally called Sunlight Flakes, Lever's third revolutionary contribution to the soap trade. Simultaneously he began to buy up other established soap companies in Great Britain, and to convert his overseas agencies one by one into manufacturing companies by which he could avoid the tariff barriers erected against imported soap. He made his first voyage to America in the same year as the foundation of Port Sunlight, and subsequently each year between 1894 and 1898. In 1892 he first travelled round the world. Wherever he set foot he left a business, or at least an agency, behind him.

As his factories increased in number, he began to acquire the sources of his raw materials, particularly of vegetable oil, in order to cut out the intervening merchants and brokers. In 1905 he bought three hundred thousand acres in the Solomon Islands for raising cocoa-nuts. In 1906 he was in acrimonious correspondence with the Colonial Office for concessions in British West Africa. In 1910 he acquired his Nigerian properties. In 1911 he entered into a treaty with the Belgian Government for enormous

B

concessions in the Belgian Congo, and at the same time purchased, almost casually, six million acres of French Equatorial Africa for £70,000. By the outbreak of the first World War, Lever had sunk £1½ million in his African enterprises alone.

At home, few of his successes came easily, but all of them came eventually. By 1913 Lever Brothers and its associated companies were producing nearly half the soap sold in Britain. In the industrially developed countries overseas, only his Japanese company was a failure. Even in Africa, where the struggle had been hardest and the investment most risky, Lever's foresight was rewarded. The war helped him. Although he temporarily lost his factories in Germany, Austria, Belgium and northern France, sales of soap boomed in the United Kingdom, now that the Government were themselves buyers of huge quantities for the armed forces, and the wages of women munition workers were added to those of their men. Glycerine, an important by-product of the Port Sunlight factories, was in great demand for explosives; and margarine, made from many of the same raw materials as soap, was manufactured by Lever Brothers at the Government's request in order to supplement the attenuated butter ration. For all these products Africa was a valuable source of vegetable oil. Leverhulme (he was raised to the peerage in June 1917) acquired a fleet of ships to transport it from West Africa direct to Port Sunlight. He had achieved what he had long intended, a vertical combine of companies leading from his tropical plantations to the British bathroom and larder; and a horizontal combine of manufacturing and selling companies extending round the entire globe. By 1918 the capital employed in the business was £17½ million.

The description of the man need not be so breathless as this description of his business. For while the only link between Lever Brothers and the Hebridean purchase was Leverhulme himself and the fortune he had made, it is only possible to explain why he bought the islands in terms of his personality, and his attitude to money and social reform.

In 1917 Leverhulme was a short, thickset man, five feet five inches tall, with a paunch that stopped well short of obesity and created a general impression of erect sturdiness. When he stood in a group, the line of faces would drop suddenly to his, as if to the embrasure of a battlement. His hands and feet were neat and small. His head, which a contemporary painter could describe without excessive flattery as Homeric, was carried proudly on a short neck. Its most distinctive features were his hair, now turning from grey to white and standing stiffly and thickly from a broad forehead, the wiry, determined hair of a worker; his letter-box mouth, wide and thin-lipped; and, most noticeably, his eyes, in which a stranger could immediately find evidence of his energy, for they were unusually luminous and penetrating, a wide area of white surrounding the bluey-grey iris, and the corners striated by lines of good humour. Journalists dubbed him 'a typical John Bull', 'like a squire out of Trollope'. There was 'a happy country glow about his face', which disarmed the ridicule of envious men. His expression altered continuously. He would throw back his head urchin-like in recoil from the explosion of his laughter; and a moment later, stare into the distance, his features firm, contemplative and serene. His appearance was compared to Gladstone's, but wrongly, for he was stern, not grave, and his gaiety was unforced. He was not unlike Herbert Morrison, except that his gestures were quicker; he found it difficult to remain still, and ideas came most easily to him as he walked up and down, 'his head pushed forward', as his friend Harold Begbie wrote of him, 'as though shoving against storm.'

His health remained good up until a week of his death. But he became deaf in middle age, and his deafness increased in his last years until it was difficult for him to hear a speech or a sermon, and conversation had to be shouted. He tried without success every form of hearing-aid which was then available. Deafness did not diminish his activity, though it was the cause of the strained expression noticeable in many of the post-war photographs taken of him, and encouraged his tendency to speak in monologues and to rely more and more on dancing for social recreation: but even though the band was instructed to play abnormally loud, there were pathetic occasions when Leverhulme would not notice that the music had stopped and continued to dance with a partner too kind or too embarrassed to break away.

He managed his personal life, like his business, according to a fixed routine. He was woken at 4.30 every morning by the night-watchman, and after exercising with Indian clubs for twenty minutes and plunging into a cold bath, he dressed and began to annotate the letters and reports that had reached him late the previous day. At 7.30 he breakfasted. While it was not a rigid rule that his guests and family should breakfast with him, they soon learned that an extra half-hour on top of the three hours of sleep that they had already enjoyed while Leverhulme worked, would be noted by him with quiet contempt. He would then disappear. Ten minutes with the newspapers, half-an-hour for personal correspondence, and by 9 am at the latest he was in his office. There he remained all day, allowing himself fifteen minutes for luncheon at his desk ('I prefer a cup of tea, two poached eggs, or a little cold meat'), and forty minutes sleep immediately afterwards. From 2.15 to 5.30, more work. At 7 pm, dinner, at which no business talk was permitted, and at 10 pm bed.

The open-air bedroom where he began and ended this austere day still survives at Thornton Manor, the house three miles from Port Sunlight where he lived from 1888 till 1919. Between two converging roofs and a bank of high chimneys, there is a small leaded platform, covered at each end by a sloping canopy of frosted glass. Under one of them Leverhulme placed his bed, but so narrow were the canopies and so wide the gap between them that the rain drove in unimpeded, and a gutter was constructed round all four sides of the leads to drain off the water. It was not unknown for Leverhulme and his uncomplaining wife to wake up under a coverlet of snow. In a far corner is the simple wooden cupboard where he kept his Indian clubs, and opposite stands a huge stone tub for his bath and a wash-basin that would be considered grim in an army hutted camp. There is no other furniture, no decoration, no view.

I stood there on a wild December night, while the rain-soaked wind syphoned in and out of this miserable cube of space, and wondered again at the nature of this strange man. Why did he choose to sleep like this? He was not in the least indifferent to discomfort or ugliness, for his houses and offices were designed without shame of luxury. It was certainly not nature-worship, since even the stars were hidden by the frosted panes of glass. If he was concerned for his health, the explanation most frequently given, one wonders how so rational a man could believe that nightly exposure to cold and damp could lengthen his already long life. Perhaps it was a form of discipline, primarily physical, but with a moral motive added. He was always preaching the virtue of self-control: he rarely drank, and after 1896, never

smoked. His career appeared to him as an endless campaign. So
he slept as a soldier would sleep, to harden himself against the
flabbiness latent in great wealth.

Outside his business, Leverhulme's main interest was in art
and architecture. If he decided to endow a church or a school, to
buy a property in England or to open up a vast tract of Africa, the
architectural or town-planning possibilities of the place were
among the first to occur to him. He was never happier than at his
drawing board sketching the outlines of a new estate which his
expert assistants would later fill in, matching the social need to
the lie of the land. He had little technical knowledge of engineering, but an excellent eye for a site; he could tell at a glance the
exact fall of a slope or the width needed for a road. The gardens
of his many houses are typical of his taste. They are interlocking
chains of vistas, gardens for movement, the flowers and shrubs
incidental to the gravel walks and stone steps descending in
graduated cascades to a summer-house, an artificial pond or an
Italianate pergola. He gave as much thought to his kitchen-
gardens as to the most herbaceous of his borders, for the walls,
the internal terracing and the pattern of paths, afforded full scope
to his delight in geometrical planning. At the same time he knew
how to blend formality with surprise. His great garden at Thornton Manor is a gradual approach to wildness; the stiff terraces
immediately around the house are softened by degrees into paths
curving through shrubbery and open out unexpectedly into water
gardens with artificial islands and a long wide canal driving deep
into a wood. At The Hill, his London house on Hampstead Heath,
he made the most of a more confined space by terracing a steep
slope and rounding it off by a lily-pond and a pergola leading to
a belvedere. At Rivington, his country house near Bolton (he called
it a bungalow, but it contained a ball-room), he created a Japanese
garden out of a moorland quarry, and erected nearby an exact
replica of the ruins of Liverpool Castle. Originality, variety,
careful planning, determined execution, a touch of deep insight,
a rare lapse into vulgarity—Leverhulme's gardens are self-
portraits.

The interiors of his houses are less successful. His set-pieces,
such as the underground ball-room at The Hill, or the music-
room at Thornton, are heavy in their proportions without
achieving grandeur. They strive too deliberately for effect. His
smaller rooms are imitations of period rooms:

'I prefer Georgian dining-rooms as the rooms in which to give large dinners,' he wrote in 1910. 'For small dining-rooms I prefer Tudor. For drawing-rooms I prefer what is called the Adam style; for entrance halls the Georgian.'

He was happy with fakes. But the detail is always superb, particularly of his doorways, staircases and connecting corridors, where the excellence of the wood and stone-work still gives pleasure to the touch of hand or foot. For much of it Leverhulme was indebted to James Simpson, son of his old friend Jonathan, who became head of the architectural department at Port Sunlight and a director of Lever Brothers. On the materials used in extending and improving his many houses, Leverhulme would not spare expense. 'Is it technically possible to do it like this?', he would ask Simpson at their almost daily conference. 'Yes, sir, but it will be very costly.' 'Never mind: do it.' Thus the interiors of The Hill, Thornton Manor, Rivington, and later, Lews Castle, became workshops for craftsmen. Lady Lever once commented that she rarely found herself in a house free from the presence of workmen. The reward for her patience came too late for her to enjoy it fully, for she died in 1913, but today, nearly fifty years later, the heavy, smooth turning of a mahogany door, the proportions of a stone chimney-piece, the run of the fingers along a perfectly tooled bannister-rail, or the neat fusion of two vaulted ceilings where passages meet at an awkward angle, recreate the pleasure of those who devised the right solutions to the original problems.

The furniture is magnificent. Leverhulme was a collector throughout his life, and there was enough left over from the furnishing of his large houses to line the walls of the Lady Lever Art Gallery at Port Sunlight with splendid antiques, mostly of the English and French seventeenth and eighteenth centuries, and tapestries and porcelain of many other periods. His taste in pictures was more pedestrian. He was a great buyer of paintings from the contemporary exhibitions at the Royal Academy. He liked story pictures meticulously painted: Lord Leighton, Sir Luke Fildes, Sargent. He bought pre-Raphaelites: Millais' *Sir Isumbras at the Ford*, Holman Hunt's *The Scapegoat*, Ford Madox Brown's *Cordelia's Portion*. But there were also Constables, Turners, Rowlandsons, and even a group of fifteenth-century Spanish pictures which stand out oddly in this Edwardian collection. He never pretended to be a connoisseur. He bought works of art to furnish his rooms, to provide focal points, and because he had an unaffected admiration for artists, like craftsmen, who could achieve what lay within his range of understanding but beyond his scope. His collections were not peacock displays of his affluence. He was a proud possessor, but he bought for his own enjoyment.

When the time came for a series of portraits to be painted of himself, Leverhulme was not in the least indifferent to the figure which he would cut in the eyes of posterity. In the early years of this century, riches acquired by personal effort were regarded as less respectable than riches acquired by inheritance. If, in addition, they were acquired by dealing in a commodity like soap, which seemed illogically absurd because the need for it was universal, the new-rich were doubly exposed to ridicule. 'Soap-boiler' was the term flung at Leverhulme by his detractors. Even his membership of the House of Commons from 1906 to 1910, his Baronetcy in 1911, his ennoblement in 1917, and the successive visits to Port Sunlight by Gladstone, Asquith and King George V, did not make him immune to this form of envious belittlement. Undoubtedly he was wounded by it, and so he deliberately had himself represented in the grandest possible manner. There was the Orpen portrait, the Strang portrait, the de Laszlo portrait (the latter in the full robes of a Viscount), all of which showed him as a man of commanding dignity. His true personality was more subtle and less assured.

In 1920 Augustus John was commissioned to paint him. This portrait went to the opposite extreme. It hangs today in the music-room at Thornton Manor, the scars still visible on the canvas which Leverhulme mutilated in anger at what he saw. He cut out the head with its florid face, drooping jaw and hard thin mouth, and pushed it to the back of his private safe, where his grandson rediscovered it thirty years later. But it was not so much the face that distressed him, as the hands, with their long, corroded, purple fingers, curved like talons. It seemed to him that Augustus John had determined to express his dislike of all big business by a vitriolic caricature of his patron. What easier way than to make his strong features appear dissolute, his unusually small, almost feminine, hands seem rapacious?

When Leverhulme had cut out and concealed the head, the tattered remains of the canvas were returned in error to the artist by the housekeeper who found it stuffed back into the packing case. John immediately informed the press: photographs were published of the portrait before and after mutilation. There was an international outcry in support of his protest that no man, whatever fee he had paid for it, had the right to destroy a portrait merely because he thought it unflattering. On Guy Fawkes Day, London art students carried a headless torso of Leverhulme in procession to Hyde Park. In Italy, according to John's own account, the painters, models and everyone else connected with the painting industry, called a twenty-four hour strike: 'A colossal effigy entitled Il LE-VER-HUL-ME was constructed of soap and tallow, paraded through the streets of Florence, and ceremoniously burned in the Piazza dei Signori (*sic*), after which the demonstrators, reforming, proceeded to the Battisteria where a wreath was solemnly laid on the altar of St John.'[4] It is only right to add that when the head was rediscovered, Augustus John gladly returned to the family the remainder of the canvas, and the two were reunited in time for the latter part of the John Exhibition at Burlington House in 1954.

John's portrait was cruel because it was untruthful. Leverhulme's failing was not greed. He enjoyed making money because it enabled him to do things, and he disliked losing it because it was proof of incompetence. Men who have acquired very great wealth are sometimes mean, but it is seldom that they retain a lust for money, in the sense of hoarding it or wishing to dig secretly into every cranny for more, as those curved fingers in the portrait were intended to suggest. Leverhulme's business and legal battles were conducted openly and on a colossal scale. Although his successes further increased his personal fortune, for he was the sole owner of the two million Ordinary shares in the Company, the struggle was what excited him, not the prize. The struggle, and the responsibility. Within a few months of his death he wrote to the Minister of the Stornoway Congregational Church; 'Continuous immersion in work is a fate I have brought to myself by having over 160,000 shareholders periodically requiring a lick of treacle. The compensation is that I find it thrilling trying to keep one's head above water.' Ten years earlier he had said: 'I work at business because business is life. It enables me to do things.'

He had enough money to do whatever he wished to do, and when he found himself with a surplus, he either gave it away, or embarked upon some new private venture. He was not in the least ashamed of his extravagance, for he considered, justifiably, that one man in a million had his particular gifts, and a very rare quality, like a very rare commodity, had a high market price. He knew that he was trebly useful to society: first by supplying a much needed article; secondly, by providing good employment for scores of thousands of people; and thirdly by using the small fraction of profit left over for himself to create something beautiful like a garden or an art gallery, or to endow a school, a church or a new Town Hall, which would never have come into existence in that particular form unless he had provided the will and the means. One of his former secretaries wrote of him on the centenary of his birth, 'The ruling passion of his life was not money or even power, but the desire to increase human well-being by substituting the profitable for the valueless.'[5] How profoundly true that is as a summing-up of his venture in the Hebrides!

But Leverhulme could also be ruthless. Most men who worked for him never got over the fear which his eyes inspired at their first interview, and since his death some of those most close to him have come forward with the admission, the accusation, that as an employer, for all his occasional sentimentality, he could be tyrannical. The official historian of the Company expresses with his usual honesty and balance their general opinion of Leverhulme in his later years: 'He gave the impression of a driving tyrant, prone to find fault with his subordinates, yet possessed still of a fighting spirit which compelled their profound admiration.'[6] Many examples of it could be quoted. There is a file accidentally preserved among Leverhulme's Hebridean papers containing the reports made personally to him on the daily movements of the manager of his New York office. The man was watched by a private detective agency from the moment he left his home in the morning to the moment he stepped on board the Brooklyn ferry for his return at night. At week-ends the agent had instructions to keep his home under constant observation. This was not because the manager was suspected of dishonesty; only of laziness. After three months the suspicion was disproved by the complaints of the firm's American salesmen that the New York office was overloading them with work.

Far less secretive was the watch that Leverhulme kept on his clerks at Port Sunlight. The lay-out of the administrative building was changed during his own lifetime, and it is now possible only to visualise the extraordinary arrangements by which he exercised personal supervision throughout the day. His private office was a glass cage mounted above and between the two long halls where the clerks worked. Every one of them could see him, standing at the high wide desk which is still shown to visitors, and he could see every one of them. At the slightest sign of inattention to work, Leverhulme was at the window looking down on the hall and speaking sharply through the internal telepone to the manager nearest to the culprit.

He could not endure laziness. To him it was not a fault, but a sin, the wanton waste of a man's precious capacity to work. 'I organise, deputise and criticise,' he once said, and one can still sense the violence with which the words were expelled. He ruled his business by constant exhortation and example. He was not above employing his phenomenal memory to set sly traps for subordinates whom he suspected of forgetfulness. He would snub the Secretary of the Company for offering advice before he had been asked for it. He was seldom generous in admitting an error of judgment. Yet it is difficult to imagine how the strength of will that had shaped such a career could have taken any other direction in his later life, unless there had been a loss of energy or a feeling of satiety. There was no loss of energy. The older he grew the harder he worked, and the more he expected from those whom he employed.

Immense driving-power by the head of any organisation may produce efficiency, but it also produces exaggerated subordination. Leverhulme did not make many intimate friends, and no member of his Board, except perhaps James Simpson, ever en-joyed his full confidence. He was a lonely man, and in spite of his autocratic methods, a shy man. He found himself surrounded by colleagues who were all too conscious of the superiority of his gifts to their own, and he was never able to break down the barriers created by his position as founder, lifelong Chairman and owner of all the equity in the enterprise on which they all depended. His brother, James Darcy Lever, who had been nervous of the rapid expansion of the business, had a mental breakdown in 1895, and died in 1910. Leverhulme's only surviving child, William Hulme Lever, was born in the year when Port Sunlight was founded. His wife, to whom he was devoted, had no knowledge of the business. During his middle years, there was therefore almost nobody with whom he could discuss it freely.

These chances, combined with Leverhulme's own temperament, produced an unhealthy dependence upon him. It became difficult for any person in his employment to take an important decision without first referring it to him for approval. As he rarely reprimanded his staff for troubling him with unnecessary detail, his correspondence mounted and their initiative waned. The volume of business transmitted to and from the Hebrides, for example, amounted to nearly 50,000 letters in the seven years of Leverhulme's proprietorship, quite apart from the decisions which he gave verbally; and his Hebridean affairs occupied only a small fraction of his total working hours. Many of these letters are openly sycophantic. He did not relish criticism of his decisions, nor even comments upon them, and in consequence he was not told many unpleasant things that he needed to know. This attitude extended from the most junior of his employees to some of the most senior. A film, entitled *Portrait of a Man*, was recently put together from shots taken of Leverhulme during his last years. In one sequence he is shown on board ship playing darts with half-a-dozen of his chief executives. Leverhulme throws a dart, and whether it hits or misses the bull (the dart-board is unfortunately out of the picture), the exaggerated applause that follows, the competitive congratulations, show all too clearly the nervous relationship that existed between him and his entourage.

Leverhulme's reputation does not rest solely on his creation of an industrial empire, but on the social and political ideas that inspired it. Though he was a life-long Gladstonian Liberal, in many ways he anticipated the later policies of both the Conservative and Labour parties. A left-wing economist has paid this tribute to him:

I was curious to see how his ideals and his expression of them in his business stood up against the sociological and economic ideas of 1951. I was amazed to find that not only had he put into practice most of our principles of social welfare, but that he had anticipated many of our problems and had pointed the way to the proper solution of them. He seemed to me to be the embodiment of the epoch into which he was born—the hundred years of social reform. . . . The strange fact is that the Labour Party in its pragmatic approach to the theory of the Welfare State probably owed as much to William Lever as it did to Robert Owen.[7]

His ideas were developed in many speeches and articles, the most important of which were collected in a book edited by Stanley Unwin, and published in November 1918.[8] They reveal an attitude which is important to the understanding of his motives in Lewis and Harris.

He was a disciple of Samuel Smiles, whose book *Self-Help*, first published in 1859, was given to him on his sixteenth birthday, and thereafter he would present a copy to any boy in whose future he was interested. From it he acquired the early conviction that there was no conflict between a man's ambition and the interests of his fellow-men. On the contrary, ambition and hard work were the sources both of personal happiness and social welfare. 'Any attempt,' he wrote, 'at limiting the powers of the individual to acquire wealth is like endeavouring to lower someone's standard of health because it is higher than the average. The healthy of a community are a source of strength to all others, and so are the wealthy. What we require to do is not to weaken the strong or impoverish the wealthy, but to show to the weak and the poor the way to become healthy and wealthy.'

He was fond of quoting John Bright's definition, 'Happiness consists in congenial occupation with a sense of progress', and to this he added his own concept of social duty: 'There is one great principle governing the world, which is that of self-interest. . . . But there are two kinds of self-interest, one the narrow self-interest, which is so short-sighted as to be blindly selfish; and there is that broad, intelligent, enlightened self-interest, which says it can only find its own best interest of self in regarding the welfare and interest of others.' Thus he reached his doctrine of service: the exercise of power and the acquisition of wealth are justifiable only by the benefits which they bring to society as a whole. If you make no money, you can do no good, and to do good is the first object of a man of business. There is a happy coincidence of interest between him and the men and women whom he employs. A bad employer creates bad workmen, and he will lose money because he will be ill-served. But if he provides them with good working and living conditions, and with the opportunity to win extra rewards by extra ability and effort, he will benefit himself, for there will be no labour-trouble in his factory, and their sense of partnership will lead to better quality and higher output.

These ideas, commonplace today, were thought sentimental at

the time when Leverhulme first began to put them into practice at Port Sunlight. The Trade Unions were as suspicious of them as his fellow-manufacturers. The word 'paternalism' was one that he much resented but never wholly succeeded in shaking off. For he did not stop short at providing decent houses, communal facilities for the enjoyment of leisure, well-ventilated factories, a share in the profits of the business, and opportunities for advancement. He required in return that his employees should live their lives in accordance with his own ethics. He was himself a devout Congregationalist, and while he was tolerant of other Christian sects, he was shocked by any departure from his nonconformist code. Gambling he would not tolerate; drinking, even in moderation, he regarded as an unnecessary lapse; he never forgave a smutty story; and at Port Sunlight, we read, girls over the age of eighteen attending the weekly winter dances 'might submit the names of men to the social department, which issues invitations to them unless there be reasons that militate against them.' Cumulatively this attitude could become most oppressive. 'No man of an independent turn of mind,' wrote a Trade Union official to Leverhulme in 1919, 'can breathe for long the atmosphere of Port Sunlight. That might be news to your Lordship, but we have tried it. The profit-sharing system not only enslaves and degrades the workers; it tends to make them servile and sycophant, it lowers them to the level of machines tending machines.'[9]

This reaction, exaggerated as it was, explains why some of Leverhulme's most cherished social schemes never quite succeeded. The very attempt to improve people by improving their conditions, and by reminding them implicitly of their debt to him, induced a feeling of obligation, a sense that they were under scrutiny, on trial. When he addressed the annual meetings of his 'Co-partners' at Port Sunlight, or wandered around the village by himself, patting children on the head, he was apt to deceive himself into thinking that the quasi-feudal greetings that he received from his tenant-employees were akin to the demonstrations of affection shown towards a much beloved bishop by his flock. But while there were very many who admired him, there were fewer who loved him. The enormous effort that he expended on his schemes for moral and material betterment did not produce a reciprocal sense of gratitude. He was, after all, still the boss. His huge fortune aroused envy, and from envy to resentment is only a short step. A trouble-maker would not find it difficult to persuade the work-people that the whole pattern of improvements was nothing more than a palliative, an attempt to divert attention from the gross inequality of their rewards.

'Co-partners': what did it really mean? It meant that a man or woman working for Lever Brothers would receive as a gift a maximum of £300 in non-negotiable Co-partnership certificates, on which the average dividend was ten per cent. But most held far fewer, and the annual addition to their wages was likely to be about £5 or as little as 30/-. Leverhulme had hoped that the scheme would spread throughout the works an attitude of joint responsibility for its success, but the dividend soon came to be regarded as a right unrelated to the year's profit. By 1923 he was admitting privately to one of his directors, 'We have all of us felt disappointed that men and women could be Co-partners, and still be quite apathetic and uninterested in efficiency and output.' There was another reason. Certificates were awarded or cancelled not only according to the holder's value to the Company: on the back of the form, there was a warning that the certificate was liable to cancellation for 'neglect of duty, dishonesty, interference, immorality, wilful misconduct, flagrant inefficiency or disloyalty.' Leverhulme, who was himself the final court of appeal, always made it clear that 'a man of high character should receive a more generous allotment than a man of equal ability, but not of the same high character'. People were graded into moral categories, A, B, C or D, and in the course of a year, it was possible to sink in the Chairman's estimation, and therefore in deserts, from an A-man to a D-man. The system, excusable though it was (for the annual dividends were nothing less than an annual gift to the Co-partners out of Leverhulme's own pocket, and he had every right to impose conditions), did not help to remove the impression of disguised philanthropy, with strings attached.

Another of Leverhulme's ideas which never met with the success he hoped for, was his belief that a man's normal working day could be reduced to one of six hours. Here again his motives were a combination of humanitarianism and self-interest. 'Men and women who get up to go to work before daylight,' he wrote in 1917, 'and return from that work after dark, cannot find life worth living. They are simply earning enough to work one day and preparing themselves to work again the next day. Their whole life is one grey monotonous grind, and soon their lives become of no more value to themselves or the nation than that of mere machines.'[10] This, he thought, was immoral, unnecessary and wasteful. If people are paid more for working fewer hours, it is wrong to assume that their employer will lose money. He will make more money, for three reasons: because his work-people will be fresher and keener; because the higher wages they earn will buy more of the goods they produce; and because machines, which are normally obsolete before they are worn out, can be more profitably worked eighteen or twenty-four hours a day by three or four shifts of six hours each, than for the eight or ten hours of a single shift. So, he argued, let the worker become 'a director of machinery'; let him produce more in shorter time for less cost and higher wages. That was the only way in which national wealth and personal well-being could simultaneously be increased.

Even at Port Sunlight itself the scheme was never introduced. There were economic objections to it. If, as Leverhulme suggested, the worker is mainly a machine-tender, the strain on him of eight hours work is not much greater than that of six hours, provided that the rest-breaks and working conditions are adequate: the machine, which is almost tireless, is doing most of the work for him, and no manufacturer could benefit by paying double wages, as it were, for the two-hour overlap. Objections to the shift-system were also raised by the Board of Trade and the Trade Unions. But the chief obstacle was a human one. The people of Merseyside were not accustomed to shift-working. The girls employed at Port Sunlight feared that when they were working on the evening shift, their young men would walk out with other girls. And they found that the two extra hours of leisure were not to be spent as the workers wished. They were to be educated. This, said Leverhulme, was to be 'absolutely compulsory.' From fourteen to eighteen, their education was to be 'of a high-school character;' from eighteen to twenty-four, 'university and technical;' and from twenty-four to thirty, 'training for military service and citizenship.' They must also grow more vegetables in their gardens. Their initial welcome for the scheme soon changed to dismay.

When Leverhulme turned his attention to Africa and the South Seas, he at once saw that there was the same need as in Lancashire for housing, hospitals, and schools to make the people happier, healthier and more useful, but with the change of climate one detects a change in his tone of voice. In the tropics he saw nothing but waste; waste of human energy, waste of land, waste of raw materials. The people only needed a leader to show them how to make the most of their natural assets. They would surely welcome skilled organisation as much as the Colonial Office would welcome the organiser. But, for a time at least, he must be given a free hand. He would revolutionise these primitive societies for their own benefit as well as for his own, provided that they did not demand the same degree of freedom from control that was regarded as a right in England. Leverhulme never formulated these conditions; he assumed them.

His first disappointment came in the Solomon Islands as early as 1906. 'The declining native population were little inclined to work: as soon as they had satisfied their very limited desire for imported luxuries, the islanders lost interest in plantation employment.'[11] His answer was to suggest importing Hindoos from India. The Government of India and the Colonial Office refused, and after years of wrangling, Leverhulme commented, in words that might have been extracted with few changes from his later correspondence with the Scottish Secretary:

I cannot understand the attitude at the Colonial Office, but these interlacing Government departments such as the Colonial Office and the India Office are very difficult to influence for the good and progress of those portions of the Empire where they feel a little in conflict. I am sure that Kulambangra is quite an ideal spot for Indians, and from there as time went on they would spread all over the Solomon Islands. We should have an increasing population instead of as at present a decreasing population. Land is valueless without men and women to live on it. It seems a pity that such good fertile rich land, as far as my knowledge goes the best in the Pacific for coconut growing, should be unused in this way.[12]

In British West Africa, he had much the same experience. Again, the parallel with Leverhulme's conflict over the proper method of developing the Hebrides is remarkable:

It was the settled policy of the Colonial Office that the native populations of West Africa under British rule should in general have secured to them rights to hold their ancestral soil without disturbance, to cultivate it as they would, and to do with its produce what they thought fit. . . . Lever saw that the production of the materials in which he was interested, by native methods, was miserably inefficient, and he believed that if he were once allowed to proceed with his plans he could improve the efficiency of the industry out of all recognition. . . . 'I sometimes wish,' he said, 'that all native Chiefs in the British Colonies, in Africa at any rate, were made dukes. In my opinion we should then take the sensible view that this land was theirs for development and the advancement of civilisation, and just as we will not tolerate a duke keeping his land for his own pleasure, or to lock it up, so I can never understand why a black man should be allowed to assume a different attitude.'

He was equally unimpressed by the arguments in favour of tribal organisation. Natives should be treated as 'willing children', housed, schooled, doctored, and moved from place to place as might be required. Above all, they should be taught the value of regular habits and of working to time. Under such a regime, how could they fail to become both healthy and industrious, and how then could they fail to be happy?[13]

The Colonial Office did not see the problem with the same eyes, and eventually it was from the Belgian Government that Leverhulme secured the concessions and relative freedom of action that he thought essential. In the Congo he had control over five large tracts of wild country, amounting to about 1,860,000 acres in all, which he was free to develop for palm-oil with native labour. He undertook to care for the medical and educational advancement of the Africans, who should live, he said, 'in comfort and happiness, cultivating their own ground in their own way.' The population was 'poor, underfed, ravaged by sickness and inter-tribal warfare, and all were cannibals.' There were no buildings and virtually no communications except the River Congo and its tributaries. The European staffs lived and worked in conditions of appalling discomfort. The huge amount of capital invested in the Congo by Lever Brothers was described by the Company's critics as an insane venture, until it proved a success, when it became 'an unwarranted monopoly.' In the Congo Leverhulme undertook his biggest gamble. He acquired his concession when he was in his sixtieth year, and visited every part of it when he was aged sixty-two, and again when he was seventy-two. His personal contributions ranged from the plan of the new town of Leverville to the design of a special boot for climbing palm trees. 'Not a palm-area was selected, nor a site chosen,' his son records, 'except on his authority; not a building was erected unless the plans had been passed by him, and very

c

often these plans were largely his own; not a piece of plant or machinery, nor a craft on the river, was ordered until he had carefully examined and passed the specifications.'[14] This was what he enjoyed doing most, creating wealth out of waste, human beings out of near-savages, and he enjoyed it as much because he was in supreme command as because it would bring him and others prosperity. He possessed to an unusual degree the capacity to sustain an initial enthusiasm.

Leverhulme had several of the qualities of greatness. His driving energy, like Henry Ford's or Beaverbrook's, exposed him to the charge of ruthlessness from those who had never dared attempt what he achieved. Certainly he could be impatient with prejudiced or slower minds. He disliked opposition because things could be done sooner without it than with it. 'He could seize the heart of an intricate proposal almost instantly,' wrote one of his close associates, 'and before the problem was fully presented to him, he had arrived at his decision upon it. His restlessly active mind was constantly turning over some new enterprise; no sooner had he reached one goal, but another and a greater appealed to him.'[15] Had that been all, Leverhulme would have been a very successful business man, and nothing more. But it was not all. He was an efficient machine; but he was also a romantic, with all the adventurous and engaging qualities that this word implies. He was, moreover, deeply religious. His life, often said, was an attempt to practise Christianity. This was not an affectation. A Lancashire slum, a hovel in Africa or in the Western Isles, seemed to him obstacles to achieving the full dignity and happiness of which men are capable. Even if he was sometimes insensitive to the different meanings that others might attach to the terms 'dignity' and 'happiness', he did more than any Englishman of his generation to demonstrate in practical form that poverty was both unfruitful and unnecessary. That is why he is remembered.

The first record of Lord Leverhulme's interest in the island of Lewis is dated 1 August 1917, when the firm of Knight, Frank and Rutley informed him, in response to his enquiry, that the property was for sale. By the end of the month he had secured an option from the owner, Colonel Duncan Matheson, and Lewis passed into his hands on 15 May 1918.

The reasons why he bought the island can only be inferred. His son states that he 'felt that the time was approaching when he should consider giving less detailed attention to the affairs of Lever Brothers,'[16] and needed a new toy to play with. If this was so, it was a passing idea, since the size of his already huge Company was quadrupled between 1917 and his death in 1925,* and at every stage of this expansion he continued to give the Company's affairs the same attention that had characterised his entire career. The Hebridean venture was an added interest, or, as many of his closest colleagues regretted, an unnecessary distraction, to a man already overloaded with work.

His previous visit to Lewis in 1884 was closely connected in his mind with the two great loves of his life, his wife and his business. It was there that he and Lady Lever had passed one of their happiest holidays, and there (or following the visit to Orkney a few days later) that the idea came to him to specialise in the sale of soap. Since those days, he had scarcely given another thought to the Hebrides. The affairs of Lewis did once come fleetingly to his attention when the Provost of Stornoway appealed to him in 1903 for a donation towards the town's new library and recreation hall. Leverhulme answered formally that so many calls were made upon him that he did not feel able to assist, and when the appeal was repeated nine months later, he again refused. Lady Lever died in 1913. When he learned that Lewis was for sale, the memory of that wonderful, fruitful holiday recurred to him. To own the island would be another link with her and with his early life. Such, at least, in sentimental moments, was one of the reasons that he gave for his purchase.

What other reasons were there? He certainly had no business motive, in the sense that he expected to make money for his Company out of the islands. There was at that time no conceivable profit for Lever Brothers in the seas and peat-bogs of the Hebrides. The idea of utilising the oil from Hebridean whales and fish-offal in the manufacture of soap and margarine came later, and at its strongest was a very slender link with Port Sunlight. 'You, my Lord, and the Duke of Sutherland and the Duke of Buccleugh are the three greatest landowners in the kingdom,' said a shareholder to him at the annual meeting of Lever Brothers in March 1918. Leverhulme replied disingenuously: 'You have

* In 1917 the capital employed in Lever Brothers was £15,693,601. At Leverhulme's death, it was £65,071,700.

far more land than I have. As a shareholder of this Company
you have ten million acres. I have nothing like that. I think you
ought to be congratulated.' 'But you have just purchased the
Island of Lewis?' 'Yes, if it had been a good purchase in a
financial sense, Lever Brothers would have had it. But it was not,
so I kept it for myself. I can't pay dividends for Lever Brothers
on that sort of investment.'[17]

How early he decided to embark at his own expense upon his
development schemes for the island cannot be determined in the
absence of any contemporary record of his inner thoughts. He
kept no diary, and wrote few intimate letters. His son believed
that his plans took root in his mind from the very start, but he
wrote to his Edinburgh solicitor as soon as the final deeds were
signed, 'You have done quite right to advise Colonel Matheson
that I do not contemplate making any changes in Lewis;' and in
a message sent to the *Glasgow Herald* as soon as the name of the
new proprietor became publicly known, he said, 'My object with
the Island of Lewis is not business, but to find a delightful home
in a beautiful island and among a people whom I greatly admire
and respect, and who will, I am certain, prove most charming
friends and neighbours.'

This was probably an understatement of his intentions for the
sake of allaying local fears. Leverhulme had never yet bought an
estate which he had not rapidly transformed. At first he may have
thought it politic to pretend that he looked no further than the
castle and its garden for the pleasure that Lewis could afford him.
He was anxious to avoid the charge that he had come to the
Hebrides in order to act the Highland chieftain. Laird of Lewis he
was, but only by purchase; and never, not even after he became
Viscount Leverhulme of the Western Isles, did he make any
claim to the dignity which goes with the traditional headship of a
clan. He moved very cautiously in his first approaches to the
Lewismen. He emphasised his Englishness. He refused to wear
the kilt. He was prepared to live quietly in his castle until the
islanders showed that they were willing to accept something more
from him. His purchase of Lewis might have no greater result
than his purchase of Rivington, a building to transform, a garden
to create, a retreat where he could work quietly. Or the Hebrides
might become in his later years what the Solomon Islands were
in his middle-age, half an adventure, half a business enterprise.
Experience would show.

Leverhulme's purchase of Lewis was therefore due to a combination of circumstances and motives, in which sentiment, both for its situation and the memories it evoked, p' ,ed a great part. He had changed the whole economic and social life of communities in several parts of the globe. Now by accident he found a British community in equal need of help, living in a part of the kingdom which by his standards was accessible, yet remote and backward enough to stir in him a romantic, pioneering sense of mission. With the island of Lewis he acquired 400,000 acres and 30,000 people. This was in the grand tradition, to which he was by no means indifferent. But it was also in the Lever tradition. He would enjoy his proprietorship for its own sake, and if the people allowed him, he would show them the way and provide them with the means to help themselves.

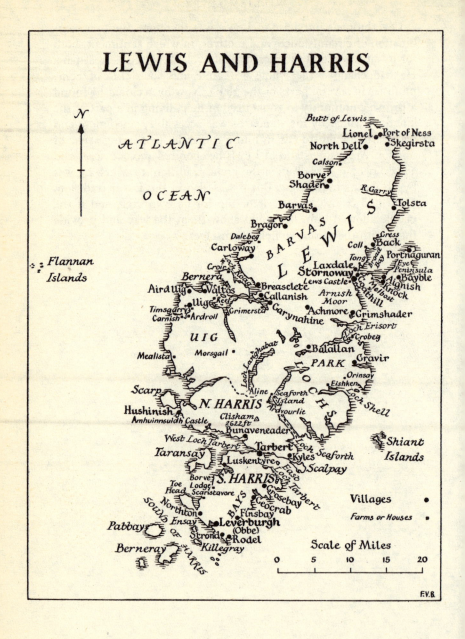

# LEWIS AND HARRIS

# Chapter Two

# LEWIS AND ITS PEOPLE

LEWIS IS PART of the string of islands that lie like the skeletal remains of a whale aslant the north-west coast of Scotland, but it is not itself an island. It is joined by a lumbar stretch of land to its neighbour Harris, which is divided into two halves by the narrow isthmus of Tarbert. The two 'islands' together form the northern half of the Outer Hebrides, the Outer Isles, or the Western Isles, for the terms are almost synonymous, varying only in their romantic associations.

Lewis (which is also known as 'the Lews') is the largest in area and population of all the Outer Isles. Its capital, Stornoway, with a population in 1921 of 4,000 is the only true town in the whole group. Harris, North and South Uist, Benbecula and Barra lead their separate existences. Divided from each other by centuries of clan rivalry, they are still capable of feeling a certain envy of their neighbours' strokes of good fortune and taking an unspoken pleasure in their setbacks. Lewis is additionally separated from all the others by forming part of the county of Ross and Cromarty: Harris and its southern neighbours are administered from Inverness. Not even the creation in 1917 of the parliamentary constituency of the Western Isles has imposed on them a unity that appears from the map inevitable, but which they do not particularly desire.

The rock of which Lewis and Harris are formed, Lewisian Gneiss, is the oldest known geological formation in the world. A nugget of it was centrally displayed on a white velvet cushion at the South Bank Exhibition of 1951, and crowds stared at it as if they were looking at the original matter from which all life developed. But it is the enemy of life. It covers the surface of the island with a shell so hard that only in a few favoured spots near the coast has a sufficient depth of fertile soil accumulated to make tillage possible. Elsewhere the barren rock is married to almost equally barren peat, the growth of only the last few thousand years. Before the peat, the rock lay bare to the gales and glaciers of the ice ages, which scoured the surface of the land into un-drained hollows and formed the innumerable lochans of the interior. The ice ravaged an already ungentle land, but it also spread over much of its surface a stiff, grey, sandy clay which is itself unfertile and contains a mass of loose stones. On it the peat gradually formed to a present maximum depth of twenty feet. This, then, is the Lewis sandwich that has so profoundly affected its economic history: harsh peat on harsher rock, with a layer of unyielding boulder-clay between them.

No country that I have ever seen, except the uplands of Nor-way, to which Lewis bears a strong resemblance, has resisted more stubbornly all attempts to change its nature. A dinosaur would not look out of place in this landscape. The peatbogs of Lewis are undulating stretches of empty, brown land, rising to a few hills which accentuate by their dull roundness the desolation of the moors. The eye searches for something sharp, something precipitous, or at least something not brown, but finds only a little loch which seems to be nothing but a reservoir for more rain. The islanders, who have never felt much love for their central moorland, have contributed to it an occasional corrugated-iron hut or pimply wooden cabin beside the road, and have run across it a telephone or electricity line, often both side by side, as if (which is indeed the truth) the peat-waste is merely an un-welcome interruption between the east coast and the west.

The greater part of Lewis is of this nature. But there are two districts which offer something more. In the southern quarter of the island near the border with Harris, the ground heaves up on both coasts into low mountains separated by narrow sea-lochs, which penetrate deeply into the land and are studded with small islands. The shore curves pleasantly on the Atlantic side to form bays of firm white sand. Here one can sit on a sunny day and imagine oneself in Greece, or walk for miles through deer-forests without seeing more than a single shooting-lodge, for the finest part of Lewis is almost uninhabited. The heather-covered slopes end abruptly in cliffs thrust like clenched fists into the sea. It is a masculine land, treeless and rock-strewn, defiantly raised above the water, and proclaiming its perpetual divorce from the main-land of Scotland.

The climate is depressing more than severe. A sunny day is a memory to be treasured; a rainy day is tolerable only because it is expected. At least some rain falls on five days out of seven. Owing to the thermostatic control of the Gulf Stream, there are no strong contrasts between heat and cold. Snow does not lie for long. Only the wind is exceptional. Round the Butt of Lewis, the northernmost cape of the Outer Hebrides, winds of gale-force rage for an average of 378 hours in the year, and because the island is almost bare and two-thirds of it are flat, the wind slices across from coast to coast, destroying crops, flattening huts, and making it impossible to establish wind-breaking belts of trees.

The people have adapted themselves to their rough land and climate. Their houses surrender comfort and elegance to expediency. The crofter's black-house had gradually been replaced over most of the Highlands, but in Lewis it was still the most common form of dwelling immediately after the First War, and examples of it can still be seen in the remoter districts. It is 'the simplest surviving homestead in Western Europe.'[18] Externally, it is a long low cabin with stone walls rounded at the corners, and roofed with straw thatch or turf fixed with ropes of heather. The walls, which are unmortared, are built double, the space between filled with earth and stones, forming a wall six feet thick and about the same height. The roof only extends as far as the inner edge of the wall, leaving room for a man to stand and walk on the wall-top during the annual renewal of the thatch. In its original form the black-house had no proper windows, for which were substituted small panes of oil-skin or crude glass let into the roof, and there was only one entrance, used by humans and cattle alike. Inside, there were no partitions: the animals used the lower half, the family the upper half. The house was always constructed on a slight slope to provide a primitive form of drainage, but the manure was allowed to accumulate until the yearly spring-cleaning. The hearth was in the centre of the clay floor, and the smoke from the peat-fire found its own way out through the thatch or open door. Furniture was of the simplest kind. A metal cooking-pot hung on a chain over the fire, and the people squatted round it with often no more than an upturned box for a chair and another for a table. They slept in box-beds at the further end, the boxes being tilted on their sides to provide some protection against the rain as it oozed through the thatch, thickened and blackened with soot. There was no sanitation, no electricity, and no piped water.

There are many people living in Lewis today who can describe without affectation the advantages of this incredibly Spartan life, and point out with pride the house itself which now lies only a few feet away from the modern 'white-house' which replaced it, the black-house having been given over wholly to the animals. It was, they say, secure from the winds, for with its rounded corners and low outline, it hugged the earth like a crouching animal, and the thick unbroken walls deadened the sound of the gale to those within. It required little timber in its construction, and timber was scarce. It was also very warm. The fire was never allowed to go out, and the air from the doorway was warmed by the byre before it reached the inner part of the single room. The stench of manure was smothered by the even stronger stench of burning peat. There was something companionable, even Biblical, about the close association between the family and their animals. They would have no partition because 'the cows like to have their company and see the fire, and as they are their great mainstay, they pet them accordingly.'[19] The hens, which settled on the roof timbers above the cows, laid more plentifully from their constant exposure to the smoke. But the greatest advantage of all was the excellence of the smoke-impregnated thatch as a fertiliser. It was stripped off once a year and laid on the fields, and the house re-roofed. When the slate and tiles of the new houses replaced the thatch, Lewis lost one of the few agricultural advantages it enjoyed over less primitive communities.

Towards the end of the last century the black-house was modified by Government order. It became compulsory to insert a partition between the byre and the dwelling part of the house, and chimneys were built into the partitions. Deep, narrow windows were also sometimes pierced through the walls. So when Leverhulme first saw the black-houses of Lewis in 1917 ('houses not fit for Kaffirs', was his private comment), they were already an improvement upon what he would have found in 1884, had he had time to extend his visit beyond Stornoway. But the chief characteristics of the black-house remained: animals and human beings still shared the same roof, which was still of porous thatch. Describing a visit to such a house as late as 1924, a medical officer from the Scottish Board of Control wrote:

It is probably a wet day, and it is necessary to wade through a sea of muck while cows jostle one another and hens fly upward in a frenzy of excitement. In the day-room the interior is obscured by a thick grey haze. The peat glows in the centre, and above hang long black stalactites, funereal streamers trailing downwards from the roof like weeds from the foul bottom of a ship—the consolidated soot of months.[20]

The effect of these conditions upon the people's health was not as disastrous as might have been expected. Although the Highlands and Islands Medical Service did not begin until 1915, and there were villages in Lewis which had previously not been visited by a doctor more than twice in forty years, the children were rarely deformed and by the 1920s the rate of infantile mortality was one of the lowest in Europe. The one serious disease was tuberculosis. In 1923 the death-rate from this cause was 2.2 per thousand, or not far short of three times the rate for Scotland as a whole. Fifty years earlier tuberculosis had been almost unknown in the island. It therefore seemed unlikely that the peat-smoke could be the cause of it, and some authorities even argued that it was a remedy, for it has affinities with tar and resinous trees, known prophylactics against phthisis. An alternative explanation was that the men brought back the disease from the Navy, and the girls from the ill-ventilated basements of houses on the mainland where they went to work as domestic servants. The black-house was thus given a fairly respectable bill of health.

But what impact did their living conditions make on the islanders' outlook? The Crofters Commission of 1884 had reported: 'Their habitations are usually of a character which would imply physical and moral degradation in the eyes of those who do not know how much decency, courtesy, virtue and even mental refinement survive amidst the sordid surroundings of a Highland hovel.' This was, and is, true. We are so accustomed by our experience of great cities to link respectability with cleanliness, that it has become difficult to explain the islanders' indifference to their surroundings except in terms of mental and moral decay. But a single visit to a Lewis village will disprove it. The houses are rough and dirty because the climate is dirty and the people are poor. It was their traditional way of life, which did not imply any decline from previously higher standards. They were peasants. They lived on the land and by the sea, each in his separate croft. They had privacy, pride of possession, and a variety of occupation that sharpened their wits and left to each man the daily decision how to make the best use of his own property and time. The self-assurance and lack of class-consciousness of the Highlander, which has been remarked on by travellers from the earliest times, is largely due to this traditional independence from orders or fixed routine. He is by nature inquisitive, but not impertinent. Quick to demand his rights and agile in argument, he is a formidable opponent, and an enmity once made, a conviction once held, are hard to dispel.

There is, however, another side to their characters. The Lewismen, as Leverhulme had frequently been warned but could never bring himself to admit, lack initiative to an extent which can drive the southerner to despair. 'Laziness' is too strong a generalization for men who toil on the sea for a whole week with only a few hours rest, or for women who daily creel heavy loads of peat and seaweed on their back for miles across the moor. But these spurts of energy are succeeded by long intervals of doing nothing. Anything additional to the annual cycle of their labour is regarded not only as burdensome, but unnecessary. In their own island they dislike change, although the British Commonwealth is peopled with Lewismen who have changed their entire lives in changing entire regions. At home they prefer their traditional discomforts, their traditionally hard way of winning a livelihood, not because they are unaware that better ways exist, but because to be the first to attempt the innovation would expose them either to the envy of their fellow-crofters if it succeeded, or to their contempt if it failed. So the black-house endured for centuries and agricultural and fishing methods advanced with painful slowness. Technical improvements could only be forced on them by an outsider, a government department or a progressive laird, and then they were accepted with a conventional show of displeasure which often concealed an inner relief that something had at last been done. Should the experiment show signs of failure, all their traditional dislike of a contract of service between inferior and superior, and their corporate suspicion of improvement in any form, flooded back as an excuse for their halfhearted response.

The Free Church, to which the majority of the rural people have adhered since the Disruption of 1843, has generally been unsympathetic to innovation. It preached a rigid form of Puritanism, denouncing music, dancing, drinking and even the traditional *Ceilidh*, the evening gatherings in the black-houses that has

done so much to create and preserve Gaelic legend and song.
Observance of the Sabbath has always been a strict rule. Even
in Stornoway, where the influence of the more liberal Church of
Scotland was stronger than in the country districts, a day set aside
for meditation and worship became a day of gloom. In our own
time, the streets are deserted except for the small family groups
making their way, morning and evening, to church. In the
autumn of 1959 I heard a Lewis child reproved for holding a
skipping-rope in her hand on the Sabbath, before she had even
skipped. No good churchman may work on Sunday, however
urgent the work may be. A fisherman must be back in harbour
before midnight on Saturday, and must not leave again for the
fishing-grounds before midnight next day. The conscientious
housewife does no cooking. Nobody may travel. Nobody may
raise his voice in anger or delight. Entertainment of any sort,
even the wireless, is forbidden. A Lowland fisherman once remarked to a Stornoway gillie on a lovely Sunday afternoon after
a week of bad weather, 'We want some days like this for the
fishing,' and received the reproof, 'Is this a day to be talking
about days?'[21]

Admiration is mixed with our astonishment. Acceptance of
such discipline on the day of rest and recreation (in its true sense)
implies great strength of will and faith as well as dogged conservatism. There was also a special reason for it. Like the early
Christian fathers, the Free Church Ministers had first imposed
their discipline as a means of combating lingering pagan superstition. The Reformed Church did not reach Lewis until 1610,
when the new Minister had found it necessary to baptize all
under the age of forty, and virtually reintroduce the institution
of marriage. 'Down to the eighteenth century,' writes the historian of the Hebrides, 'the real religion of the people was simply
saint-worship, strongly diluted by the pagan rites inherited from
their Norse forefathers.'[22] Until about 1880 healing-stones were
built into the houses, spells were cast on a neighbour's cattle,
wax-effigies of enemies were slowly melted, and old women in
Stornoway would sell favourable winds to mariners. Many outsiders considered that the Church had merely substituted one
form of superstition for another, one fear for another. The people
thought it unlucky as well as immoral to offend their Minister,
and in their minds they carried over to the 'new' religion many of
the taboos associated with the old. 'Everything that dark super-

stition and a severe creed can do has been done to oppress the
minds of the people,' wrote a late nineteenth century observer.[23]
Today our judgment need not be so stern. The people do not
give the impression of living in terror of their Church; they
respect it more than fear it. But certainly the Church did not
exert its enormous influence on the side of experiment in the
period immediately after the First War. The Ministers kept aloof
from public controversy, and there is no record of any open
clash between them and Leverhulme on the central issue.
Privately they may have advised caution both to him and to their
people, for the whole spirit of their teaching during the previous
two hundred years had been against material self-seeking which
might lead to an even more obnoxious form of paganism. They
could have found in Leverhulme himself proof that even great
riches can be acquired without any loss of Nonconformist
faith.

The rapid spread of education favoured Leverhulme's schemes
just as Church influence implicitly condemned them. Lewis
children make bright scholars, and many of them have achieved
distinction on escaping the heavy hand of island tradition by
emigration to the mainland or overseas. Lord Macaulay was of
Lewis stock, and Sir Alexander Mackenzie, who discovered the
great Canadian river which bears his name, was born in Stornoway. Since the Education Act of 1872, there has been a primary
school within reach of every parish, and towards the end of the
century the Nicolson Institute at Stornoway was founded by a
Lewisman to provide a secondary education for the cleverest
children from the town and country. For many of the latter it was
the first time that they had ever entered a building larger than
their local chapel, and they could be seen clinging to the ban-
nisters with both hands, so novel was the idea of a second storey.[24]
By 1900 the courses at the Institute included science, classics and
commercial work, and its leaving-certificates were accepted for
entrance to the Universities, the legal profession, and the civil
and armed services. Many of the Nicolson pupils made their later
careers outside the island, but a good proportion returned to the
croft where they were born. Their education was in a sense
wasted, but it had its effect upon the relationship between Leverhulme and the islanders: their innate shrewdness was supplemented by some learning, and he could talk to them in a language
which they would understand.

It was also true in a more literal sense. Gaelic was still the native language of the people, and outside Stornoway it remains so today. But English was the first subject to be taught in the schools, and when Leverhulme arrived in Lewis, he found that the language difficulty was one of the least of the barriers between him and the people.* Most of the middle-aged or younger men and women in the country districts, and almost all in Stornoway, were bilingual. Previously, one official survey after another had deplored the survival of a separate language. 'The Gaelic language may be what it likes,' commented the Census Report for 1871, 'both as to antiquity and beauty, but it decidedly stands in the way of the civilisation of the natives making use of it, and shuts them out from the paths open to their fellow-countrymen who speak the English tongue.' It was argued that the difference in the standard of living between Shetland and Lewis was due at least in part to the difficulty which the Gaelic-speaking Lewismen had in dealing with merchants from the mainland and in making their way if they emigrated. But by 1918 it had been proved that the children quickly learned the second language, and in that year Parliament responded to a petition signed by 18,000 people in the Highlands and Islands by making provision for Gaelic to be taught in Gaelic-speaking areas. The argument had been turned on its head; now Gaelic was to be put in an oxygen-tent. Advanced tuition in Gaelic was given at the Nicolson Institute itself, although it was obvious that the pupils who took the subject would be least likely to benefit from it, since the best scholars were the first to join professions away from their birthplace. Still, the policy had its effect; the language survives, as an asset and not as an obstacle.

This summary of the island's character has been full of contradictions, but contradiction is itself a leading island characteristic. The Lewisman is alert, yet given to indolence; welcoming to strangers, yet resentful of any trespass on his privacy; the most home-loving of men, yet prepared to take up his roots and replant them in the furthest corners of the world. The ugliness of his possessions and the complete lack of any visual taste in the

* The 1921 Census of Lewis indicates very clearly the rapid advance that had been made during the previous forty years in teaching English:

| Percentage who spoke Gaelic only | Age group | Per cent |
|---|---|---|
| | 3–4 | 65·5 |
| | 15–19 | 0·8 |
| | 45–49 | 11·1 |
| | 75–79 | 61·2 |
| | 80 + | 65·6 |

layout of his croft and village are in curious contrast to his responsiveness to literature and music. He admires leadership, but takes a perverse pleasure in its failure. Deeply angered by any wrong done to himself, he will nevertheless try to outsmart his neighbour or his benefactor. He is extraordinarily cautious even for a Scotsman, for he fears ridicule even more than he desires success.

There is something in the Lewisman's temperament that prevents him from making the most of his opportunities and intelligence. It may be nothing more than Celtic pessimism. He expects the worst to happen; it so often has before. Shipwreck, famine, sickness, blight, accident, war, have inured him to disaster, and it no longer seems worth while to take any special precautions against it, except those ordained by his Church. Life is hard, so keep it simple: there will be less to lose, fewer disappointments. This was the philosophy which Leverhulme found so difficult to understand. It was utterly alien to his own.

But there was something even more important—the Lewismen's turbulent history, and their resulting attitude to land.

There are just over a hundred villages (townships) in Lewis, and all but two lie within a mile of the sea. The land is kinder near the shore. It is better drained, the wind-blown sand improves the soil, and seaweed is easily available as an additional fertiliser. There were no roads in the island until 150 years ago, and communication was mainly by coastal boat, particularly in and out of the deep lochs of the Uig and Park districts, where the many crofters who were also fishermen could draw their boats up the beach opposite their crofts. For all these reasons we find that the townships ring the coast-line, and the interior is left empty. As many as fifty crofts can form a township, or as few as six. In three districts (the immediate neighbourhood of Stornoway, the Eye Peninsula, and the north-west coast) the townships are crowded so close together that only the road-signs enable the stranger to distinguish one from another, but on the southern part of each coast they are spaced widely and romantically apart where the mountains meet the sea. It is these that are normally photographed for commercial calendars.

The crofts, of which there were some 3,400 in Lewis in 1917, average six acres. The houses usually stand in a ragged line beside the road, each at the foot of its strip of land, and separated from its neighbour by a post-and-wire fence or rough stone wall. The typical croft is divided internally into three roughly equal areas, one for growing hay, a second for oats or barley, and the third for vegetables, mostly potatoes. It is a little less than the smallest farm, a little more than the largest allotment. There may be a chapel and its attendant manse, and the bigger townships also have a school, and a post office or a small shop. There is never an inn. It is quite unlike an English village in appearance and character, for there is no true centre to the township, and no division of labour. Each head-of-family is his own master, his own mason, cobbler, fuel-merchant, dairyman, and often his own weaver. His croft is his capital as well as his home.

At the back of the row of crofts stretches the hill-moor. It is held in common by the people of the township for peat-cutting and grazing, and although there will often be a fence between the common grazings of one township and another, there is never any internal fencing, because the cost of it would be too great in proportion to the number of sheep and cattle which it would enclose. The moorland is poor, undrained and untreated. As many as ten acres are sometimes needed to provide summer-feed for a single sheep. Each crofter is regulated by a township committee as to the number of stock he may pasture on the moor, and his entitlement is known as his *souming*.* Thus the croft-system combines intense individualism with a form of communalism. The crofter jealously guards the few acres which he cultivates privately, and shares with his neighbours the many hundreds, even thousands, of acres which are untamed.

The system is not older than the later part of the eighteenth century. Before then, all the township's arable land, as well as the moor, was held in common, and it was divided annually into strips by ballot, each crofter working the strip allotted to him for the year. By the beginning of the twentieth century this old 'run-rig' system had been all but forgotten. Most crofters assumed that the pattern of individually held crofts had existed since the remotest time, and that although he paid a small rent for it, it was as much his own property as Lews Castle was the laird's. In this misapprehension lay trouble for a succession of nineteenth and twentieth century owners of Lewis, and particularly for

* A typical *souming* for a crofter from the township of Reef in 1924 was: two cows, one three-year old heifer, one two-year old heifer, two stirks up to one-year old, and ten sheep.

Leverhulme. It meant that the crofter regarded any alteration or criticism of the crofting system as an attack upon the rights that his ancestor had won by centuries of service to their lords and struggle against outsiders.

The temptation to trace this attitude to its roots in the Norse occupation of the Hebrides between the eighth and thirteenth centuries must be resisted. It need only be said that the Highland and Island society that emerged from the middle ages was one based on tribalism. The chiefs of the clans, successors to the Norsemen, like the famous Macleods of Lewis, maintained standing armies of their kinsmen, and in return for their support allowed them, between battles, to make a living from the land. Their rent was their service, and the chief obtained his income by pillage. It was a horrible period of Highland history. 'There was no idealism behind these feuds. . . . They were conceived by primitive passions of greed and revenge, and their fruits were wholly evil.'[25] Tradition and prestige demanded that the rest of Scotland should be treated as a hostile foreign power, and when in 1598 the King sent his Gentlemen Adventurers under the Duke of Lennox 'to plant policy and civilisation in the hitherto most barbarous Isle of Lewis', the colonists were set upon in Stornoway Castle by Neil Macleod and '200 barbarous, bludie and wicket Hielandmen' who cut their throats by the light of a lantern.

By the middle of the eighteenth century, the Macleods had given place as lords of Lewis to the milder Mackenzies, Earls of Seaforth, and the failure of the '45 finally transformed the island character. In 1773 Samuel Johnson found, to his apparent regret, that he and Boswell had arrived in the Hebrides,

too late to see what we expected, a people of peculiar appearance and a system of antiquated life. The clans retain now little of their original character; their ferocity of temper is softened; their military ardour is extinguished; their dignity of independence is depressed; their contempt of government subdued; and their reverence for their chiefs abated. Of what they had before the late conquest of their country there remains only their language and their poverty.

There followed what later generations considered to be the golden age of Lewis. At last there was peace, and for a few years there was plenty. The land, arable and pasture, was held in common by the townships at moderate rents. For the people's simple needs there was enough to go round. On the vast unappropriated waste they could pasture a great number of their livestock. The potato, introduced from Ireland by Clanranald in 1743, had become accepted, after some initial opposition, as a main source of sustenance. The game of moor and river was theirs for the catching. The cutting and burning of seaweed for the manufacture of kelp (an alkali then used in the glass and soap industries) provided them with the money to pay their rent. 'The intervals of leisure were passed with great cheerfulness among a primitive people . . . whose minds were not embittered by an intelligent envy of the welfare of others, or by belief in rights from which they were debarred.'[26]

This happy picture was soon to alter. The cause of the change was the impoverishment of the lairds; its symbols were sheep and deer; its consequences were eviction, mass emigration, and universal distress. It is important for the full understanding of the Leverhulme incident that this cycle of events should be described, for when he came to Lewis the bitter memories that it left behind profoundly influenced the islanders' attitude towards him.

The abolition of the clans after the Jacobite rebellion weakened the links between the people and their chiefs, who had no further claim on their military service and often went south in search of the elegance and pleasures that the Highlands could not provide, leaving their estates for most of the year to the management of unscrupulous factors. The natural leaders of the people no longer lived among them. Instead, they began to look to their factors to provide them with the means to support their extravagancies, and did not enquire too closely into the methods which they used. At first, it was done by raising rents and from the profits of the kelp industry. But there was a limit beyond which indigent peasants could not be squeezed for more, and the kelp boom collapsed early in the nineteenth century. The lairds then resorted to two expedients, often in rapid succession: they replaced their crofter-tenants by sheep-farmers; or sold their ancestral estates to strangers. All the islands of the Outer Hebrides were disposed of in this way by the middle of the century,* yet it was

---

* *Harris* was sold as early as 1779 by Norman Macleod to Alexander Macleod, a former captain of an East Indiaman, whose descendants re-sold it in 1834 to the Earl of Dunmore. *Barra* was sold by the Macneils in 1838 to Col. John Gordon of Cluny, who later offered to sell it to the Government as a convict station. In 1844 *Lewis* was purchased by Sir James Matheson from the Earl of Seaforth (Mackenzie), and in the next year *South Uist* and *Benbecula*, the property of the Macdonalds, were also sold to Col. John Gordon. *North Uist* was the last to go, in 1856, sold by Lord Macdonald to Sir John Campbell Orde.

not so much the arrival of the new lairds that caused the later troubles (for they were often more solicitous for the islanders' welfare than their immediate predecessors), as the arrival of the sheep.

As soon as it was discovered in the late eighteenth century that southern breeds of sheep, like the Cheviot, would thrive in the Highlands, many of the lairds seized the chance to make quick profits from their wool. The sheep-farmers from the lowlands or northern England could pay twice the rent of the crofters, and the landlord did not need to spend a penny of his diminishing capital on preparing the ground for the sheep: the moor was ready to receive them. But not only the moor. They took the crofter's arable land as well as his summer-grazing, and he was evicted at short notice. The sheep-farmers were in fact super-crofters, taking over the croft-lands of several townships. As strangers to the island, with a much higher standard of living, their only link with the crofters was that both rented their land direct from the same laird. The farmer held by legal right what the islanders regarded as their own by custom.

The next stage was the substitution in some districts of deer for sheep, when the sporting-rights of the forests were found to be even more profitable than the grazing. This did not lead to many more evictions; the deer simply took over the moors from the sheep. The people, however, saw in the exchange a further outrage to their birthright. Rich Englishmen and lowlanders invaded the islands for two months in the year, paying huge rents for the right to pursue deer and salmon, occupying the lodges that the proprietor built as an investment, employing very few of the local men, and treating the remainder as little more than potential poachers.

The anger aroused by the evictions can best be illustrated by three examples of the verbal evidence given to the Crofters Commission in 1883:

Is it just, my Lord, that a few strangers should possess more than half the soil, and that the best of it, mostly for rearing sheep and cattle, while the descendants of the original possessors, a race of hardy and industrious men and women, are crowded together on the most sterile portions of the soil?

*Malcolm M'Ritchie, Minister of Knock, near Stornoway*

This is the cause of it all—that we see the land which our fathers had brought under cultivation by the sweat of their brows put under tacksmen (farmers), or as they should more properly be called, desolators of the land, and ourselves heaped upon one another on the very worst portions of the land. . . . I fear there is a danger that they may rise as the clans of old rose, if they don't get hold over the land of which they are deprived for the sake of sheep, deer and grouse.

*Donald Martin, Crofter of Back, Lewis*

It appears that when Britain becomes involved in a struggle with another nation in the future, they must send for the deer and sheep of Harris, as well as its young men, and then they can see which is the best bargain.

*John Macleod, Cottar of Ardhassaig, Harris*

The evictions were carried out with the utmost ruthlessness. The heath pasture was set on fire to deprive the stock of their only sustenance, and so accelerate the crofters' departure. While the younger men were away at work, the black-houses were pulled down over the heads of the old people and children, and the ruins burned. Many of them died from exposure. The survivors had only two choices. They could either rebuild their township on the already overcrowded and over-stocked land of the neighbouring township. Or they could emigrate.

Thousands of them chose emigration. It was the government's, as well as the landlords', policy to encourage them to do so. The Highland clearances were represented as being in the people's best interest. The land was too poor to support so large a population, and their energy could be used far more profitably in the New World. The sheep-farms and deer-forests made economic sense; present crofting conditions did not. These arguments, together with the destitution of their land and the known welcome for emigrants in America, induced many of the crofters to put down the 10/- or 20/- needed for a trans-Atlantic fare. It was not the first wave of migration, for as early as the 1770s, thirty thousand Highlanders had settled in America. In the mid-nineteenth centry, however, it was resumed at an accelerated rate. Many of the migrants made good, and their descendants still return, in some unfamiliar disguises, to visit the land from which their families were eradicated a hundred years ago. Other more pitiful stories are hinted at by records such as this: 'My sister and her husband did not get much satisfaction or comfort in America.

They were but young at the time, and the proof of their discomfort was that their heads were as white as a seagull, mourning for the land that they had left behind.'[27]

Lewis and Harris did not suffer from the clearances as much as the remainder of the Highlands and Islands. Their populations continued to increase until 1911, while in all other West Highland areas, the population had been declining since about 1830.[28] This was partly because the Northern Hebrides had the fishing and the tweed industries to fall back on. But they were also more fortunate in their lairds. The Captain Macleod who bought Harris in 1779 was the first to take real pains for his tenants, and Earl Dunmore followed his example. In Lewis the sixth and last Earl of Seaforth, who died without sons in 1815, and his successor James Alexander Stewart-Mackenzie, were much loved. But in both islands clearances took place, although on a smaller scale than elsewhere. Every crofter in the west of South Harris was evicted from his home, and those who did not emigrate were resettled on the poorer land of the Bays district on the opposite coast.[29] Nearly 35,000 acres of Lewis were taken for deer-forests, and when the Seaforth fortunes were failing, crofts were replaced by three sheep-farms in the Stornoway district, Coll, Gress and Aignish.[30] The first two are names that will recur frequently in this narrative. Coll and Gress came to symbolise for Lewis, and indeed for the whole country, the struggle between Leverhulme and the crofters, between the island's future and the island's past.

Lewis had the further advantage that the island was purchased in 1844, at the height of its distress following the final collapse of the kelp industry and a succession of harvest-failures, by a man of exceptional wealth and vision, a proto-Leverhulme. Sir James Matheson, a native of Sutherland, had made his fortune in the Far East as one of the founders of the firm of Jardine, Matheson and Co, and for many years after his return he was Member of Parliament for the constituency of Ross and Cromarty, in which Lewis lay. He bought the island from the Mackenzies for £190,000, and spent an additional £380,000 on its improvement.[31] Part of this enormous sum represents the cost of building Lews Castle and several shooting lodges in different parts of the island. But he also sunk much of his fortune in extending the island's road system, building schools, providing quays and fish-curing stations, establishing a chemical works for extracting paraffin oil from peat (this experiment failed), assisting crofters with meal and seed, and with bulls to improve their stock, and subsidising the emigration of over two thousand Lewismen to Canada. He was also one of the first to found model-farms and to experiment with land-reclamation on a scientific basis.

Leverhulme examined the records of his predecessor with the deepest interest, for Matheson had attempted many of the experiments which Leverhulme wished to repeat, and his failures were as instructive as his successes. He must have observed that Matheson's major investments never paid a dividend, not even from the reclamation of land, and that the extra employment that he provided was not always accepted by the crofters. Labourers had to be imported from the mainland although islanders nearby were in arrears of rent and destitute, and this apathy nullified all his efforts to help.[32] But Leverhulme approached the problem of Lewis with an object quite different from Matheson's. Fishing, not the land, was to be the basis of the island's future prosperity; immigration, not emigration. So he was not in the least disturbed by the smallness of the impact which Matheson's vast expenditure had made on the island's economy. As for the alleged apathy of Lewismen, Leverhulme's eye may have fallen on this explanation by a Stornoway solicitor in the Crofters Commission's Report:

The late Sir James Matheson was a great man, a public benefactor, a resolute pioneer of progress, the architect of his own colossal fortunes, most hospitable, and sometimes profusely benevolent. . . . Alas, there was another side to this picture. The policy of the estate was a tortuous, subtle, aggressive one in pursuit of territorial aggrandisement and despotic power, so absolute and arbitrary as to be almost universally complained of.

The eulogistic half of this assessment of Sir James could be applied almost word for word to Leverhulme. He was determined that the second half should never be.

Lewis was a profoundly discontented island on Matheson's death in 1878. All expenditure was halted. The factor, Donald Munro, a name still spoken with loathing in Lewis, ruled the island with utter disregard of the crofters' legitimate grievances. The evictions continued. By 1883, the crofters had lost 160,000 acres to sheep and deer. Several hundred men from the Uig district marched on the castle to demand the restoration of their grazings, and although on this occasion Donald Munro was able to satisfy them, it was clear that the island, like the larger part of the Highlands, was on the verge of a serious uprising.

In response to this unrest, Parliament appointed the Crofters Commission, which heard evidence in every part of the crofting Highlands, including Lewis. The report of the Commission was published in 1884, the very year in which Leverhulme first visited the Hebrides. We owe to it a detailed picture of the islands after the clearance policy had done its worst, and a series of Acts of Parliament that brought some relief to the people without removing the accumulated grievances of the past hundred years.

The crofters attributed all their troubles to the evictions. They believed that if they could return to their old townships, and be protected by law against any further clearances, all would be well. The Park district, for instance, had been cleared of twenty-four townships to accommodate 11,000 sheep, and the population distributed between America and unfertile or overcrowded corners of Lewis. The Park lease, they told the Commissioners, had now expired, and the widowed Lady Matheson could not find a new farmer to take it over. She had refused to consider their application for its return to the townships, because, she said, 'it was unsuitable for that class of tenant', and she had taken it into her own hands. The crofters did not claim the land to be their own by law, but by 'custom' admittedly unknown to the Statute Book, yet none the less binding on the proprietor. Their right to occupy their small patches of land was, in their view, inalienable. Moreover, when they were evicted, they were given no compensation whatever. From crofts reclaimed from the moor, built upon, manured and tilled, they were suddenly compelled to shift to rough bog or bare rocky land, and there again to reclaim, build and cultivate, only perhaps to be moved again. It was intolerable that when a man bought the island of Lewis, he should buy the rights and liberties of the people with it. This argument was reiterated with passionate eloquence as the Commission moved patiently from one township to another throughout the western Highlands and up the length of the Hebrides.

The Commission did not accept the claim for security of tenure of individual crofts. They said that it would encourage a reckless increase in population, and 'aggravate the indigence, squalor and lethargy which too much abound already'. The crofters' appeal to the custom of their ancestors 'cannot be seriously entertained. The clan system no longer exists. The chief has in many cases disappeared. The relations of ancient interdependency have vanished.' The Commissioners did, however, recommend that the townships and common grazings should not be further reduced in size without the agreement of the crofters, and that the proprietor should be obliged by law to give up sufficient land to enlarge existing townships, where enlargement was essential to relieve congestion. But this, they recognised, would not solve the main problem of an estate like Lewis, where the population had increased so much, in spite of the evictions, that even if all the farms and deer-forests were returned to the people, and half of them made their main living by fishing, there would still not be enough land for the remainder. According to the people's own estimate, fifty-seven acres per head was the minimum necessary to maintain a family, and all the land in the Western Isles would not provide more than 19.3 acres per head. 'We are therefore of the opinion,' the Commissioners concluded, 'that a resort to emigration is inevitable.'

Parliament enacted many of these recommendations over the next thirty years. It set up the Congested Districts Board with powers to enlarge existing holdings, fix a fair rent for crofts and settle the boundaries of grazings and townships. It also provided financial aid for local rates and public works. In two important respects, however, Parliament disagreed with the findings of the Commission to the crofter's advantage. By the Act of 1886, the crofter was given security of tenure on his own holding. He could not buy or sell it, for it remained the property of the landlord, but he could leave the tenancy to his heirs, and he could not be evicted unless he allowed his rent to fall a year in arrear, grossly neglected the croft, or subdivided it against the regulations. Secondly, the crofter was entitled to compensation for any improvements he had made to the croft, if at any time he wished to give it up of his own free will.

These were important gains, which were to have a great influence on Leverhulme's plans, but they did not remedy the fundamental grievance. The farms and forests remained in the hands of strangers or of the laird himself. They could not be obliged to surrender them to form new crofts, and the land-hunger of the younger men was not abated by conferring on those who already held land a legal right to retain it indefinitely. For many years the two sub-classes of crofter, the cottar and the squatter, had been increasing in numbers, particularly in Lewis, where overcrowding was more serious than in any other part of the Highlands. The cottar was usually the son or a close relation of the crofter, who allowed him to erect a small hut on his land and scratch a living from part of it. The squatter was a man without family, or one evicted from another township, who appropriated a corner of land and lived a precarious existence, without legal rights, as a burden on the others. Neither cottar nor squatter paid any rent or rates. Together they formed the surplus population of the islands which the Crofters Commission had wished to drain off by emigration. But two assisted-passage schemes, in 1888 and 1906, both failed because of the reluctance of the Lewis people to leave their island. By 1914 there was one cottar or squatter in Lewis to every two genuine crofters.

The growing congestion had already led to outbreaks of violence. In 1887 a body of landless men had attempted to seize some of the former croft-lands in Park, and following the acquittal of some of the raiders, Lady Matheson thought it wisest to grant them fourteen small crofts.[33] Two months later three hundred men marched to the castle to petition her for land on the sheep-farm of Galson, and another group drove the sheep off Aignish farm and demolished the fences. A battalion of marines was ordered to Lewis to keep the peace, and the raiders were either imprisoned, or quietened by the grant of small fishermen's holdings. The land-agitation in Lewis then lay almost dormant for two decades.

On the outbreak of the Great War, thousands of Lewismen joined the services, many of them as Naval reservists, and others as recruits for the island's own regiment, the Seaforth Highlanders. One sixth of the entire population served their country in some capacity, a higher proportion, it was said, than in any other part of the British Empire. Scarcely a man was left in the island capable of bearing arms. The young women were away in munition factories, and the crofts were tilled by the children and the old.

Far from forgetting the problem from which the war had temporarily relieved them, the soldiers and sailors from Lewis renewed their demands for a fair deal. Letters began to appear in the local newspaper, of which the following, from a leading-seaman, is typical of many:

We hope your paper will help us to get the land of our forefathers, that they were deprived of cruelly to make room for sheep and grouse and the sporting Sassenach. All Lewismen can now plainly see that they have been quiet too long.[34]

An even more threatening note began to creep into the statements of land-reformers who were agitating at home on the service-men's behalf. This letter reached the newspaper from Edinburgh:

I would say to those landlords and dukes with millions of acres, 'Your turn has come. What would have become of your estates if the Germans had come over here?' Let there be a combing out of such wealth as originally and naturally belonged to the people. Much of the land in our beloved country has been obtained by the power of the sword. Surely, then, our warriors who have defended this land have by the same law a right to share it. Conscription of wealth is a natural sequence to conscription of life. Our brave lads shall not be compelled for want of land to emigrate again.[35]

One further example must suffice; this from the island itself. On 19 December 1917, a speaker addressed a Barvas audience as follows:

What are we going to do with our soldiers and sailors? We must look after the men who have fought for us. We must see that they get the land. (*Loud applause*). It is morally theirs. Is there a landlord in the British Empire who would grudge them the soil which they so bravely defended from the savage and brutal Huns?

So a new and even more inflammatory argument was added to the old. The farms must be reconverted into crofts because they were wrongfully taken from the islanders; and because the island-ers had now defended them with their lives. The Government responded sympathetically to this double appeal. In 1911 they had passed an Act which permitted the compulsory purchase of land for new crofts, but it was difficult to administer and it had barely nibbled at the problem before the outbreak of war put a stop to all further action. Now stronger legislation was promised for the particular benefit of Highland ex-servicemen who wished to return to the land when the war was over. On 11 October 1917, in a speech at Inverness, T. B. Morison, the Lord Advocate, gave this undertaking on the Government's behalf:

We are entitled to expect that the land-question in the Highlands should be settled once and for all. The evils of the old system are now admitted practically on every hand, and everyone is agreed that the people of the Highlands must be placed in possession of the soil. . . . It has been demonstrated that farms when broken up carry a larger stock and support a larger population, while the unchecked expansion of deer-forests has been nothing short of a national scandal.

In November 1917, the Secretary for Scotland, Mr Robert Munro, let it be known that he was considering a suggestion put to him by the Lewis Crofters Association that the Government should purchase the island of Lewis as a 'colony for crofters, fishermen and cottars to settle thereon, and to make the best use of it in cultivation after the war'.[36]

It seemed that the crofters' long battle was won. But it was about to enter its most interesting phase. For on 17 October 1917, less than a week after the Lord Advocate had given his pledge at Inverness, Lord Leverhulme had landed semi-*incognito* in Lewis with very different ideas for its future.

## Chapter Three

# 'A POOR LANCASHIRE LAD A LONG WAY FROM HOME'

THE OWNER OF Lewis was Lieutenant-Colonel Duncan Matheson, great-nephew of Sir James Matheson. He had succeeded to the estate in 1899. The accumulated burdens of taxation and death duties had made it impossible for him to sustain the heavy financial liabilities of Lewis in addition to his other properties at Ullapool, Dingwall and Achany. The castle had been rented before the war to a succession of sporting tenants, but the revenue from the island still did not meet the annual expenditure. In November 1913 Matheson offered to sell it to the nation. The idea was still under consideration by the Scottish Office in 1917, when Colonel Matheson advertised the island for sale in *The Times*, and it was this advertisement that first aroused Leverhulme's interest.

Before deciding on the purchase, Leverhulme arranged with Matheson to visit the island accompanied by his English agent, Frank Clarke. The whole northern and western Highlands were at that time a prohibited area, and military permits were necessary for both of them. It was a grim wartime journey by rail through Edinburgh and Inverness to the Kyle of Lochalsh, and thence by the antiquated MacBrayne steamer *Sheila* to Stornoway. Twenty-eight hours after leaving Port Sunlight, Leverhulme and Clarke landed in Lewis to be greeted by Matheson's factor, Charles Orrock ('Chamberlain of the Lews'), who was the only person in the island to be told the secret. Duncan Matheson himself was away in Perth, commanding one of the reserve battalions of the Seaforth Highlanders. He had offered to put up the visitors at the castle, but out of delicacy for the existing owner's feelings, Leverhulme decided that they should stay at the Royal Hotel in Stornoway. He registered himself as Sir William Lever, a name that he had abandoned four months earlier on his elevation to the peerage as the 1st Baron Leverhulme of Bolton-le-Moors. He was anxious to avoid ostentation, but his method was strange, since his former name was even better known at that time than his new title.

The secret of his visit was well kept. He remained on the island from 17 to 21 October 1917, travelling by road in atrocious weather to every corner of it with Clarke and Orrock, and it was only on the last day that his presence became known to a few of the leading men of Stornoway. He went to a stationer's shop in Point Street, and asked to see some views of the interior of Lews Castle, which he had not yet visited. The stationer produced some photographs from his pre-war stock, and because they were shop-soiled, offered them to the stranger ('a dapper little man', was the first impression that has remained with him) for 9d each, 3d less than the original price. 'I'll take the lot for 6d apiece,' replied his customer. Amused, the shopkeeper agreed. 'To what address shall I send them, sir?' Leverhulme would not give his name. 'Just send them to the Royal Hotel; they will reach me.' As he left, the stationer followed him to the door, and watched him walking with short steps up Point Street. At that moment Charles Orrock came out of the Chamberlain's office opposite. 'Who on earth is that?' asked the shopkeeper. 'That,' replied Orrock, 'is Lord Leverhulme. He has just bought the Lews.'

For dramatic effect, Orrock was anticipating the fact. Leverhulme did not become the actual owner of Lewis until seven months later. But his tour of the island, even though he had seen Lewis at its wildest and most hideous, had confirmed his intention. He took away with him a copy of the report of the Crofters Commission for 1902 (the Brand Report), and in his letter thanking the manager of the Royal Hotel for the loan, he wrote, 'I presume that it is hoped to let a little daylight and advanced ideas into remainders from a bye-gone age.' In this guarded sentence one can detect something of the plan that was already forming in his mind.

As soon as he returned to England he initiated active negotiations for the sale. Colonel Matheson obtained leave from his regiment and met Leverhulme at Port Sunlight on 29 October 1917 in the presence of their solicitors. Matheson had originally asked for £200,000 as the purchase price. Leverhulme had thought it 'not an attractive proposition even at the figure I named (£152,000), but beyond that it is impossible.'[37] In fact, as he discovered during his visit in October, Lewis was not a financial proposition at all, for the proprietor's half-share of the rates, the upkeep of the sporting estates and the expenses of the Chamberlain's office, exceeded the rents from all the crofters, farmers and sporting-tenants combined. The island had 3,400 crofters who paid an average rent of £2 each, some as little as 25/-, and nearly 2,000 cottars and squatters who paid no rent at all. There were only twelve farms of any size, and in wartime it was not easy to let the shooting and fishing. Leverhulme was therefore in a strong bargaining position. He was offering to buy a property which had become an impossible liability to the owner.

The purchase price which they eventually agreed was £143,000, compared to the £190,000 which Sir James Matheson had paid for the island to the Mackenzies in 1844, since when the property had been much improved by the building of Lews Castle and the lodges. Leverhulme also bought from Colonel Matheson for an additional £10,000, the seven Gobelin tapestries at the Castle which today hang in the Lady Lever Art Gallery at Port Sunlight. He purchased the boats and other movable property belonging to the estate for £7,000, the crofters' £10,000 arrears of rent for £2,750, and the farm-stock for £4,226. His initial expenditure thus amounted to just under £167,000.

The formalities, including the disentail of the estate, were completed in time for Lewis to change hands on Whitsunday, 15 May 1918. Leverhulme received two large boxes containing the three hundred and sixty title-deeds, some of which dated back to the fifteenth century. He had come into possession of one of the oldest and largest estates in the United Kingdom. On its seven hundred square miles lived nearly 30,000 people. It included the Flannan Islands in the Atlantic and the Shiant Islands in the Minch. The whole estate was freehold, except for a few isolated properties in the town of Stornoway. He could do with it whatever he wished, if the people of the island would support him.

The intended sale became public knowledge in February 1918. In its issue of the 8th of that month, the *Stornoway Gazette* printed in an obscure corner of the paper, under the passive headline *Reported Sale of the Island of Lewis*, the following inaccurate and pitifully brief statement:

A report comes from Edinburgh that the island of Lewis has been purchased from Major Matheson by Messrs Lever Bros., the world-known soap-firm of Port Sunlight, near Liverpool.*

* Duncan Matheson had been promoted to Lieutenant-Colonel some time before, but he continued to be known in the island by the affectionate nick-name of 'the Major'.

The formal announcement, naming Leverhulme and not his Company as the purchaser, and giving Whitsunday as the transfer-date, was published in the *Scotsman* a week later.

There was an immediate clatter of excitement in the national press. What did Lord Leverhulme want with Lewis? Was it peat? Fish? Feudal grandeur? Leverhulme replied to all these enquiries with dignified, but not quite truthful, denials. All he wanted, he said, was a 'residential retreat.' To the London correspondent of the *Scotsman* he added: 'I feel that I can take a great interest in the life of the isle, and if there are any economic problems, I shall be glad to work with the people for their solution.' Privately he wrote to the Edinburgh solicitor who had acted for him:

You will know that some of the Scotch papers have said that I may put any amount of money I like into the Lews, but it is quite certain I shall never get a penny out. . . . However, as I know I never had the knack of making money, and as profitable investments are quite beyond my range of foresight, I am quite content, for I hope to get happiness and health, if I cannot get wealth, in the Island of Lewis.[38]

Further than that he would not go. He had no comments to make on the land question, and gave scarcely a hint of the conclusions he had drawn from his first visit.

The people of Lewis were puzzled and excited by the news. They all knew Leverhulme by reputation. *Sunlight* was almost the only soap sold in the island, and many of them had personal connections with Liverpool, from where cargo boats sailed regularly to Stornoway. Even if he did nothing else for Lewis, it would be an advantage to have a wealthy laird at the castle again. They felt genuine regret at parting from Duncan Matheson, who was a kindly man and a loyal Highlander, but the impoverishment of his family after Sir James' death had prevented him from improving his estate as he would have wished. There was no vocal protest in the island against the buying and selling of their homes behind their backs. The Hebrides were too accustomed to it. Nor did they share the indignation expressed on their behalf by Scottish nationalists on the mainland that a self-made Englishman should have thrust himself into one of the most historic of Highland fiefs. A leading social historian of the Highlands has written: 'Although the external income-earning laird may be a figure of fun in the novels and a butt for political execration, the crofter knows if he is well off with such

a man. . . . His contempt is profound for a rich man who is a
skinflint towards a Highland estate.'[39] It matters more to the
crofters what a man is, than from where he comes. Leverhulme
was recognised as an enlightened employer. He was known to be a
Liberal in politics, a Nonconformist by religion, and abstemious
in his private life—all of them virtues extolled in Lewis. He was
also known to be very rich. Perhaps this was the biggest virtue
of them all:

> I tell you, lad, the place will be
> The garden of the west,
> The northern Venice by the sea,
> With milk and honey blest.
> Geraniums growing in the glens,
> An' gold-fish in the burns,
> An' Sunlight medals for the hens
> That show the best returns.
>
> For kelp we'll get £10 a head,
> Now, what d'ye think a' that?
> If *Leverhulme* comes down our road
> By Chore! I'll lift my hat.
> What's more, our rents will now include
> Free food, and coal, and gas,
> Although of course it's understood
> We'll 'please keep off the grass'.[40]

There were also more formal messages of congratulation from
the Stornoway Town Council, the Lewis District Committee,
and, most remarkably, from the Lewis Crofters and Cottars
Association, which had been proposing only a few months before
that the Scottish Office should buy the island and administer it
as a state colony. Their President now wrote to Leverhulme:
'The smallholders and cottars of Lewis are delighted that your
Lordship has purchased the island, and beg to congratulate him
on this historic occasion, assuring him of their hearty goodwill
and support. Lord Leverhulme's fame as a just and model
employer of labour has reached Lewis before him.' Letters
addressed to him personally or to the local newspaper from the
trenches in France and from naval ships were equally enthusiastic. It seemed as if the land agitation had been forgotten in the
excitement of imagining what Leverhulme might do. Few people
took seriously his threat to do nothing except enjoy his leisure

E

at Lews Castle, yet his tactful pretence that this was his sole object pleased the inhabitants. They awaited with intense curiosity his first public appearance amongst them.

He came for Easter, with his son William Hulme Lever and James Simpson, and remained a week, from 28 March till 5 April 1918. He was not yet the proprietor—there were still six weeks to elapse before Whitsun—and he again decided that it was more fitting, and probably more comfortable, for him to stay at the Royal Hotel than at the castle. It was in such small details that Leverhulme was most careful to avoid giving any offence to island susceptibilities. On this occasion he did not again tour the whole of the island, but made a few short journeys out of Stornoway, commenting to Simpson on what he saw from the car. ('These aren't farmers, Jim,' he said at one point. 'They're fishermen.')

There was no official demonstrations. Leverhulme was deliberately self-effacing, and the formal welcome was postponed until after the property had actually changed hands. But there were many private encounters between him and leading men of the island, at which little more was exchanged than courtesies on one side and some shrewd questions on the other.

There was also one public meeting in Stornoway, in support of the Scottish war-savings campaign, at which Leverhulme made his first speech to the islanders. He was received with loud applause when he mounted the platform erected in the Old Post Office Square, and again when he rose to speak:

I am a poor Lancashire lad a long way from home, but I want you to look on me as out and out a Lewisman for the future. . . . I am looking forward to sharing with you all the joys and sorrows of life in Lewis. When I was here last autumn I saw it—Mr Orrock tells me—under the worst weather conditions, and I have seen it in fine weather like today. And I like it whether it is rough or smooth, warm or cold, and I am glad that fortune has so smiled on me as to give me a place among you. You were happy before I came, and you would be happy if I went. (*Laughter.*) We will show the adjacent island of England and Scotland what can be done. (*Laughter and cheers.*)

The remainder of the speech was about the war, the Germans ('those brigands'), and the need for bullets and money. At the end he offered to double whatever Lewis raised for war-savings up to £20,000. The speech, and the offer, created a favourable impression. A humourist, evidently; a man who didn't give himself airs; an Englishman who could appreciate the dank beauty of the island; and no skinflint, for he had given a staggering earnest of benefits to come. Leverhulme returned to Thornton Manor, followed by baskets of island oysters and salmon, equally satisfied with this first encounter.

His next visit was on 29 June 1918, and he stayed for three months. It was the third time since October that he had made the long journey to Stornoway, but it was his first visit as proprietor. He had asked that any official celebrations should be put off for a few days, as the ladies in his party, which included two of his sisters, would be exhausted by the train journey and the crossing of the Minch, and the *Sheila* was not due to dock until late at night. Nevertheless, the quay and South Beach were gay with bunting and evergreens, and a large arch had been erected, with a banner reading WELCOME TO YOUR ISLAND HOME. Hundreds of people thronged the quay, and a pipe-band stood ready at the landing-place. An unfortunate delay then upset the arrangements. 29 June was a Saturday. As the minutes passed, the *Sheila* still did not arrive, though the sea that night was calm. The waiting crowds strained their eyes through the semi-darkness of mid-summer towards the gap between the long horns that enclose Stornoway harbour. The steamer's lights at last appeared a few minutes before midnight. She docked as the hour struck. It was the Sabbath. To everyone in that large assembly it was unthinkable that the rehearsed programe of welcome should now be carried out in full. The pipe-band was dismissed, and the new laird stepped ashore to muted greetings from the Provost. His party then drove off to Lews Castle through crowds which could not restrain their cheers, and Leverhulme spent his first night under his own roof and flag.

Three days later, Provost Maclean presented Leverhulme with an address of welcome at a large meeting convened in the Masonic Hall at Stornoway. It referred to 'the high trust imposed on you, and our sincere hope that you may long be spared to carry out in our midst those enlightened Christian principles by which we are glad to know your Lordship has been inspired in the past.' Blunter and more significant was the supporting speech made by ex-Provost Anderson: 'There are very serious problems to be solved, and your Lordship will have to tackle them bravely after he has obtained personal knowledge of them. If there is to be any progress, traditions must first disappear. Great remedial measures are needed if the boys of Lewis are to be satisfied.'

Leverhulme had taken great pains with the preparation of his reply, although he was a natural orator. He had the rare ability to snatch phrases out of the air, alternately responding to the mood of his audience and creating it by the warmth of his manner and the vigour of his gestures. He put his audiences at ease because he was seen to be so completely at ease himself. His speeches had a certain literary flavour; the sentences were usually well carpentered. But their effect was due to his radiant goodwill, his evident pleasure at being there, the effortlessness with which he swung between grave and gay, and even the conscious absurdity of his anecdotes, which made his hearers forget for the moment his immense reputation and achievement.

On this occasion he had not only to make friends of his audience, but to strike the key-note of his future proprietorship. It was the time to speak out. He had already had enough evidence that the people of Lewis bore him no resentment for his intrusion into their affairs. Indeed, as ex-Provost Anderson had just pointed out, tradition took second place in their minds. They were looking to him for action. He was ready to supply it. From this moment onwards he made no further mention of seeking a residential retreat; and the reception of his speech showed that he had not miscalculated the effect of his modest entry into the life of the island, nor the moment for him to disclose his real motives.

He began:

I am quite overwhelmed with the warmth of the reception you gave me, my sisters and friends—forlorn English folk (*laughter*)— last Saturday night or early Sunday morning. I have come a long way from home to live amongst you, and my future happiness depends on your goodwill. If you receive me coldly or with indifference, though I live in the castle, I shall be more miserable than if I lived in a summer shieling.

A title can only be justified on the grounds of service, and you have always looked upon your laird as one who can render you services that could not be rendered by any other person. Only to the extent that I can render service should I consider that there was any reason for my becoming possessor of this island. (*Applause*).

Then came the hint for which they were waiting:

I want to say to you that I do feel that we in this island have been drifting a little away from the modern line of march of science and art. We have not kept up with all that science has placed at our disposal for the improvement and development of the resources of the island. We have here surrounding us wealth beyond the dreams of avarice (*loud applause*), and so far from Lewis being considered an outlying part of the world, it is really, as far as the harvest of the sea is concerned, what you may call the hub of the universe. (*Applause*.)

There are two ways of dealing with a community: one method called philanthropy—muddling sentiment I call it. (*Applause*.) The other method is by availing oneself of the means placed at our disposal by science to enable people to live for themselves and work out their own destiny. (*Loud applause*.)

While the war lasts, there is little that we can do, but we can be thinking and planning. We should not be true to those men and women, if we did not consider carefully what can be done in the time of peace to ensure that they shall come back to a better Lewis than ever they knew. (*Loud applause*.)

Working on the lines of commerce I hope we can solve this problem in Lewis by providing full occupation at wages not a whit inferior to those paid elsewhere. We cannot carry on industries successfully unless we can compete in the open market. If you have got the right material (and we have got that), and if you have got wealth at the door waiting to be harvested (and we have that), it is for us to see that we prepare it for the market in such a way that it shall fetch the highest price, and out of that we can pay the highest wages. (*Applause*.)

That is roughly the idea of how I think we can work together. No government, not even by the laird of Lewis, whatever limited power he may have (*laughter*), can be exercised without the consent of the governed fully and completely given. (*Applause*.) On such lines I believe we can work out such a condition of things here as will make Lewis the envy of less happy lands. (*Loud applause*.)

Continuing in what the reporter called 'a lighter vein', Leverhulme remarked that when the war was over, he hoped to have 'a flying machine, which leaving the Mersey at 2 o'clock, would land him in Stornoway after a few hours run, in time to have dinner at the castle. (*Laughter*). Lewis might in future become a starting-place for New York. (*Renewed laughter*).' He ended with the words that were often to be quoted in later years:

All I can do will be done. We will work on business lines, and we will have nothing to do with philanthropy. We will be able to look each other in the face, and you will be able to say to me, 'We thank you for nothing but the opportunity you have given us, and that is all we want.' And I shall say to you, 'We are good friends; it is a pleasure to live amongst you, and I hope we shall have a long and happy life together.' (*Loud and continued applause.*)

The speech had succeeded beyond his hopes. He had planted the seed of the idea, without actually mentioning it, that the agitation for land was old-fashioned and irrelevant. The future prosperity of Lewis lay in fishing, not in crofting. His reference to 'business', 'commerce' and 'industries' had passed without comment; his mention of science had raised a cheer. It was a good beginning. But Leverhulme was too astute an orator to be unaware of the power of his oratory, and he remembered that his audience included the most far-sighted men of the town, many of whom were themselves in business, and they were gathered there specifically to welcome him. Often in his career he had found that other men's enthusiasm waned quicker than his own. He would immediately follow up his success at the Masonic Hall by a practical demonstration that he had meant what he said. He wanted to see, as soon as possible, machines moving earth, men laying foundations and building roads, and watch the town and harbour of Stornoway emerging at his inspiration from the habits of centuries.

During July, August and September 1918, Leverhulme remained at Lews Castle, making frequent expeditions to Stornoway and every district of the island, and arranging in detail the execution of his master-plans. But before describing them, the more personal side of his life in the island must be outlined, in order to indicate the way in which he adapted himself to the novel role of a Highland laird.

The best place from which to see Stornoway as a whole is from the top of Gallows Hill, which rises in the southern part of the castle's park. The town, harbour and castle lie at your feet. The broad bay, enclosed by two low fingers of land, gleaming like baize in the sunlight, terminates in a small stubby peninsula, where the older part of the town was built. It is quayed on all three sides, and seals off the inner harbour, which tails away northwards as a lagoon separating the castle from the town. Individually there are few beautiful buildings in Stornoway, but the browns, whites and yellows of the houses, set at slightly different angles or on curves, form a pleasant pattern in combination with the continual movement of seagulls and small boats. Often I have sat at a window overlooking the harbour and wondered what part of the scene below me has remained quite unchanged by the passage of forty years. I could only be certain of the birds and the water, the tilted, sweeping flight of the gulls and the small wrinkles on the protected sea.

The castle stands in baronial isolation opposite the town, the arm of the harbour acting like a moat between them. A glacis of lawn, flanked by huge banks of rhododendrons and grazed in Leverhulme's day by herds of deer and Shetland ponies, leads up from the harbour's edge to a castellated Victorian pile. There is nothing forbidding about Lews Castle. Sir James Matheson built it on the site of Seaforth Lodge as a laird's home, not as a feudal castle. It was intended to balance but not overawe the town, and it does so very effectively, the grey granite backed charmingly by the only wood of any size in Lewis, its turrets breaking the silhouette in a way that suggests romanticism more than grandeur as its builder's motive.

Inside it is more disappointing. Today the castle is the island's technical college, and it is not easy to visualise its original appearance now that the ball-room has been converted into the main lecture-hall, and the corridors are floored with linoleum and lined with models of trawlers in glass cases. But nothing has altered the surprising meanness of Matheson's central staircase, nor the weak proportions of his long hall-corridor on the ground floor. It was a big house, and the many living-rooms were extended by two conservatories, demolished after the second World War. Upstairs a turret-stairway rises to the leads, from where on a clear day it is possible to see above the roofs and masts of Stornoway a hundred-mile stretch of the west coast of Scotland, at its nearest point thirty-five miles away, and in the other direction a wide expanse of the Lewis moor, unbelievably empty in contrast to the fuss of crofts extending up the coast.

When Leverhulme first saw the castle, his mind turned at once to the possibilities of improving it. The Mathesons' furniture was not included in the sale, apart from the Gobelin tapestries in the ball-room and some lovely glass chandeliers which today hang in the drawing-room at Thornton Manor. Leverhulme refurnished the house from top to bottom, concerning himself personally

with such details as the colour of the radiators in the maids'
bedrooms, and the exact position in which the door-knob should
be fitted to a wardrobe. Internally he made two major alterations.
He enlarged the ball-room by throwing into it an adjoining room;
and he equipped the house with electricity, central heating,
additional bathrooms, and internal telephones and bells. None of
this work could be carried out until the winter of 1918-19, and
consequently Lews Castle was not a comfortable house during
the three months of his first long visit. His niece, Mrs Macdonald,
remembers that 'it was dimly lit by flickering gas jets, which
burned lower when the geyser for Lord Leverhulme's bath was
turned on.'[41]

James Simpson was instructed to draw up plans for doubling
the size of the castle, but the work was never even started. Nor
was the garden ever fully developed. It remained much as the
Mathesons had created it, a carefully planned wilderness of oak
and rhododendron, with paths branching to every corner. To this
Leverhulme added a terraced kitchen-garden, a cinder tennis-
court, and (one of his chief legacies to Lewis) the carriage-way
known as the Arnish road which wound along the water-front
to a point just short of the River Creed.

Even in the first year, while the war continued and before his
alterations to the house were begun, Leverhulme entertained
lavishly. The summers of 1919 and 1920 saw Lews Castle
transformed into a brilliant centre of hospitality. His guests were
of three sorts; associates and employees of Lever Brothers;
friends unconnected with his business; and the people of the
island.

The latter were invited to the frequent balls and garden-
parties held at the castle. In the main they were the townspeople,
for outside Stornoway the island had almost no middle-class, and
Leverhulme evidently felt that the crofters' families would be
embarrassed by sudden confrontation with luxury that they could
never have imagined. In the town invitations were so eagerly
sought after that he soon found himself unconsciously giving
offence, as when he invited in error all the tenants of a particular
house, but not the landlady. He appealed to the Provost's wife to
help him out. Mrs Maclean asked to be excused from compiling
a list, 'as it would bring a hornet's nest about my head'. The task
was handed over to the Chamberlain's office, and sooner or later
every person of any consequence in the island had spent one or

more evenings at the castle, dancing to Mrs Logan's band from Inverness or sitting out in the conservatories. Stornoway had never before experienced anything like it. There was a ball on 11 August 1918 for 140 guests from the Fortrose Masonic Lodge; another the next night for 200. The naval officers stationed at Stornoway were entertained the following week, and whenever there was a visit from an outside cruiser or distinguished guest, Leverhulme would seize on it as an excuse for yet another party. He danced every reel, choosing the plainest partners first, and in the intervals, managed to make himself agreeable to every person under his roof. He was the perfect host, the perfect suitor.

His English guests were helped with their difficult journey by the transport department at Port Sunlight. They would find lunch-baskets waiting for them at different stations *en route*, seats booked for them on the train and cabins on the steamer. On arrival they were expected to stay one week at the castle, and another at one of the shooting lodges. Their hostesses were Leverhulme's sisters, Emily and Alice Lever, and in later years, a third sister, Mrs Paul. The non-business guests would be left to amuse themselves, fishing, shooting, walking or sight-seeing in cars; a favourite occupation was to wander round the quays at Stornoway when the island girls were gutting the herring. For the guests in Leverhulme's employment it was not quite such fun. One of them has recalled, 'You were not invited to come to Stornoway. You found a note on your desk telling you exactly when you were expected. You would find there three or four directors of Lever Brothers and their wives, four couples from the executive side, and a strange assortment of other guests, including, perhaps, Sir Harry Lauder, Mrs Kennedy Fraser (the authority on Hebridean folk-song), Olga Nethersole (the actress), Sir Edwin Lutyens, and a Norwegian expert on sea-weed. The staff-members never felt that they were on holiday, for Lord Leverhulme might suddenly send for them to demand an explanation of some letter that they had written three months before and quite forgotten. It was a relief to escape to a shooting lodge.'

In the evening, however, Leverhulme was at his best. His guests might not have seen him all day. He would appear for dinner at about 7 pm invariably in evening dress, brimming over with charm, and behaving as if he had not a care in the world. Even before the island was legally his, he had engaged a piper.

The piper was not always as popular with the guests as he was with Leverhulme. Mrs Macdonald has recorded:

We were piped into dinner by Pipe-Major Macleod in full regimentals, and at first he remained in the room throughout the meal, playing at intervals. This, however, precluded all conversation while he was playing, and although he was a master of his art, it was too noisy a performance at such close quarters, so he was persuaded to stand in the doorway with the drones of his pipes facing the long hallway to the front door.[42]

When the pipes had been muted, Leverhulme dominated his end of the table with anedcotes and chaff. He was not ungenerous in conversation, but his deafness made it one-sided and he was determined to enjoy himself. He kept in his waistcoat pocket a slim notebook in which he would jot down any story that amused him, under the headings 'Scotsmen', 'Lawyers', 'Doctors' and so on, and retail them at his dinner-parties. They were of the simplest kind (shy young man telephoning to his girl: 'Is that you, Miss Brown?' 'Yes.' 'Oh, Miss Brown, I do love you so, and want to know if you will marry me?' 'Why, yes, I should be very pleased. Who are you?' Another favourite was: 'I have spent the best years of my life in the arms of another man's wife—my mother'), but they delighted Leverhulme, and even the most superior of his guests soon found themselves enjoying his enjoyment.

One visitor to the castle, a civil servant who had come on grim business from the Scottish Office, has left this picture of him on one such occasion:

His management of the mixed elements in the party was a master-piece. He seemed to exercise a sort of mesmeric power over his guests, that bent them readily but unconsciously to his will. . . . There was music, dancing and some very good singing—in English and Gaelic—and much merriment. At one stage a few of the young girls called for a song from Lord Leverhulme. 'Ladies! Ladies!' he protested. 'You know I cannot sing. I just croak!' But the lassies jingo-ringed him, chanting:

> 'Lord Leverhulme for the bathing-song!
> Lord Leverhulme for the bathing-song!'

He pretended to be shocked. 'That dreadful song!' But the insistent chant continued. Then with dramatic suddenness he agreed. 'Very well; if you insist, I shall sing a song—and I shall sing the bathing-

song.' It was quite true. He couldn't sing; he could only croak. And
that versatile little man croaked heartily through a song which would
make an Irish navvy blush.

As *encore*, in the Irish dialect, he gave an excellent recitation, dis-
playing real humour and histrionic ability of a high order. Soon after
the recitation, when everything was going noisily and merrily, I felt a
firm grip on my bicep, and a quiet voice said in my ear, 'Let us go over
to a quiet place, behind the pillars. I want to have a word with you.'[43]

At the end of the evening he would run up the stairs two steps
at a time, even when he was over seventy, to show how young
and vigorous he was. His bed-time did not lift a weight from the
party; it extinguished a light.

Few people ever saw his bedroom at Lews Castle while he was
still alive. It is now the book-store for the technical college, and
the walls are lined with shelves. But it is not so greatly altered
that one cannot visualise the horrid little cupboard in which he
chose to sleep. It is not quite so exposed as the open-air bedroom
at Thorton Manor. At least there are four walls. But there is only
one window, six foot from the floor, and even if Leverhulme had
been tall enough to see out of it, he would have had no view
(from a castle in that incomparable position!) except of a back
yard closed by a high granite wall. There was no glass in the
window and no ceiling below the loose tiles. The rain drove in
from both directions, and the present caretaker, who was there in
Leverhulme's day, points out the runnel in the asphalt floor
which connects with a gutter to drain the water off. Opposite
this cell, down a short flight of steps, was his dressing-room,
equally plain; it is still fitted with the shelves where he put his
clothes.

The private office, or 'sanctum', was, however, a spacious room
at the front of the castle, overlooking from its windows the 'hub
of the universe', the fishing-quays of Stornoway. The window-
frame cuts the town to about its size during the Cromwellian
period. Next to it was a larger room for the secretaries. In his
sanctum Leverhulme started his working-day at his usual hour
of 5 am, sipping a cup of tea, and preparing his reports and
letters for dictation after breakfast. He usually dictated at great
speed to three shorthand-writers simultaneously, so that what
one of them missed, another might catch, and he would be spared
the distraction of repeating it. A fourth secretary waited in the
background for verbal instructions, and from time to time an

expert was called in from next door or from more agreeable occupations below. In the last three years of his life (it is curious that he did not think of it earlier) he saved his time by a system of coloured labels, a different colour for each secretary, which he attached to a letter or report, putting a tick against the form of answer that he wanted—'Acknowledge', 'Accept', 'Will not', 'Précis', 'Translate', and so forth—from which the secretary would draft for his signature a suitable reply.

It should be remembered that Leverhulme was followed by his colossal business interests wherever he went, and that when he was in Stornoway he was not on holiday, nor dealing exclusively with his Hebridean schemes. He insisted on receiving reports weekly, in some cases daily, from about fifty of his chief executives, and it was these that he read from 5 am onwards, scoring them with remarks in blunt red pencil or green ink. A single example will show how he burned up his energy, and that of his staff, by this constant process of written cross-examination. The Secretary of Lever Brothers, L. V. Fildes, reported to him that the Company had lost a very minor court case, involving £15. Leverhulme scrawled on the letter:

In my experience, cases are lost for one of three reasons: (1) Because the case should never have been brought at all. (2) It was badly presented. (3) It was badly prepared. Report to me under which of these three categories this case falls.

Fildes replied:

There can be a fourth category: that the case was wrongly decided. We are appealing.

Leverhulme minuted:

Approved. Let me have further details.

Such concern for every facet of his business may seem absurd, and to many it did. But it was his way of working. He refused to let mere distance weaken his control. He awaited the daily post with hunger. Sometimes, by elaborate arrangement, it was delivered to him at intermediate stations on a railway journey; or a member of the staff would be instructed to join a long-distance train for a ten-mile journey and a fifteen-minute talk with 'the Chief', until they reached the point on the line where the next member of the staff was waiting to take over; or a group of employees would follow his car in another, to be called forward one by one for consultation. The method only worked because Leverhulme had a superlative memory as well as great zest. Obviously he could not carry with him the vast files of current correspondence stored at Port Sunlight or Lever House in London. So he carried them in his head, and it was very rarely that he was found contradicting himself or sending for a figure.

The estate staff at Stornoway, particularly the Chamberlain, Charles Orrock, and his successor after September 1920, Captain A. M. Fletcher, adapted themselves with astonishing ease to the human tornado which had hit the sleepy island. To read through the fat folders of their letters to Leverhulme forty years after they were written, is a lesson in equanimity, efficiency and patience. His own letters to them were correspondingly appreciative and to the point. But the letters were incessant. When he was in the island, and his Chamberlain was available for immediate interview, the stream showed no sign of abating. From his room across the strip of water (he had only to walk to the window to see the office to which he was addressing all these urgent enquiries), Leverhulme wrote twelve separate letters to Orrock in the course of the single morning, 26 September 1918, and it was not exceptional. They dealt with the following subjects:

1 The use of donkeys for carrying peats.
2 List of bonus-payments to the game-keepers.
3 Government proposals for taking over farms.
4 Design of the Lewis war-memorial.
5 Extermination of rats.
6 Town Clerk to be thanked for an illuminated address.
7 This letter dealt with several subjects:
   i Site for Sanatorium.
   ii Reclamation of waste land.
   iii Title-deeds of the estate.
   iv Stornoway harbour development.
   v Contract of service for game-keepers.
   vi Applications for crofts.
8 Come to tea this afternoon, bringing a one-inch map.
9 Leases in Stornoway.
10 The Pipe-Major is entitled to free fuel.
11 Export of peat to Port Sunlight.
12 'I have bought the Stornoway Gas-Light Company.'

These letters were not mere notes. The letter about donkeys, for example, extended to five pages. ('Each donkey ought to carry two creels of peat on each side—total four—being the burden that four women can carry. One woman would be required to lead the donkey—therefore one donkey and one woman would do the work of four women. I do not want the donkeys to have special creels made, but. . . .' And so on). How many letters were dispatched all over the world that day, if this was the quota for one small office in one small island!

He would have had no time to shoot or fish, even if he had enjoyed it. As it happened, he hated it. He had thus described duck-shooting at Thornton Manor: 'Up goes 10/-, bang goes 2d, down comes half-a-crown!' For a man who had just bought one of the most famous sporting estates in the world, Leverhulme showed remarkable indignation at the waste of time and money that the sport involved. He had quite enjoyed engaging a head-keeper, for he wished to do everything expected of his new status; but when he discovered how large was the retinue which the keeper had gathered about him, even Leverhulme was appalled:

I am not at all enamoured with the game-keeping side of life here in Lewis. It does not appeal to me at all to keep a number of strong healthy men looking after pheasants, rabbits, deer, salmon etc., when the country is wanting men to make roads, cultivate the soil for food and carry on the life of the nation. I feel myself entirely out of sympathy with it.[44]

During the first three years, however, he kept all the sporting rights of the estate in his own hands, except the beautifully situated lodge of Eishken on Loch Shell, which he allowed Mrs Platt, the sitting tenant and widow of the builder of the lodge, to retain together with the 42,500 acres of the Park deer-forest. The other lodges in the island had all been built by Sir James Matheson: Grimersta, with salmon-fishing said to be the best in Europe, and worth £2,000 a year in rent; Morsgail near Loch Langhabat; Uig on the Atlantic coast; and Soval, with its grouse moor. Leverhulme found them useful annexes to the castle, and a means of amusing his guests and repaying business obligations. But by refusing to let them, he was depriving himself of the laird's chief source of revenue. He could not have demonstrated more effectively to the islanders that his purpose in coming to Lewis was not to make money.

Every afternoon Leverhulme excaped from his office and visited some part of the island. While the war lasted he was rationed for petrol, as if, he said, he wanted it for joy-rides. But this did not prevent him from acquiring a fleet of open Ford vans, later painted yellow to give warning of his approach, in which he travelled with Orrock or a guest from the castle, exposed to the biting winds of the wide moors. On these expeditions he wore the same old-fashioned clothes as he did at Port Sunlight, the cut-away frock-coat. spongebag trousers, white bow-tie, high Victorian collar and tall grey bowler, adding to his wardrobe only an overcoat of Harris tweed and, later, a plus-four suit of the same material. He never adopted a tartan, which was in any case little worn by the people themselves. His appearance became familiar throughout the island.

He was welcome everywhere, not only for what he was, but for what he might bring. In Stornoway, he had many official duties to perform and his difficulty was to confine his engagements to the minimum that would not give offence. As proprietor he was *ex officio* chairman of such bodies as the Stornoway Harbour Commission, a position which provided him with his initial opportunities to discuss with the public men of the island his plans for its development, without giving the impression of intrusion into their affairs. Later there was no question of intrusion: he became the island's leading businessman and counsellor, as well as its sole landlord, and he was able to request special meetings of all the public bodies whenever he had some special announcement to make. He soon became the person to whom they instinctively turned when any matter arose affecting the island as a whole. Thus he lent the castle grounds for a great garden-party in September 1918 in aid of war-savings, and persuaded Lord Strathclyde to make a special journey to Lewis to address the gathering. (A telegram from Leverhulme to Strathclyde survives: 'Could we have visit from flying-machine? Enormous stimulus and attraction. Tank impossible on Lewis Island.' The answer was No.).

A good example of Leverhulme's method of approach is provided by the discussion on the Lewis war-memorial. Even before the war was over, he invited himself to a meeting of the special war-memorial committee, and laid before them his 'thoughts'. He suggested that they should consider a combined memorial for both soldiers and sailors, and that it should take the form of a work of art, not a utility building like an ex-servicemen's club or welfare centre, which in the course of years would become little more than a familiar rendezvous, its original purpose forgotten. The site, he went on, observing that the first suggestions had gone down well, should be one where the memorial would be visible from every part of the town and to every ship entering the harbour: perhaps on the South Beach itself. Then came the sweetener: 'a resident in the island' was willing to give £5,000 as an opening contribution to the fund. There was laughter and applause. A week later, Leverhulme appeared before the committee again. 'A distinguished architect who happened to be staying at the castle' had made a rough sketch of the sort of thing he had in mind, but he proposed that the final design should be open to competition among all the architects of Scotland. The memorial, he suggested, should be 'a tower with five storeys, and a room on each, in which the names of the dead could be recorded, not on vellum, which could decay, nor on stone, which could be chipped, but in bronze, which would last through the centuries.' (*Loud applause*). The idea was carried out, and the memorial was dedicated by Leverhulme in 1924 on his last visit to Stornoway. There the tower stands today, not, it is true, on the South Beach, but on a hill a little way out of the town, a memorial to the dead, but in a lesser degree, to Lever-hulme's tact, initiative and generosity.

When he visited the country districts, his arrival was often unheralded and even unpremeditated. He would knock on the door of a black-house like a conscientious parliamentary candidate, and compliment the family on 'their comfortable cottage', stifling the indignation and nausea which the sight and smell aroused in him. At other times, it was arranged for him to meet the entire male population of the township in the school-house. Often he was presented at the start of such meetings with a written statement of their needs—a road, a fence, a jetty, a mill for grinding corn. On these occasions Lewis seemed to him almost mediaeval in its backwardness and feudal reliance on its laird. He would address the people with equal simplicity, speaking with deliberate slowness to an audience unaccustomed to the English language, and still less to hearing it spoken with a Lancashire intonation. He was sometimes able to promise what they asked. Yes, he would send his surveyor to mark out the route for a road to Grimshader; he would try to arbitrate between the

4. The peat-bogs of Lewis, looking south to the mountains of Harris

5. Crofting-lands, looking north from near Stornoway

6. Lews Castle, Stornoway, in 1960

7. Stornoway seen from the window of Leverhulme's study in Lews Castle. Foreground, the inner fishing-harbour; centre, Goat Island, linked to the mainland by a modern causeway; background, the Beast of Holm (on which the *Iolaire* foundered), facing the Arnish light across the harbour entrance

conflicting peat-claims of neighbouring townships in the parish
of Lochs; he would see what could be done to repair the harbour
at Ness and at Bragor. But whether he was able to satisfy them or
not, Leverhulme never met with any hostile demonstrations
during these progresses through the island. The children
gathered in knots by the road to wave as he passed, and there were
pathetic displays of bunting. Even in the districts which had been
most severely hit by the evictions, he was not held to blame for
past history. The land-question was scarcely raised in his
presence at the village meetings. Their demands, politely reiterated in township after township, were for the minimum
facilities to help them live their ancient way of life. 'Let us hope
that his Lordship's visit to Tolsta will be a means of giving us a
road through the village.' 'We hope Lord Leverhulme will give
us new peat-cutting grounds.' 'We explained to him that our great
need is for a cart-road; we have only a path, more like a peat-bog
than a road.' Such was the tone of the weekly reports sent in by
the outlying country districts to the local newspaper. They reveal
neither sycophancy nor a spirit of unrest. During the summer of
1918 there was an atmosphere in the island, for the first time in
a century, of optimism and trust.

Leverhulme did everything he could to foster it in the short
time before the soldiers returned. At this stage he did not speak
much in public about the details of his schemes, while intensi-
fying his private surveys and consultations. He concentrated on
making himself acceptable as a person. 'I am not so foolish, as to
think I can teach people who have lived here all their lives,' he
told the Masonic Lodge on 10 July. 'I can teach them nothing at
all. I have to learn everything, and you will find me a very willing
and attentive pupil.' He kept his word. He learned so rapidly
that soon he overtook his instructors. The complexities of
Scottish land-law, the tortured history of the island, the secrets of
the fishing and tweed industries, were mastered one by one. He
began to use naturally in his daily conversation and correspond-
dence words quite unknown to him a few weeks before: to say
'manse' for vicarage, 'Provost' for Mayor, 'policy' for park,
'park' for field, 'feu' for lease. He interested himself in every
detail of the island's life, whether it was the proprietor's responsibility or not. Sometimes he purchased his right to be consulted
by a donation, but more often he achieved his object by taking
infinite pains to make friends. Here are three examples. When,

F

by an oversight, he once failed to put a contribution in the collection-box at the United Free Presbyterian Church which he attended every Sunday, a cheque for £5 was sent to the Minister on Monday. A Stornoway solicitor who had disagreed with him over a small point of law was at once invited to dinner at the castle, and when he declined on the grounds that 'I should be sorry to mar by my presence what I am sure will be a pleasant party', Leverhulme replied, 'For myself, I always make it a rule never to close a door. Life is short and quarrels long, so away with them.' The solicitor and his wife were at the castle next day. When an old crofter-woman called on him with some petition, Leverhulme received her 'like a duchess', invited her to have tea with him and his guests, and when she demurred, had her served in a room apart.

The multiplication of such small incidents, which immediately became known throughout the island, combined with his generosity, energy, and the evident delight that he took in his new property, gradually transformed welcome into near-adulation. One of the most level-headed of Stornoway's public men was quoted as saying: 'I believe that in the person of Lord Leverhulme, humanly speaking, the redeemer of our island has come amongst us'; and when Leverhulme presented certificates to the children at the Nicolson Institute, the chairman remarked, 'he is in danger of being saintified' (*sic*). The news of his success spread as far as Lewis exiles in America, where at a dinner in Boston on 18 December 1918, 'the enthusiasm which prevailed when the toast of Lord Leverhulme was proposed was striking evidence of his popularity among Lewis folks in all corners of the globe.'[45] They regarded him as the prototype of a new twentieth-century laird, one who lived the part but did not act it, and who scorned to consider his task complete when he had acquired a castle and a piper, surrounded himself with ghillies, and distributed a little free fuel to the poorer tenantry. If here and there in the island misgivings were expressed in private, they have not been recorded. An echo of the agitation for land was still reaching Lewis from men serving overseas, who tended to regard Leverhulme's schemes as an added benefit, not as an alternative to the land; and the agitation was to swell in volume during the succeeding autumn and winter of 1918–1919, when political controversy was stimulated by the General Election and the servicemen began returning to their homes. The reaction forms the central part of this narrative. But a reaction it was. When Leverhulme left the island on 27 September 1918 after three strenuous months, he did not doubt, whatever the attitude of the Government might be, that he had succeeded in winning the respect of the people. He knew that it would take longer to win their hearts.

He heard of the Armistice as he sat in his London office, and wrote at once to the Chamberlain:

I have just received the glad news that fighting ceased at 11 a.m. today. So the war is now over, and we can get down to business with a light heart, and with determination to overcome all difficulties and obstacles in bringing prosperity and success to Lewis and its people.[46]

The news was given to the people of Stornoway by the sounding of the ships' sirens in the bay. Leverhulme telegraphed to the Provost offering to pay all the expenses of the celebrations, and gave an additional week's wages to his staff. He returned to Lewis for six days at the end of November, in the middle of the Election campaign, and in an important speech outlined his proposals for the future. But scarcely had there been time for the people to grasp the enormous implications of his plan, than the island was hit by the greatest disaster in its history, an event which sent a shudder of horror throughout the world.

On 31 December 1918, a party of five hundred servicemen, the great majority of them from Lewis, were waiting at Kyle of Lochalsh to complete the last stage of their journey home on leave. Five hundred passengers were beyond the capacity of the little mailboat *Sheila*, and HM Yacht *Iolaire* was sent to Kyle by the naval authorities to bring the remainder to Stornoway in time for them to spend New Year's Day with their families. The soldiers in the party, and a few civilians, embarked on the *Sheila*. About 260 men, all naval ratings, were assigned to the *Iolaire*, which sailed from Kyle at 7.30 pm, an hour ahead of the other ship. By midnight a gale was blowing from the south, but as all on board were sailors, and for some this was their first leave since the beginning of the war, the weather did not greatly disturb them, and they celebrated the passing of the old year with immense enthusiasm. The ship had then reached the middle of the Minch, just short of the Shiant Islands. Less than two hours later they sighted the familiar Arnish light, marking the entrance to Stornoway harbour, and began assembling their gear for the great welcome that they knew awaited them at the quay.

At 1.55 am on 1 January 1919, the *Iolaire* struck the rock known as the Beast of Holm at the eastern side of the harbour entrance, opposite the Arnish light. The cause of the disaster was never established for certain, in spite of an exhaustive public enquiry, since all the officers perished. The rumour that the captain and navigating officer were drunk was exposed at the enquiry as quite baseless, and it was eventually decided that 'an over-running of the course, a mere error of judgment, was sufficient to account for what had happened.'

Immediately after the impact, the ship listed heavily to starboard, and huge waves broke over her. Some sixty men were washed into the sea, or jumped to save themselves. None of them was ever seen alive again. The stern of the *Iolaire* was only a few yards from dry land, but there was a great rush of water between the ship and the rocks, and in the total darkness, it was impossible for a man to see in which direction safety lay. By the light of rocket-flares many more were tempted to risk the jump, only to perish by drowning or being dashed against the rocks. Two boats were lowered, but both were immediately smashed to pieces. As the ship settled down, she turned broadside to the shore, breaking the force of the sea and allowing a few of the survivors to struggle ashore. One of them, Seaman J. F. Macleod, managed to swim to the rocks with a life-line, followed by a hawser, by which several more lives were saved. An hour-and-a-half after striking, the ship foundered. When the first rescue party arrived from Stornoway, all that could be seen of the *Iolaire* were her masts, to one of which a man was clinging. The storm was still so violent that he could not be brought off until dawn.

Of the 285 men on board, including the crew, 206 lost their lives. There was scarcely a house in the island not mourning the death of a son, husband or close friend. No list of passengers had been compiled in the hurry of their departure from Kyle, and many of the seamen had not been able to warn their families that they were returning home. Consequently people went to express their sympathy to their neighbours, only to find, when the remaining bodies were washed ashore, that they too had lost their men. 'This unspeakable tragedy', as Orrock described it in an immediate telegram to Leverhulme, numbed the island. The great crowd which had assembled at the harbour to greet both the new year and their returning friends remained in ignorance of the terrible event taking place barely one mile away from where they stood, until the first stragglers from the wreck reached the town. When the people gazed at the scene of the disaster in daylight, it seemed unbelievable that so few had managed to cross those twenty feet of water to the shore. All this had taken place almost within their own harbour, on a point of land at which many of them had looked every day of their lives. That the men should have died like this after surviving four years of war was hard enough; that they should have died on their native rocks was unendurable.

What could Leverhulme do? Of course he telegraphed his deep condolences. Of course he contributed generously to the relief fund, and spoke at many public meetings in England and Scotland in support of it. He also travelled north as soon as possible, and had himself rowed to the site of the wreck. But this was a tragedy beyond the solace of any proprietor. It is still talked of with horror in the islands.

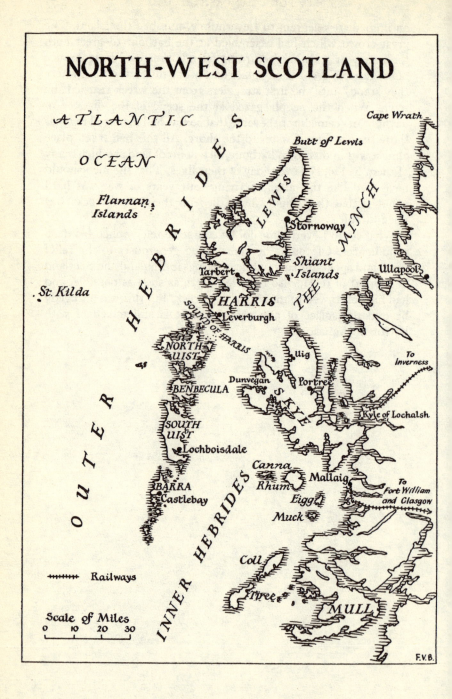

# NORTH-WEST SCOTLAND

ATLANTIC

OCEAN

Cape Wrath

Butt of Lewis

Flannan
Islands

LEWIS

THE MINCH

Stornoway

Shiant
Islands

Ullapool

Tarbert

St. Kilda

HARRIS
Leverburgh

SOUND OF HARRIS

NORTH
UIST

Uig

To
Inverness

Dunvegan

BENBECULA

Portree

SKYE

Kyle of Lochalsh

SOUTH
UIST

Lochboisdale

OUTER HEBRIDES

Canna

Rhum

Mallaig

To
Fort William
and Glasgow

BARRA
Castlebay

INNER HEBRIDES

Eigg

Muck

Coll

Railways

Tiree

MULL

Scale of Miles
0   10   20   30

F.V.B.

# Chapter Four

# FISHERMEN, NOT FARMERS

ALTHOUGH INITIALLY HE concealed, even from his friends, his deeper motives for coming to Lewis, Leverhulme's own mind was made up soon after his first exploratory visits. Subsequently his purpose never wavered. When circumstances forced him to leave Lewis, he transferred precisely the same ideals to Harris. He expressed them over and over again, publicly and privately. As it would be a pity to dilute his words by paraphrase, his main argument will be given here as far as possible as he stated it himself, in interviews, speeches and letters spread over a number of years.

He started from the assumption that the abolition of poverty was among the noblest of human undertakings:

Surely our ambitions are a better life for each of us, more equal distribution of wealth, higher wages in order to attain to a better living, more plentiful supply of all that we require in the way of boots, shoes and clothing, better houses—homes with gardens, homes that are really places in which a soul can live and expand, and not caves in which we can crouch out of the light.[47]

In the Hebrides he had found a degree of hardship and poverty which shocked him:

At the present time you see young men leaving the island to escape poverty; you see children watching the cattle all the live-long day on the wind-swept grazings; you see women carrying creels of peat on their backs, a weight of 80 lbs, while in the Congo no negro woman is allowed by law to carry more than 44 lbs; and you see the men coming back from the sea with fish that must either be consumed in the village or salted and packed in barrels—the least remunerative way of selling that hard-won harvest. These people are not adding to their happiness. They are merely existing.[48]

His purpose was to rescue the people from this needless indignity:

75

The service I wish to render is that of an attempt to introduce a higher scale of living and of greater opportunities for happiness and well-being to the fine people of the Western Isles. I have travelled around the world and I find Lewis and Harris men honoured and respected and filling the highest positions in Canada, Boston, New York and elsewhere throughout our colonies. It is only in their own native island that they are living under conditions of squalor and misery.[49]

These conditions had previously existed elsewhere in the United Kingdom, and had been remedied without resort to mass emigration, almost the only 'policy' that Lewis had ever known:

I have recently been reading up the history of my native town of Bolton, and I have been much struck by the similarity in some respects between it and Lewis. In about 1790 the people had to get their meal from Preston and Manchester. So they were led to turn their attention to industrial pursuits, with a result that Bolton became more prosperous than any other district of Lancashire. . . . If the Lews were peopled on the same scale as Lancashire, it would have a population of about two million. Of course we do not want that, and I grant that if Lewis is to remain a purely crofting community, it is already over-populated. But the point I wish to make is that those who say that Lewis has a greater population than it can sustain, are talking through their hats![50]

Following the same train of thought, he told a press-reporter two months later that he hoped 'to show that it was possible to do for Lewis what Samuel Crompton did for Lancashire'.[51] He considered that the answer to the island's problem was not emigration, but an actual increase in population, say from 30,000 to 60,000, sustained by some degree of industrialisation. What degree? Certainly not the conversion of the whole population into factory-hands, but the introduction of reasonably modern methods into their existing native industries. The islanders considered that they had no industries. But they had; fishing and weaving. The men took naturally to fishing, the woman to weaving. The only reason why they remained so poor was that they added to these two occupations, a third—their crofts. A croft was clearly uneconomic. The value of its produce averaged 8/- a week, far less than the value of the labour spent upon it, and the constant subdivision of crofts by cottars and squatters reduced it still further. Crofting prevented a man from giving his full attention to what should be his proper job, fishing. The crofter's year was a succession of compromises with competing claims on his time; in the early spring he was line-fishing off Lewis; he broke off to prepare his land for the sowing; in June he went herring-fishing; in the late summer he was back on the land harvesting his croft; in the autumn he returned to herring-fishing. To Leverhulme such a dispersal of energy was fantastic:

At present the Lewisman is only what I call an amateur fisherman. Stornoway people tell me that they won't employ Lewismen on their boats, because the crofter must leave his trawler or drifter in the springtime to attend to his croft. Fancy running a newspaper on those lines! Imagine what it would be like if all the reporters and sub-editors of the *Scotsman* had crofts, and went away to tend them for two or three weeks at a time![52]

So if they wished to improve their standard of living (as surely they must), they would have to choose between crofting and fishing; and of the two, they should choose fishing. Of this Lever-hulme was in no doubt. 'Crofting today is entirely an impossible life for these fine people.'[53] He would help them to shake them-selves free of its crippling conventions:

The great wealth of Lewis is in the surrounding sea, and not in the land. The only recovery, it seems to me, can be reaping the harvest of the sea and establishing industries in the island; and so gradually find employment for the people, apart altogether from their small crofts, out of which it would be impossible under any circumstances whatever, even freed of all payments of rents or rates, for the people to make a living. On the other hand, out of the harvest of the sea there ought to be a basis for solid prosperity in the island.[54]

There was another point-of-view on crofting, held with equal intensity by some of the crofters and their supporters outside the islands. It will be given its proper place and emphasis in this account. For the present purpose, only Leverhulme's attitude is important, for it governed his entire approach to the Lewis problem. 'These are fishermen,' he had said to James Simpson, 'not farmers.' Later he attempted under stress to deny that he was an opponent of the crofting-system. His letters, and some of his early speeches, make it clear that he regarded it as the cause of all the island's troubles. He did not wish to evict any man from his only home. He had been horrified by his reading of the events

of fifty and more years before. But he hoped to provide opportunities that would induce many to leave the crofting life of their
own accord, and he foresaw that their success and evident
happiness would lead eventually to the abandonment of crofting
throughout the island.

Leverhulme estimated that it would cost £5 million 'to give
Lewis a fair start.'[55] Who was to pay? There were only two
possibilities, himself or the Government. Few people in the
island had any spare capital, and the budgets of the local authorities were already overstretched. Lever Brothers could not help,
for his purchase of Lewis had nothing to do with his Company.
He was very willing to provide a large proportion of the initial
capital out of his own pocket, for he feared that if he left it to
government departments to carry out this revolution in the
island's economy, even should they agree with him that it was
soundly based, only confusion, delay and parsimony would
result:

Reports from Royal Commissions and visiting Commissioners, thick
as leaves in Valombrosa, have been the dominating feature of Government policy in the Highlands and Islands of Scotland. The invariable
rule seems to have been, where expenditure of public money was
recommended by such commissions, for the Government either to
ignore such reports or to cut down expenditure so penuriously as only
to result in the waste of public money by not spending the full amount
required. . . . Lewis and Harris have been too long the Cinderella in
the Government pantomime.[56]

But he did not refuse under any circumstances to accept aid from
public funds. Indeed, for the improvements to Stornoway harbour
and the projected island railway, he invited the Government to
carry the whole capital cost. He was not successful in either of
these two applications.

He was also anxious for contributions from island businessmen,
not because he expected to obtain much money from this source,
but in order to involve them in his schemes as closely as possible.
He was most scrupulous in his dealings with them. He would not
set up any new industry in Lewis which would be in direct
rivalry with an existing one; and he refused to exercise that
remarkable option of a Lewis laird, to prevent the establishment
of any new business in local competition with one owned by the
laird himself. He hoped that Lewismen would invest in his

companies, but he did not want them to stand the risk, 'for there is a strong element of uncertainty in every one of them.'[57] He therefore offered to put up a minimum of sixty per cent of the capital required for each company, and any capital needed beyond sixty per cent that was not subscribed. He went even further. He guaranteed to buy back at par the shares of any subscriber who wished to sell them within a period of two years after purchase. The local shareholders were also to have representatives on the Boards. 'Thus there is really no speculative element for people in Lewis, and I am very anxious to avoid anything which looks like company promotion in this undertaking.'[58] It is significant that this handsome offer, combined with Leverhulme's unrivalled reputation as a man of business, did not lead to a rush of applications for shares. He found himself having to provide eighty-eight per cent of the capital for his main company; and some of the original applicants cried off before it was even launched. But there were others more confident. The Provost of Stornoway, Murdo Maclean, wrote to him in August 1918, 'My intention is to take shares for myself, my son and daughters, and also for three of my employees. To use a Scotch expression. "I wish to dip my laddle in them all".'

. Leverhulme at first found no difficulty in providing the enormous sums required. He had simply to sell out some of his preference shares in Lever Brothers, or to lodge them with his banks, where his credit in 1918 stood as high as any man's in the country. There were some mutterings among the shareholders of Lever Brothers that the Chairman was risking their money as well as his, because if he met with disaster in the Hebrides, the Company was bound to suffer too. Leverhulme waved these objections aside: Lewis was much less of a risk than the Congo, and look what had happened there! He did, however make a genuine effort to keep his Hebridean accounts quite separate from his main Company's, and gave instructions that 'on no account must the business of Stornoway interfere with the business of Port Sunlight.' He was the first to break the latter rule. A succession of experts from Merseyside and London were ordered to report to the Chief at Lews Castle—geologists, architects, engineers, naturalists, chemists, ichthyologists, agronomists and gas-men, as well as innumerable secretaries and special advisers, who may or may not have been on Lever Brothers' pay-roll. Some of them stayed for months, a few for years. Others, like James Simpson, the head of the architectural department at Port Sunlight, Sir Edgar Sanders, who was in charge of Leverhulme's personal office in London, and Carl Holmboe, an indefatigable Norwegian who knew about everything, paid fleeting visits to Stornoway and at other times kept in touch with Leverhulme by correspondence.

Leverhulme was fond of repeating that his object in the Hebrides was neither philanthropy nor money-making. In fact it was both. He was laying out a great slice of his personal fortune on projects like island roads which could not possibly show a return on his capital, and more directly he made princely gifts to the island, like the site for a tuberculosis sanatorium and his many donations to local funds, quite apart from his large expenditure on the upkeep of the sporting estates from which he derived no personal enjoyment or profit at all, but which kept many men in employment. His offer to guarantee the investors in his companies against any loss, and the uneconomic terms on which he leased the houses that he built in Stornoway and elsewhere, were not the actions of a man unmoved by sentiment.

But equally, he expected to make an eventual profit from his enterprises. By any standards, particularly his own, a failure to make money would mean the failure of his idea. He would show the world what could be done to raise a primitive community from the torpor of centuries, but it was little use doing so if his achievement depended on the constant injection of fresh capital; and who was to inject it when he had gone? Nobody can seriously doubt the idealism of Leverhulme's work in Lewis and Harris; but he had a strong business incentive too. That he sometimes (but not quite always) denied it publicly, was a measure of his sensitiveness to criticism. The soap-boiler gibe still hurt. Now he was to become a fishmonger too. He did not want it to be said that he was exploiting the Outer Hebrides, which held such a special place in British affections, as it had been hinted that he had exploited the Solomon Islands of the Pacific. So he played down both the money-making and the philanthropic sides of his work almost to the point of self-contradiction; by rejecting philanthropy, he was saying that he intended to make a profit; by rejecting the business motive, he was engaging in philanthropy. The only effect of this contradictory disavowal was to make his detractors scoff the more.

When Leverhulme bought the island of Lewis, he knew as little about fish as he had known about soap when he rented his first factory at Warrington. 'I never thought about fish until I came here,' he admitted.[59] However, by intensive reading and questioning, he soon acquired a sound working knowledge of the catching, curing and marketing of fish, and within a few months was suggesting ideas which amazed men who had spent their whole lives in the industry. To make it clear why Leverhulme saw such immense possibilities in the Lewis fisheries, it will be necessary to describe briefly the nature of the Hebridean industry, and the position as he saw it in the early part of 1918.

Edible sea-fish are of two sorts: the white-fish, like cod and haddock, which feed near the bottom of the sea; and the 'pelagic' fish like the herring, which shoal near the top. White-fish are caught in two ways: by local line-fishing near the coasts; and by deep-sea trawlers which scoop up the fish in great bag-nets, venturing as far as Iceland for their catch. Herring are caught mainly by drifters, which are rarely absent from their home-ports for more than twenty-four hours; the drift-nets are lowered into the water so that they float vertically about eighteen feet below the surface, at right-angles to the direction taken by a shoal of herring, which swim into the net and are caught in the meshes by their gills.

All three types of fishing, line, trawling and drifting, were carried out in Hebridean waters, but of the three, drifting for herring was about ten times more important, in terms of the weight and value of the catch, than all the other forms of fishing combined.* Stornoway was not even listed in official publications among the major Scottish white-fish ports. Its treasure was the herring, and three herrings appear in the town's armorial device, above the words 'God's Providence is our Inheritance.' Leverhulme was delighted when he first discovered this motto. It concisely expressed his own thoughts.

The advantages of Stornoway as a herring port were four. It had the longest fishing season of any British port; the herring was the finest in quality of any caught in European waters; the fishing grounds, except for those in the Clyde area, were the most sheltered in Britain and the most economical to work; and

---

* In 1919, the figures for landings at the Hebridean ports were:

|  | Herrings | White-fish |
|---|---|---|
| Weight | 341,283 cwts. | 37,972 cwts. |
| Value | £271,479 | £19,256 |

Stornoway harbour was safe and accessible in all weathers.[60] Each of these claims needs examination.

The best herring fishing in the Minch fell in two seasons: the winter fishing of January, February and March; and the summer fishing of May, June and July. Before the first World War the summer fishing was the more profitable, but owing to changes in fishing policy due to the war itself, the winter had now become the peak season in the Minch. This did not mean that the summer herring had disappeared; it was simply not being pursued so vigorously as before. Leverhulme was advised by his experts that 'fish are in fact available all the year round, and it only requires local fishermen to go out regularly.'[61] This advice was to have a great influence on his plans, for it meant that Stornoway might become an all-season fishing harbour, just as coastal holiday towns do their utmost to establish a reputation as all-season resorts. It attracts a broader range of customer and ensures continuity of local employment.

But, of course, no large fishing port depends mainly for its trade upon boats based locally. All herring boats follow the fish in their predictable but unexplained migrations, and temporarily use the port nearest to the best fishing grounds of the moment. Drifters from the east coast of Scotland and England crowded into Stornoway harbour during its best seasons, and migrated to the North Sea during the later summer and autumn. The richest fishing of all was off Yarmouth and Lowestoft in October and November, when not only the few local drifters from Stornoway joined the great Scottish fleets in East Anglia, but thousands of Lewis girls went with them, travelling, living and working in conditions of acute discomfort, to gut the herrings and pack the barrels. Leverhulme could not alter this annual cycle: the majority of the boats would continue to follow the majority of the fish. But he hoped to prolong the Stornoway season sufficiently at each end to make it worth while for many of the men and girls to work for him all the year round, and to attract to Stornoway other types of boat, like the deep-sea trawlers, which would make it a main port-of-call, if not their base.

Stornoway's second advantage is the quality of its fish. The Minch summer herring is known as the 'matje' or 'maiden' herring, caught late in May and during the whole month of June before the formation of the roe. It is a luxury herring, not very large, but fat and particularly rich in oil. As a food it is greatly esteemed. In many places all over the world, it is still sold under the distinctive name of the 'Stornoway herring', and before the first war, it was said to be the only cured herring which the Americans regarded as a delicacy.

There are several ways of eating the matje. It can, of course, be eaten fresh within twenty-four hours of being taken from the sea. But owing to its unusual oiliness, it deteriorates rapidly and must then be cured by one of several methods. In Leverhulme's day, before quick-freezing was known, the most usual form of cure was by pickling. The herrings were gutted and tightly packed with salt in barrels. After the matje had formed its roe from July onwards, it was subjected to a harder form of cure. Seventy-five per cent of the herring catch was dealt with in one of these two ways before 1914. It was the main industry of Stornoway, from where hundreds of thousands of barrels were shipped annually, mostly to destinations in eastern Europe through the Baltic ports. In Germany and Russia, particularly, it was regarded as a cheap but excellent diet. It was eaten raw (although pickling was itself a form of cooking), and it would not have been considered strange to serve a cured matje in the best restaurants of St Petersburg. The British people, however, would not eat it in this form. They considered that pickled fish was a degrading diet. They would only eat the matje fresh, 'klondyked' (boxed in salt and ice), kippered, or, if they were gourmets, as bloaters. It is not necessary to describe these other methods of cure. It need only be emphasised that pickling had been the usual pre-war method; that it was carried out all over the country almost entirely by Scottish girls; that three-quarters of the product of the Hebridean herring fishing was exported in this form; and that Leverhume felt it to be wasteful of the excellent quality of the fish.

The harbour at Stornoway is the only completely sheltered stretch of deep water on the east coast of Lewis, and it is ideally situated for fishing both the Minch and (by a short journey round the Butt) the Atlantic as well. It is the last harbour between the north-west of Scotland and the Icelandic and Newfoundland trawling grounds. It is an outpost, and yet a centre; a short run from the mainland, but within easy reach of the ocean. Only Castlebay in Barra provided any competition to Stornoway among the harbours of the Hebrides, and Castlebay's contribution in 1917 was only one-fortieth part of Stornoway's.

Leverhulme may therefore have given a wrong impression to outsiders when he so frequently spoke of developing the potential wealth of the Hebridean fishing. 'All the people I have spoken to in this neighbourhood,' he wrote to James Simpson in August 1918, 'confirm that the sea surrounding the island is simply teeming with fish of all kinds, and that only a fraction of the wealth of the sea is being reaped.' He repeated the same idea in many of his public statements. Most people would have deduced that the Lewis fisheries had hitherto been almost entirely neglected. They would have been surprised to see Stornoway at the height of the season, when the drifters were packed in hundreds and four-deep against the piers, and the quays were lined with teams of girls gutting the herring and packing the thousands of barrels that occupied every available square yard. It had been a thriving port for centuries before Leverhulme came, and in the years immediately before the outbreak of war, its trade had boomed. During the war itself the Admiralty commandeered many of the fishing boats for mine-sweeping, a large number of the fishermen were called-up, and the German and east European markets for cured herring had entirely disappeared. But what Stornoway had lost in its export trade, it had immediately regained in the home market. Aided by government propaganda, herring became an important British war-time food, not pickled, but 'freshed' (packed loosely in ice) and kippered. Stornoway temporarily abandoned pickling for these other methods*, and in 1917 the Commissioners were able to report a record revenue from harbour dues. Thus Leverhulme had not come to create, nor even to rescue, an industry; he had come to expand one which was already prospering, and to direct more of its profits to the people of the island itself.

The possibilities fascinated him. In the first few months of his enthusiasm, he published a map of the northern Atlantic marked off in fifty-mile circles up to five-hundred miles, with Stornoway as the centre. Armed with this map he descended on the Harbour Commission. 'Look,' he said, 'if you take Lowestoft as the centre, there are 150,000 square miles of sea within a radius of 500 miles. But if you take Stornoway as the centre, with the same radius, there are 700,000 square miles of sea!'[62] The lesson was self-

---

* In the period October 1917 to September 1918, 54,000 crans of herring were freshed at Stornoway, 30,000 kippered, and only 2,700 pickled. (*Fishery Board for Scotland Report.*)

8. Stornoway from Gallows Hill. Left, Lews Castle. Broad Bay in the distance

9. 'Stornoway of the future', a visionary sketch drawn to Leverhulme's design by Raffles Davison RA in 1920. Left, bridge linking the town with the Arnish road; right centre, war-memorial on South Beach; beyond, town-hall and art gallery; right, railway station. None of these were constructed

10. Leverhulme's houses in Anderson Road, Stornoway, as they appear today

11. Cromwell Street, Stornoway, on a Sunday morning

evident to him: more sea, more fish. It only remained to persuade more people to eat it. Further, his raw material cost nothing. This was an aspect of fishing which struck Leverhulme with great force:

It is a harvest which man neither plants, nor sows, nor ploughs, but only reaps; and I see that a high authority on fishery has stated that the seas around our coasts—and this must apply more especially to the coast around Lewis—contains a hundred times as much food for man per acre as the best agricultural land in the United Kingdom.[63]

As he soon came to realise, there were some flaws in this cheerful argument. The most serious was the isolation of Lewis from the great centres of population on the mainland. Stornoway might be ideally situated for catching fish, but it was at a heavy disadvantage when it came to selling them. This had not mattered greatly before the war, when three-quarters of the catch was cured for export, and shipped direct from Stornoway to the Baltic; nor during the war, when the home market was virtually guaranteed by the Government. But was there any certainty that the foreign trade would revive when the war was over, with the Germans penniless, the Russians bolshevised, and the Scandinavian fish-curers established in the market from which the war had cut out their British competitors? The possibility must be faced that Stornoway would have to sell most of its fish in Britain. Would the acquired taste for kippers and freshed herrings survive the coming of peace? Even if it did, Stornoway's handicap was obvious. Fresh fish commanded the higher prices. So the skipper of an east coast drifter, owing no particular loyalty to Stornoway, would be tempted to take his catch from the Minch direct to the mainland rail-heads instead of returning with it to Stornoway. There had already been warning signals that this was likely to happen:

Stornoway was, as usual, the principal centre of the west coast fishing in 1917 . . . but forty per cent of the catch was landed at Mallaig, Kyle or Oban, owing to the demand for herrings in the home market; whereas in 1916, when the catch was much smaller, only seventeen per cent was landed at those ports.[64]

If Leverhulme read this passage in the key survey of the industry for the year in which his fish-interests originated, he

G

would have understood its deep significance. He was confronted by the great drawback of an island base. The fish must be off-loaded twice before they reached a fish-train, once in the island, and a second time at the rail-head: there was a double loss of time and money. At certain seasons herring were accordingly selling at Kyle for twice or even three times the price that they fetched at Stornoway. When this information reached Lever-hulme, he commented, 'It is a most interesting but highly speculative proposition.'[65] Exactly the same disadvantage operated in reverse: the extra transport costs inflated the price of everything that could not be produced locally in Lewis. Materials for building, boat-stores, coal for steam-drifters, ice for freshening the fish, all carried this surcharge. Ice, for example, which sold for 12/- a ton in Aberdeen, cost £3 in Stornoway.

The problem became particularly acute during times of glut or scarcity. The public are always indignant when they read of fish being thrown back into the sea. They immediately assume that the only object is to keep up the prices. But that is not the reason. It is because fish are sometimes landed in quantities beyond the capacity of the local transport and curing yards to dispose of them. Herring will not keep unless they are either eaten or cured within twenty-four hours. 'To cope with the gluts would require the maintenance at herring ports of emer-gency staffs and appliances which might never be employed, or only once or twice in a season, and the cost of the organisation would be out of all proportion to the value of the herring saved.'[66] Any glut in the fish-market was first felt in Lewis, where the fish were unsaleable because the curing capacity was limited, and they could not be transported cheaply. The advantage of any scarcity of fish, with a corresponding rise in price, was also minimised by distance. So losses reached Lewis first, and profits last. It is not surprising that fish-curers from the mainland began to ask them-selves whether it was worth their while to retain depots at Stornoway; and if the curers went, the drifters would certainly stay away too, for then there would be an even smaller sale for their catches.

Besides, the mainland crews found Stornoway dull. There were only four public houses in the island, and an indifferent cinema worked by gas. The Sabbath was unendurable, and made efficient fishing impossible. No herring could be landed at Stornoway on Sundays (because the boats would violate the Sabbath by their return in the early morning), nor on Mondays (because they would violate it by leaving for the fishing grounds in the early evening). A journalist, who was not unsympathetic to the Hebrides, reported:

One Minister told me that he had known instances of boats coming in from the fishing on a Saturday night too late to be unloaded. The crews left them on the beach till the Monday morning, and then, as the catch had gone bad, the fish were all thrown back into the sea. 'You'll never get Lewismen to work on Sundays,' a Stornoway fish-curer told me, 'and you'll never get outsiders to stay here unless you provide more public houses and other attractions.'[67]

Such was the state of the Stornoway fishing industry when Leverhulme formulated his revolutionary ideas. He had good fishermen to work with, and good and plentiful fish to catch. He had an excellent natural harbour. And he had inherited a centuries-old asset in Stornoway's reputation. On the debit side, he had three major problems to solve; the disadvantage of an island base at a time of rising costs; the possible loss of Storno-way's traditional export market; and the urgent need to modernize boats, harbour and fishing methods immediately after a great war. His summing-up was typically courageous:

I am convinced that there is no reason why Lewis should not be one of the greatest centres of fishing in the whole world.[68]

He intended to develop a chain of companies under his own control which would bring the fish from the sea to the breakfast table. He would cut out the middleman by his fish combine, just as he had cut out the traders and brokers who had originally supplied him with the raw materials for his soap. He could not buy concessions in the sea by the same methods as he had bought concessions for palm-oil in Africa and the Pacific; but he could provide every other link in the chain. He could have his own fishing-boats, his own curing-factories, his own transport, his own mainland depots, and, finally, his own fish-shops.

In developing this basic idea, Leverhulme tackled each problem simultaneously. In describing it, a more intelligible account can be given by taking the various stages in their natural order, beginning with the fish in the sea and ending with its sale to the person who ate it.

The herring, Leverhulme discovered, is the most vulnerable of fish. The female does her best by laying 100,000 eggs at a time, of which perhaps two mature: the rest are eaten by haddock and whiting. Later in life, the herring is pursued by every bird and fish, including other herring, for they are cannibals. As many as twelve herring, he was told, can be found in the stomach of one cod-fish. He was horrified by this rate of mortality; and picking on two of the worst offenders, he wrote: 'We must have an energetic campaign against porpoises and dog-fish, which devour far more herring even than gulls and whales.'[69] (The whales' turn was to come later.)

He also turned his mind to the increasing destruction of the spawn of the white-fish round the coasts of Lewis. There were constant complaints from local line-fishermen that their living had been ruined by trawlers sweeping illegally over the ling and haddock beds within the three-mile limit. If the Fishery Board's cruisers could not keep these 'foreigners' at their proper distance (most of them came from the east coast of Scotland), then the limits must be extended from three to thirteen miles, which would close almost the whole of the Minch to trawlers. Here Leverhulme was in a difficulty. He wanted to help the line-fishermen, but he also wanted to attract trawlers to Stornoway. If he persuaded the Fishery Board to close the Minch to British trawlers, he would uselessly infuriate them, for the ban would not apply to Norwegian, German and Dutch trawlers, against whom the international three-mile limit could not be raised. Besides, it was by no means certain that the line-fishermen were right in attributing the decline of the white-fishing to this cause. The spawn of the white-fish floats to the surface, where it would not be affected by trawls; and if the trawlers came as close to the shore as was alleged, their nets would be damaged by rocks. The argument continued throughout Leverhulme's proprietorship. No action was taken by him except constantly to appeal to the Fishery Board to enforce the existing limits. That he did no more was one of the minor grievances which local fishermen held against him. They claimed that he was putting his interests before their own.

When Leverhulme turned from the difficulties of protecting the fish to the more manageable problem of catching them, he said that he intended to have 'the best and best-equipped fishing fleet the world has ever seen.'[70] For this purpose, towards the end of 1918, he formed a company known as MacLine Drifters and Trawlers Co, which was to purchase and operate out of Stornoway about ten drifters and ten trawlers, later to be increased in number.[71] He was prepared to buy them second-hand, if they were cheap and good enough; otherwise he would build them to the most modern design. Owing to the high cost of coal at Stornoway, they would be oil-burning. As soon as this information was published, Leverhulme was inundated with offers of ex-enemy trawlers, ex-minesweepers, semi-derelict drifters, and some good boats for which prices were asked which he considered wholly unreasonable, as much as three times their pre-war value. To each offer he replied 'not interested' or 'premature', while making private enquiries in Norway for a type of boat he thought most suited to the Hebrides.

There are two further aspects of his fishing plans that should be mentioned. He never intended to buy boats to rent to Lewis fishermen. If he allowed them to fish on their own behalf with the same degree of freedom from control as a farmer who rents his land, he feared that he would never achieve the results he wanted. Nor was he willing to make loans to fishermen to install engines in their pre-war sailing wherries. Many of them did so from their own resources, and the beautiful Zulus and Fifies finally disappeared from Stornoway harbour quite soon after the war. Leverhulme did not want to discourage the crofting system on land only to create a new type of crofter on the sea. He needed men to crew his boats, and they were the same men who now asked him for drifters on hire or loans to modernize their own boats. They did not get them.

In catching the fish his skippers were to be aided by two modern instruments, the wireless and the aeroplane. In 1911 French companies had already begin to equip their trawlers with radio for communication between different trawlers of the same fleet at sea, so that one might call another towards an area rich in fish; and for communication between ship and shore, so that the fleet could be directed with their catch to the most profitable market. Wireless had not been widely adopted by British fishermen, and Leverhulme was proposing to make the maximum use of it in combination with spotting aircraft. This was how he intended the system to operate:

I am prepared to supply a fleet of aeroplanes and trained observers who will daily scan the sea in circles round the island. An observer from one of these 'planes cannot fail to notice any shoal of herrings over which he passes. Immediately he does so, he sends a wireless message to the harbour master at Stornoway. Every time a message of that kind comes in, there is a loud-speaker announcement by the harbour master, so that all the skippers at the pier get the exact location of the shoal. The boats are headed for that spot, and next morning they steam back to port loaded with herrings to the gunwales.[72]

Stornoway's harbour was a good one, but Leverhulme intended greatly to improve and enlarge it, both for the increased herring catches that he expected, and for the white-fish industry that he intended to revive. In August 1918 he laid his plans before the Stornoway Harbour Commission. First, the old derelict hulks littering the shore-line were to be broken up for piles or fire-wood, and the piers, which were in only fair condition, were to be made good. Next, a completely new fishing centre was to be constructed on the east side of the harbour. A small islet known as Goat Island, which carried nothing but a few sheep, would be linked to the nearest part of the mainland by a causeway six hundred feet long and eighty feet wide. The island itself would be ringed with quays, and in the area enclosed by the causeway, a new inner harbour would be formed. This group of piers and quays would be the centre of operations for MacLine drifters and trawlers. Railway lines would be run along the top of the causeway to link the off-loading points direct with the fish-factories just inland, and at one stage he had it in his mind to erect a factory on Goat Island itself. The causeway would serve the additional purpose of providing extra protection for the whole harbour against south-east gales.

All this, he estimated, would cost at least £250,000. He would ask the Government for an interest-free loan for forty years, the loan to be repaid out of the increased revenues of the Harbour Commission. After detailed plans had been prepared by the chief engineer at Port Sunlight, B. P. Wall, they were turned down by the Government on the grounds that the cost was likely to be double Leverhulme's estimate, and the public advantage of the scheme was not great enough to justify this huge expenditure.

Although it was always his intention to concentrate his efforts on Stornoway, which he wished to develop into a true metropolis for the island, he did not neglect the smaller fishing harbours around its coasts. He was anxious to encourage whole-time

fishermen at Ness, Barvas and elsewhere, as there were local
fisheries of great potential value to the island, like the lobsters
of the west coast, and there would not be room for all the
fishermen to live in Stornoway, nor space for their small boats
once the great fleets flooded in from England and Scotland.
Sometimes a great benefit could be conferred at small expense
on these country districts, such as the winch that he provided
at Bayble to haul the boats up the beach. But he had more
ambitious plans for them:

I am not greatly impressed with the possibilities of Bayble, but after
seeing Portnaguran at low water, and having previously seen it at high
water, it seems to me that Portnaguran does offer possibilities for a
harbour in conjunction with one at South Tolsta on the opposite side
of Broad Bay.[73]

Other fishing villages which he visited during the first summer
included Carloway, Shawbost, Ness and Skegirsta. Plans were
drawn up for the repair or enlargement of the harbours at all
these places, and several of the smaller townships heard that
their requirements were also being carefully considered by the
engineering department at Port Sunlight, which must have
seemed even remoter to them than the inland villages seemed to
the draughtsmen.

These plans took up a great deal of Leverhulme's energy, but
he devoted an even larger share of it to considering what should
be done with the fish once they were landed. It has already been
explained that this was the core of the problem. He did not wish
to interfere with the business of existing curers and kipperers,
but he hoped to find a new way of selling a highly perishable
product in a distant market. He soon reached his conclusion:
he would acquire a fleet of refrigerated ships to take the fresh
fish to the mainland; and he would can the surplus.

Hardly any of the fish caught by British boats was canned in
1918. Sardines and tinned Canadian salmon were popular, but
the public disliked the idea of eating any other form of tinned
fish, because they had never tried it. Leverhulme thought that
he could persuade them. He had some sample tins made for him
and wrapped them in labels of various designs, each bearing the
words LEWIS CANNED FISH. These he set up in a row on a
downstairs window-ledge at the castle, and looked at them from
outside, imagining that he was a woman shopping in the High

Street. The one that he preferred was a label with red lettering on a white ground, the name printed in italic capitals three times in the full round of the can. 'I have looked at it from every angle,' he told Colin Macdonald, 'from just outside the window and from twenty yards away. It strikes me in the eye from every angle and from every distance. I cannot escape it!' Leverhulme went on to describe to Macdonald in verbal strip-cartoon the effect that his label would have on a passer-by:

The light from the window shows up LEWIS CANNED FISH most attractively. It catches Mary's eye.

'I say, John, what a lovely label! Lewis Canned Fish. I like the look of it. . . . Just a minute. . . .'

'What *is* this Lewis Canned Fish?' she asks.

'Madam,' says my salesman, 'it *is* Lewis Canned Fish, and very delightful too.'

'Can you recommend it?'

'Thoroughly, madam. I believe it is the best canned fish in the world.'

'Thank you. Will you please send along a tin? . . .'

On Monday morning, Mary is in the back green hanging up the washing. Mrs Brown is over the wall.

'Mrs Brown! Do you know! I made the most *wonderful* discovery on Saturday. . . .'[74]

'It is impossible,' commented Macdonald on this remarkable performance, 'to convey in mere writing the force, the eloquence, the abounding self-assurance that radiated from this visionary as he expounded his plans. He was as an evangelist preaching the gospel.'

The drawback of canning was that although a canned fish is less appetising than a fresh one, in the season it is more expensive. On the other hand, it will keep indefinitely in a larder, it doesn't smell in a kitchen, and it can be bought all the year round. Leverhulme thought it important that his fish should look as attractive as possible when decanted from the tin. He intended to decapitate them, fillet them, and pack them three to a tin in oil or jelly, for he considered the traditional tomato sauce to be messy and harmful to the fish. The tin would sell for 6d. His mind ran on:

It will cost about 4·28d. per tin to produce. At 120,000 tins a week, at, say, 1d. profit, it will be £25,000 net profit a year, or 25 per cent on £100,000 capital.[75]

If the British public refused to buy his tins (and he had little fear of that, for they had bought everything that he had ever produced), he would export them all over the world. The new industry would bring enormous benefits to Lewis. Stornoway had never canned a fish in its history. The nearest cannery was at Aberdeen, and that was small. By adding canning to the kippering and freshening processes, Leverhulme would solve all Stornoway's problems simultaneously: gluts, scarcities, isolation, and the possible failure to revive its export trade in pickled herring. His factories were designed to deal with every type of fish in the largest quantities that could be foreseen. In the herring season they would can herring; at other seasons they would can the white-fish brought in by the local boats, his own trawlers and visitors from other ports. Stornoway would become an all-season harbour. It would have an unperishable product, against which there was almost no competition from elsewhere. The island people would never go short of work, because what they had to offer to fishermen and public alike would always meet an existing demand.

It was his policy to use all the fish; he also intended to use the whole fish. There would be no waste. Dog-fish, usually rejected by fishermen ('I never saw a more delicate fish') would become fish-cakes; fish-bones and fish-heads would make jelly or glue; herring-roes would be separated and sold in bottles as delicacies or to make fish-paste. The offal would be treated with equal respect: there was a possibility—his chief chemist was investigating it—that oil might be extracted from the herring-guts and be used in the manufacture of margarine (this was the only direct link between Lewis and Lever Brothers); the residue would make guano, a fertilizer which was much used in the Kentish hop-gardens, and fish-meal for animals.

Within weeks of conceiving these ideas, Leverhulme began to give them practical form. He needed, as a start, a canning factory in Stornoway; machinery to gut the herring, and to make, fill, and close the cans; a power-house to run the machinery; an ice-making plant to supply ice to the long-distance trawlers and for freshening the herring; and a factory to render down the offal. Of these, the simplest to acquire was the last, for an existing Stornoway Company was willing to sell out. In October 1918 Leverhulme bought for £4,750 the plant and premises of the Stornoway Fish-Oil and Guano Co. The other factories must be built, and to build required a Government permit. Leverhulme pulled every string he knew. He put in his first application to the Ministry of Food on 14 August 1918, arguing that the need was urgent, for as soon as the war was over he must be in a position to offer work to the demobilised men. He wanted to put up 'some simple sheds' to deal with an estimated 100 tons of herring a week. The canned fish would form a first-rate diet for the armed services and for prisoners of war. It would cost only £20,000. On 2 September his application was refused: the building was 'not clearly in the national interest,' since the fresh fish landed at Stornoway already had a market and the balance could be cured by existing methods, especially kippering. Leverhulme next appealed to the Fishery Board for Scotland and to the Scottish Office. From both he received strong support, and the permit was granted on 22 November. But without even waiting for the answer to his original application, he had already acted. The workmen began levelling the site, in a virgin field near the landward end of his proposed Goat Island causeway, in the third week of August.[76] Shortly afterwards, work was started on an ice-producing factory, and on a power-house to supply both factories with electricity. All these buildings, including the fish-oil works, stood at the eastern edge of the town within a short distance of the water, forming the nucleus of an industrial zone.

One of the cannery's 'simple sheds' still exists. Today it forms a bay of Macdonald's tweed factory. It is large, light and airy, a fine example of industrial building of its period. Standing at its central point, surrounded by the whirring carding and spinning machinery, I remembered that this surviving bay is only one quarter of the factory which Leverhulme erected, and from it I gained a remarkable impression of the scale of his undertaking. It was a deliberate challenge to the island's past, a symbol of his confidence in its future. He was planning an output five times that which he had dared mention to the Ministry of Food. An average of 500 tons of herring would be canned each week of the season, or 10,000 tons a year,[77] and in the off-season the factory would be kept in full production with mackerel and other fish. The machinery he ordered from Stavanger in Norway, where Carl Holmboe had been making enquiries on his behalf as early as April 1918. It cost £10,900, and included machines for cutting and splitting the fish, cabinets for smoking them, machines for stamping out the cans, sterilizing them, packing them and filling them with oil, and for putting in the lids. This great battery stood in its cases on the quayside at Stornoway for months before the factory was ready to receive it. The people stared at it and wondered.

Just as Stornoway was to be only one, though by far the biggest, of the Lewis harbours, so its canning factory was to have satellites in different parts of the island. Each would be run by a separate Company:

I want to interest the people in the locality where the industry will be carried on. The Stornoway people will have their Company at Stornoway, but there will be another Company with a canning factory at Port Ness, and a third at Carloway, and so on, to a final number of possibly a score of Companies with canning factories all over the island.[78]

The two Stornoway Companies were registered in November and December 1918. They were called the Stornoway Fish Products and Ice Co Ltd, (capital £200,000) and the Lewis Island Preserved Specialities Co Ltd, (capital £500,000). The first was to deal in ice and offal: the second in canned fish and 'fish-delicacies'. Half the shares in each Company were Ordinary shares owned directly by Leverhulme; the other half were preference shares, and every person who bought a preference share received an Ordinary share as an added incentive. Leverhulme was Chairman of both Companies, as he was of the Mac-Line; his son, Sir Herbert Morgan and Frank Clarke were directors; and the remaining members of the Board were island businessmen.

Sir Herbert Morgan was to play a great part in Leverhulme's projects. He stood in an unusual relationship to him. Only forty-two years old in 1918, he had had a varied and important public career in the Ministry of Munitions and service recruitment, and had been general adviser to the firm of W. H. Smith. He did not join the staff of Lever Brothers until later, but Leverhulme used him as a companion-help (though socially he was often ill at ease), while entrusting to him great responsibilities. Mingled with their correspondence on high business policy, one finds this sort of appeal:

*Leverhulme to Morgan (cabled)*: Have received letter from Princess Marie-Louise. Please wire immediately correct style of address, titles, etc.

Send me a list of Trade Union leaders to whom I can address a copy of my speech on Reconstruction.

Would you like to become a member of the Worshipful Company of Gardeners? If so, I should be very pleased to propose you.

A relative of mine has asked me to obtain for her the name of a nerve-specialist in London. Can you help?

Can you recommend a London hosier for white shirts and underwear?

It was to this man, extremely able and exceptionally favoured by Leverhulme's confidence and affection, that he gave the task of distributing the enormous catches and mountains of tins that were soon to accumulate at Stornoway.

With the tins he anticipated little difficulty: they could be fed slowly into the British market. But the fresh fish must be disposed of at once. There was already a fish-transporting firm at Stornoway, which combined this trade with a small fleet of drifters and a coal-importing and curing business. Its founder and owner was Duncan Maciver. Leverhulme admired and liked him more than any other native of Lewis. At first he had tried to persuade Maciver to join him in his fishing ventures: 'Whatever I do in the way of trawlers and drifters, I desire to be associated with yourself.'[79] When the purchase of boats was postponed, Leverhulme held out to him even more alluring prospects on the curing and transport sides; but of course he would require a fifty-one per cent interest in Maciver's Company. Maciver replied:

I should be quite averse to any other businessman having an interest in my business. It is only natural that one should prize one's independence. That is one of the features that one enjoys most, and it should be jealously guarded.[80]

Leverhulme was amused and impressed. He side-lined the last sentence in red ink. At a meeting between them a few weeks later he offered Maciver a fifty-fifty partnership. Maciver, in spite of his son's pressure on him to accept, again refused.

Leverhulme then decided to go ahead alone. With Sir Herbert Morgan acting as his adjutant, he planned and forged the last two links in his chain. From Stornoway the fresh fish would be transported by a fleet of refrigerated carriers to Fleetwood on the coast of Lancashire. Each fish would be 'wrapped in waxed paper and stored in boxes in the insulated refrigerated chambers of the carrier steamer.' At Fleetwood the Stornoway pattern would be duplicated. He took over from the railway company in May 1919 a huge disused granary and its adjoining wharves and warehouses, which he converted at great cost into a centre for canning, curing and fish-oil extraction. With Fleetwood in mind, he also began to experiment, thirty years ahead of his time, with quick-freezing, a process (had he but realised it) which was an even better method of preservation than canning, for it keeps the fish, fresher than fresh' indefinitely. Unfortunately Leverhulme was discouraged by experiments on his own digestion:

I had the frozen herring for breakfast yesterday, and neither myself nor any of our guests could distinguish the difference between this herring and an ordinary herring; but I did notice throughout yesterday that it did not digest as readily. It interfered with my work throughout the day.[81]

He then had another idea: 'Could we can fish in glycerine?' And then, dazzled by the sudden thought: 'Could we keep them *alive* in ice?'[82]

Neither suggestion was thought practicable. So the main function of Fleetwood was to act as a depot for Stornoway's refrigerated herring. It was within easy reach of the big markets of industrial England. Nothing would be lost by bad transport facilities, for he had cut out the little Scottish mainland ports with their distant rail-heads. Nothing would be lost by gluts, for the capacity of Stornoway and Fleetwood combined was infinite. And the public would be protected against scarcities, for Leverhulme could always release part of his great store of cans. Fleetwood was to be the key-stone of the whole system.

The last stage was the chain of retail shops, which was Morgan's particular responsibility, What should he call them? Leverhulme had for some time been toying with various names for his fish-products. He rejected in turn, 'Silent Deep', 'Island Deep', 'Lipsco' (Lewis Island Preserved Specialities Company), 'Silvascale', 'Wavecrest', 'Deepcast', 'Snack', 'Shoal', and 'Siren'. On 21 January 1919, he wrote to his patent expert at Port Sunlight:

Could you have a search made to see whether the letters MAC have been registered for fish? Sir Herbert Morgan has suggested it. For instance the particular brand of fish might be 'Mac Herring', 'Mac Turbot', 'Mac Cod', 'Mac Lobster', etc.

Then:

I prefer Mac to Mc.

In this strange way one of the most familiar names in the modern British High Street had its origin. Leverhulme did not press the unhappy idea of attributing to every breed of his fish a Highland ancestry, but he used the label for his chain of fish-shops. For a very short time he called them 'The Island Fisheries'. They then became 'Mac Fisheries'.

Mac Fisheries was incorporated on 11 February 1919, with its headquarters in London. The starting capital was £210,000, all supplied by Leverhulme personally, who became Chairman. By November of the same year the Company had grown so rapidly that the capital was increased to £2 million, and five months later to £3 million, of which £2,500,000 was issued.[83] With immense zest, Mac Fisheries was launched by Sir Herbert Morgan and Captain G. N. Crisford, the general manager, and the first shop was opened in February 1919 at 25 Hill Street, Richmond. Existing fish-shops in the best positions were quickly bought up in all the chief towns of the country, the previous owner normally remaining as Mac Fisheries' manager. By April 1919, about eighty shops had been acquired;[84] by the end of 1921, three hundred and sixty. When the total reached four hundred, Leverhulme called a halt. He had created the biggest fishmongery ever known.

The originality of Mac Fisheries lay not only in the number of its shops and the proposed link through Fleetwood and Stornoway with its sources of supply, but in the way the fish were sold and advertised. The shops were all designed in the same pleasant colour-scheme of blue and grey, and great trouble was taken with the appearance and cleanliness of the fish on sale. Elaborate designs were made on the sloping counters with fish of different shapes and colours, to which Leverhulme, never shy of borrowing useful ideas, contributed his own suggestion from as far away as America:

We saw in Seattle the finest dressed window for fish I ever saw in my life. Large white-fish, such as cod, were gracefully grouped together standing on their bellies, their mouths wide open and small lemons in their mouths.[85]

Mac Fisheries dared to invade even Bond Street, where a luxury shop was opened resembling more an aquarium than a fish-shop; the fish were displayed in tiers of artificially cooled glass containers, behind an entrance-front as splendidly embellished as the baths of Caracalla. In the country districts, the Company's vans sold fresh fish from door to door, creating a demand for fish where fish had never been sold before.

The original purpose of Mac Fisheries was to sell the fish caught by the fleets operating from Stornoway, including fish canned in the island, 'so that when the MacLine drifters and trawlers are fishing, they may have a steady regular market at a fair price for their fish of all kinds.'[86] Mac Fisheries would never have come into existence but for Leverhulme's interest in the Hebrides, and today it is the only survivor of his island schemes. But soon it became something very different and very much larger. Stornoway was almost forgotten in the astonishingly rapid development of the Company, for Lewis could supply only a fraction of the daily quantities of fish that it required for sale. The fish were bought in all the main fish-markets of Great Britain, and by 1924 Mac Fisheries was not only the owner of multiple shops, but a holding company on a huge scale.

It had bought fishing fleets in England and north-east Scotland (Bloomfields of Great Yarmouth, and the Aberdeen Steam Trawling and Fishing Company); it acquired the firm of T. Wall and Sons, with its sausages and ice-cream; it took a long lease on the Duchy of Cornwall's oyster-beds in the Helford River; it owned the biggest lobster-pond in the country, at Warsash, near Southampton; firms like Woodgers (the originator of the kipper), Isaac Spencer (specialists in the production of meal from fish offal), and Stanley Pibel (wholesale fish-merchants of Billings-gate) passed into the Mac Fisheries group well before Lever-hulme's death. Although all these companies retained a great deal of their independence, Leverhulme's was ultimately the directing hand. 'I am proud to be a fishmonger,' he said at a Mac Fisheries dinner in November 1919. 'In coming to Mac Fisheries I am in no way being disloyal to Lever Brothers.' Three years later there could be no question even of a conflict of loyalties; for in 1922 Mac Fisheries was incorporated in the Lever Brothers family itself, and the story of its unusual origins had already begun to fade in men's minds.

The framework of Leverhulme's great plan was complete. He

had companies for catching fish, preserving them, transporting them, selling them. At each stage he proposed an important innovation: radio-links and spotting aircraft for the fishing; canning for preservation; a mainland depot for storage and distribution; a long chain of shops for retail selling. All this was conceived with the dual purpose of rescuing an island people from the poverty induced by their own traditions, and of establishing in the fish trade the same sort of vertical organisation that he had so successfully applied to the manufacture and sale of soap. He summed it up in this way:

Whatever I am doing is jointly in the interests of the people of Lewis and the consumer. . . . I want to establish a regular fishing industry on sound commercial lines. As far as I am advised, the lines that have been adopted are the most certain way of securing this. The undertaking is more or less hazardous, and there are those who have been in the trade all their lives who state that a successful fishing business cannot be built up on the Island of Lewis on the lines we are endeavouring to follow. On the other hand, there are those, like myself, who are enthusiastic in the belief that success can be achieved.[87]

# Chapter Five

# THE TOWN, THE COUNTRY
# AND HARRIS

LEVERHULME'S GRAND DESIGN for Lewis included much else besides the development of its fishing industry. Stornoway was to be transformed, and the country districts revitalised by changing an economy based on haphazard crofting to one based on the scientific use of land and the manufacture of tweed. He was planning a new order, to be completed within as few years as it had taken centuries to create the old. He was in a hurry. He had always been in a hurry: but now he feared that he had only ten more years to live, and there was nobody, not even his son, on whom he could rely to round off his work for the island exactly as he planned it.

Stornoway was noticeably different in character from the remainder of Lewis. It resembled a mainland town like Oban, with its customs-house, assembly-rooms, town-hall, churches of several denominations, two-storey slated houses, its fashions, tea-parties, politics, business and gossip. 'It smells of fish and reeks of education,' commented a traveller in 1901, and the description was still apt twenty years later. To Leverhulme, however, Stornoway was not a worthy capital of his island. It must become 'the chief town of the Western Highlands', 'The Venice of the north'. He persuaded the town council that this was no mere figure of speech: 'In Venice the interests of art and the interests of commerce were in competition. So what did the Venetians do? They decided to make their city a centre both of the arts and of commerce. Working together, we can carry out the same idea in Stornoway.'[88]

Encouraged by the applause which greeted these remarks, Leverhulme began to work out a detailed plan for the rebuilding of the town. To help him he called in James Simpson and Raffles Davison RA, the former to prepare the plan, the latter to draw a bird's-eye view of the new Stornoway for the delight and instruction of its people. Leverhulme himself sketched the basic idea during his first summer in Lewis ('I am working very closely and very persistently on the town-planning of Stornoway,' he wrote to Provost Maclean in September 1918), but it was not published until March 1920, when Raffles Davison's view was exhibited in a local shop-window, and attracted enormous crowds.

The first impression which it made on the inhabitants was that Port Sunlight had been transplanted to the Hebrides. Many of them had by that time been on organised excursions to Merseyside, and returned with picture post-cards which were passed from hand to hand. In the Stornoway plan they recognised the same basic idea of wide avenues leading up to dominant public monuments and buildings, and groups of houses encircling grassed squares and ovals. Port Sunlight had been constructed on an almost flat site, and Leverhulme had been obliged to move thousands of tons of earth to create a third dimension. Stornoway was much more promising, for it sloped gently upwards from the water's edge, and the harbour, with its constant movement and interlocking views, provided him with a perfect background for a formal, even classic, design. The older quarter, on the peninsula and along Cromwell Street, he proposed to leave untouched. But he intended to sweep entirely away the nineteenth-century grid of streets behind it, constructing a new grid at an angle of forty-five degrees to the old. The main axis was no longer to run west-east up Point Street and Francis Street, but south-west to north-east up a central avenue that was to begin at the harbour, approximately where Kenneth Street meets the South Beach Quay. Here the war-memorial was to stand, a great tower immediately visible to all incoming ships. Walking up the avenue, the visitor would next come to the new town-hall, lying at the junction of the present Keith Street and Francis Street; and beyond it, still on the central axis, to a large art gallery, sited at the eastern end of Church Street. Two broad roads, from the Town Hall and art gallery respectively, would lead eastwards, meeting at a roundabout just north of the point where Lifeboat Street joins Betts Road. Here the railway station was to be built. within easy reach of the quays and the new industrial zone beyond.

Simpson immediately pointed out the objections to this fabulous plan. The main avenue, and the streets parallel to it, would run up the steepest gradient, and while the effect would certainly be impressive, it would be hard on pedestrians.

Secondly, by cutting across the existing grid, Leverhulme would involve himself in unecessary expense and trouble. Why not lay his avenues along the same axes as the present streets, and rebuild the houses one by one? His ultimate plan would be evident from the start, but it would be obscured for decades by the clutter of old houses if he insisted on a completely different alignment.

Leverhulme would not be persuaded. The dignity he wanted could only be achieved by a radical plan. He began at once to acquire for demolition the properties which lay in the path of his great avenues. He had no power to requisition them, but as proprietor he had the first option on every freehold property in the town when it came into the market, provided that he matched the highest price offered. The Town Hall and public library had been totally destroyed by fire in March 1918, and he could claim the insurance money when the time came to re-erect them on their new sites. Otherwise he intended to bear the entire expense himself, standing any loss and returning any profit to the Council.[89] It was an immensely bold scheme, for a single recalcitrant who held out against selling his property could ruin it. Leverhulme persisted in his idea year after year, colouring-in on the plan the properties as he gradually acquired them, the outlines of the future roads and buildings showing through the existing town-plan like bones and organs in an X-ray photograph. By 1923 he had obtained possession of about half the total he needed, but destroyed nothing until its replacement could be begun.

At the same time he began to build houses for the people on town-sites a little way from the new centre. The need was urgent, for not only was there an existing waiting list for accommodation in Stornoway (two out of every five townspeople were living more than two to a room), but as the men returned from the war and his industrial plans matured, so the population of Stornoway would increase very rapidly. There were as yet no proper communications in the island: the people, whether fishermen or factory workers, must live within walking distance of their work, and it was impossible to attract them away from their crofts until some alternative was waiting for them in Stornoway. As fast as he built houses in the town, so crofts would become available in the country, and those who could or would not take the leap, would at last find more room to spare around their own villages. Leverhulme announced that he would continue to build town-houses 'until I have erected sufficient so that every man who wants to live in Stornoway can have a house in Stornoway, and every man who wants a croft can have a croft.'[90]

He promised to build three hundred houses a year, beginning in 1919, until he had completed 1,200, thus increasing the population of Stornoway from just under 4,000 to nearly 9,000. As he was allowing for an optimum island population of 60,000 (though in fanciful moments he was apt to vary this figure upwards to 200,000), the relative smallness of his capital-town was one answer to the critics who complained that Leverhulme intended to strip the countryside of its people to concentrate them in Stornoway.

He took great pains with the design of the new houses. They must be quite different from the black-house, but must have 'a Scotch feeling,' as he told an enquirer, 'but not too pronounced. For instance, red tiles, which are quite suitable at Port Sunlight, would be out of place in Stornoway, where green slates are more appropriate.' Inside, there must be several rooms, including a bathroom—the lack of any privacy in a black-house was to him among its most barbaric features—and they should be built to at least two storeys. Ambrose Poynton, the London architect, was invited to prepare designs for a group of cottages on these lines.

One can still see them. About a mile from the centre of Stornoway, on what is now the eastern edge of the town, the visitor will easily find Anderson Road. This road (though many of the present inhabitants do not know it) is composed entirely of Leverhulme's houses. They are still among the most attractive in the island, and at that date must have seemed astonishingly commodious. They are built on the shoulder of a spur, over-looking the width of the Eye peninsula, the sea visible on both sides, and inland a long stretch of brown moor. Immediately below them is Goathill Farm. Anyone who has also seen Port Sunlight will immediately identify the guiding idea behind them. The houses are built in blocks of four dwellings each, no block precisely the same as any other, but all characterised by heavy hipped roofs, gardens back and front, and tunnels piercing the block to give access to the back-doors. The only complaint now voiced by those who live there is that the plaster was applied directly to the inside face of the main walls, without laths, so that in wet weather the rooms are apt to be damp and cold. Leverhulme himself wrote a sharp letter to his contractors on this very point: he had carefully considered the heating of the houses, and

it was charcteristic of him that the gas-fires were removable, so
that the grates behind could be used for burning peat.

In addition to the Anderson Road houses (or the Goathill
cottages, as he knew them), he built a number of houses in
Matheson Road. Although these were larger and detached from
each other, being intended for the managers of his various island
projects, they are not so successful architecturally, having a lump-
ish outline and bearing little relation one to the other. But from
the two roads in conjunction, one can form a good idea of the town
he planned. It was certainly not Venetian. Its colour was subdued,
matching the normally sombre sky. The brilliance on fine days
would come from the water of the harbour and distant sea, not
from the buildings. There was a deliberate heaviness about his
design, the heaviness of permanence, prosperity and defiance of
storm. Stornoway was to be a fine town more than a splendid one,
reflecting, as far as Leverhulme could visualise it, the sturdiness
of the Highland character more than its gaiety and charm.

To the town he gave three additional benefits: a greatly improved gas supply; a laundry; and a dairy. Although all three
involved him in considerable trouble and expense, it is not
necessary to describe them closely. Each in its own way illustrates his approach to the island's problems. He wanted to make
the people more comfortable and more self-sufficient. Was it not
absurd that their money should be wasted by antiquated and
leaking gas-producing equipment? So he bought the whole
concern, and modernised it at his own cost. Was it not equally
unnecessary that those townspeople who did not do their own
washing, should be obliged to send it to Inverness? So he
installed a modern laundry in the neighbourhood of the tweed
mills, where it could also be used for dyeing and washing wool.
The purpose of the dairy is self-evident, and was to assume great
importance in his mind at a slightly later stage. One further
intention was never carried out: he hoped to light the streets by
electricity. The cost was too great for him to give the idea
priority over his many others, and electricity, except for a few
private plants, like that at Lews Castle, did not reach Stornoway
until 1932, seven years after his death.

At a very early stage of his planning, he turned his mind to the
communications between Stornoway and the mainland, and
between Stornoway and the rest of the island. Both were of great
importance to its development. He wanted to draw the Outer

Hebrides much more closely into the network of Highland communications, so that businessmen from as far away as Glasgow would consider Stornoway an important and accessible market instead of a remote and indigent community, whose needs could be satisfied by an occasional coastal steamer. As for internal communications, Leverhulme believed that the proper relationship between town and country could only be established by a proper system of roads and railways which would break down the isolation of the townships, and enable them to draw their supplies from the town and contribute their produce to it.

The passenger, mail and freight services to the Hebrides is still a subject of frequent parliamentary controversy. At the end of the first World War, it was a grievance that tended to dominate all others. At one stage, all the members of public bodies in the island threatened to resign *en bloc*, and refuse to stand at the subsequent elections, unless something were done to improve the service. Leverhulme himself bought a £10,000 share in Mac-Brayne's in order to influence their policy, and addressed to one government department after another letters of complaint which were worded with exceptional anger. 'Anything more callously indifferent to the interests of a section of the community I have never experienced,' he told the Postmaster-General. 'You may be able to make an economy, but the economy achieved will be a disgrace and not a credit to the Government.'[91]

The steam-boat service was worse than it had been forty years before. In all but the four summer months, there was a sailing from Stornoway to Kyle only three times a week. The pre-war steamer service to Edinburgh, Aberdeen, Liverpool and Belfast had entirely ceased. There was only one steamer to Glasgow every ten days, instead of twice weekly. Island correspondence was subjected to delays that made efficient business impossible. Imported milk was dangerously stale on arrival; exported fish often went bad by the time it reached the mainland rail-heads. The passenger steamers were old, mechanically unreliable and disgracefully uncomfortable: it was no uncommon sight to see the saloon deck occupied by cattle, and the steerage, which was certified for 180 passengers, had accommodation for no more than twenty.[92] MacBrayne's received from the Government a subsidy for the island services that was too low to make much improvement possible. Leverhulme consistently pressed for an increase in the subsidy, threatening to start a rival service of his own unless he was given satisfaction. During this prolonged and almost fruitless controversy, in which he spoke up as champion of the islands as much as in his own business interests, he detected a Government plot to thwart his schemes. The charge was not justified, but the row provided a strong bond between him and the people. He pursued his argument with the utmost vigour.

His additional motive was to open up Lewis to tourism. The island was *terra incognita* to the tourist. The people had no incentive to provide accommodation for visitors, for almost the only foreigners they ever saw were the English tenants of the sporting rights, who hurried quickly through Stornoway to the outlying lodges, and it seemed that few others would ever be tempted to Lewis by its scenery. Leverhulme did not believe this. He foresaw great profit to the island from this source, but first the visitors must be assured of comfortable and frequent communications to the island and within it. He wrote to his traffic-manager at Port Sunlight:

It seems to me that the programme for myself (not for the guests, few of whom would care to travel by air) would be to go up and down from Stornoway by flying-machine. Can you ascertain what the cost would be from Liverpool or Hooton Aerodrome to Stornoway, and what facilities would be required at Stornoway to make this possible?[93]

His idea did not materialise. He flew for the first time on 23 May 1920, from Paris to London ('the passage was not at all what I anticipated. It was not a smooth gliding motion, but a rough tossing, pitching motion, like a ship in a storm, only worse'), but he never landed by air at Stornoway, which did not see an aeroplane on the ground until 1933. Today it boasts one of the finest aerodromes in the country, constructed during the last war, and a regular air service to and from Inverness and Glasgow.

Leverhulme's most ambitious proposal for improving the island's internal communications was the construction of an electric railway system. The idea of a Lewis railway was not entirely new. The Crofters Commission had suggested it in 1884, and the Hebrides Light Railway Company was formed soon afterwards to lay down 130 miles of track in Skye and Lewis, but the project was still-born. Leverhulme revived it with enthusiasm. He saw in it several advantages indispensable to his plans: the people of the outlying districts could commute daily to his tweed and canning factories in Stornoway; the milk, meat, vegetables and other produce of the farms could be marketed easily in the town; the sacks of wool could be taken to the weavers, and their rolls of tweed returned; above all, the fish of the west-coast harbours could be rapidly transported to Stornoway before it went bad, and so encourage the fishing in those districts as well as supply the Stornoway carriers and canning factory from an additional source. As the idea took root in his mind, almost every other project was related to it. His electric generators in Stornoway would be fuelled by island peat brought by rail; with rail transport the people themselves would be able to win their peats from ground more distant from their townships; the tourists would spread over the whole island; the reclamation of the land would be facilitated by bringing truckloads of better soil from the richer to the skinnier regions. The very existence of a railway would bind the island together and impress on outsiders the determination with which its problems were being tackled.

With his chief engineer, B. P. Wall, Leverhulme marked out the routes which the railway was to follow. Stornoway, of course, was to be the main terminus, and from it three separate lines were to radiate. One was to go south through Balallan to Aline on the Harris border, with a later extension to Tarbert. A second was to serve the west-coast fishing harbours of Callanish and Carloway and return to Stornoway via Barvas. The third was to branch northwards from this line at Barvas to serve the group of townships near the Butt of Lewis and return down the east coast through Tolsta to Stornoway. Only the thinly populated parishes of Uig and the eastern part of Lochs were to be skirted by the system. The total track required for the three lines amounted to over a hundred miles. The gauge was to be three-foot, and Leverhulme proposed to obtain the rails from the light-railway system built to serve the trenches in France, and now offered for sale as surplus Army stores.

His power was to be hydro-electric. Carl Holmboe, who was his chief adviser on this subject as well as on canning processes, told him that while it would be technically possible to generate enough electricity by building a dam at the northern end of Loch Langhabat, it would be very uneconomical. Electric power, he said, cannot compete with steam unless the trains ran very frequently. If they ran at long intervals, the power generated would be largely wasted, and the freight and passenger traffic would never repay the great expense of erecting the dam and the overhead cables. As Leverhulme proposed to run no more than two passenger trains and two freight trains a day in both directions on each of his three lines (a total of twenty-four trains a day, and of course none on Sundays), he must use steam if the system was to pay. Wall agreed, adding that there would only be one or two steep gradients in the whole system, and the hydro-electric plant would have to generate sufficient power to enable the engines to overcome these gradients, a degree of power which would be quite unnecessary elsewhere, and therefore wasteful. Leverhulme remained unconvinced. The hydro-electric station, he said, would also supply power to the island's industries. Think of the bootmakers, the printers, the satellite canning factories, and all the private householders who would benefit from it, besides his own bigger factories in Stornoway. He had other, aesthetic reasons for objecting to steam power: 'I should hate to see the smoke of a locomotive across the fair scenery of Lewis.'[94] Holmboe replied that it would take 2,000 more tons of coal to run the railways by electricity and the factories by steam-power, than *vice-versa*. Leverhulme insisted that both must be run by electricity, and returning to his romantic argument, which was strange in view of his familiarity with the Highland railways and their inoffensive intrusion into the landscape, he added: 'We shall gain the immense advantage of leaving the beautiful valleys and lochs and rivers of Lewis without a black pall of dark smoke polluting their fair surface.'[95] But his power-lines would have looked far more out of place; and in any case, his proposed routes scarcely penetrated the more beautiful part of the country.

He was as happy with his railway-system as a boy with model trains. He set aside six months for completing the surveys, six months for obtaining Parliamentary powers, and told Holmboe that he intended to start on the actual construction in the spring of 1920. As time passed, he added new ideas. There was to be wireless communication between engine-driver and guard: perhaps, after all, the engines should be oil-driven; he would organise an island-wide laundry service, the trains to shuttle back and forth to Stornoway with the black-house washing. Then came the realisation of its appalling cost. It was estimated that the construction of the lines alone would require £1½ million, 'and I can see no revenue adequately to compensate for such an outlay.'[96] Some of the crofters objected on the grounds that the lines would run across their common grazings ('our in-alienable heritage'), and would endanger their stock. The railway scheme began to look less practicable, and Leverhulme, tempor-arily discouraged, turned back to the possibilities of the roads.

Before he came to Lewis, there was almost no motor-transport in the island. In 1919 the roads (Sir James Matheson's main legacy to Lewis), were surprisingly numerous, although the surfaces had been neglected during the war. But there was no bus or carrier service, apart from the small mailcar which went out daily from Stornoway along each of the five main roads which radiated from it. The crofters either travelled on foot or with a pony and cart, taking a whole day to cross the island.[97] Several of the more distant townships were without any road at all. They lay a mile or more off the coastal roads, and every sack of peat, every item of stores, had to be carried across rock and bog on the backs of men and women. Leverhulme himself tried to lift a creel of peat: 'It almost swung me off my feet.' It was one of the most enduring impressions made on him by his first visits. Always a road-builder (the countryside around Port Sunlight is striated by his avenues), he saw an opportunity to provide immediate relief to local unemployment and at the same time to redress an intolerable hardship.

Some of his roads were purely local, such as that which he built to Grimshader across the southern part of the Arnish moor, or to the site of the new sanatorium at Laxdale, near Stornoway. Another, much more ambitious, was designed to complete the circuit of the northern part of the island by linking North Tolsta with Skegirsta, and was started at both ends simultaneously, more to give employment in those two districts than to fill any desperate need, for it would shorten the journey from Ness to Stornoway by only two miles in twenty-six and pass through wholly uninhabited country. Yet another road, known as the Arnish Road, passed along the foot of Lews Castle itself, making for the base of the peninsula which enclosed the harbour, where he intended to build a suburb of Stornoway. This, though relatively short, was the most ambitious of them all, for it was necessary to blast the route through rocks overhanging the water's edge, and two great new bridges were projected, one over the mouth of the Creed River, and a second, opposite the end of Kenneth Street, over the lagoon of the harbour which divided the castle policies from the town. The total length of these island roads amounted to sixteen miles.

It is, however, surprising that he did not undertake a survey of
the island's traffic needs to match his road-making. There is no
record that he ever contemplated the introduction of fleets of
buses and lorries to improve the communications of Lewis until
his railways were built, itself always a long-term project. He
imported several light vans for the use of himself, his guests and
his agents. His main contractors, MacAlpine's, brought in
heavy equipment for carrying out the various works and they
built a light railway to transport building material to the sites
from a quarry at the foot of the hill where the war-memorial now
stands. But of general carriers there was little sign until several
years after Leverhulme had gone, although the need for them
was so obvious and could have been met at comparatively small
cost. As subsequent history has proved, motor-transport was a
a better solution to the problem than light railways, for its capital
cost would have been trifling by Leverhulme's standards, its
employment economic, and its effect on the island's life instan-
taneous, as the road-network was on the whole already adequate.

The pattern of Leverhulme's plan was slowly emerging. A
great fishing harbour would be attached to a rebuilt capital-
town from which a network of roads and railways was to spread
prosperity all over the island. Stornoway was to become an island
metropolis, but not by means of robbing the country districts
of their people or local industry. On the contrary, Leverhulme
always visualised town and country as complementary. He wished
to increase the population of both, raise the living standards of
both, and make one more truly dependent on the other. If he
had his way, the crofts would gradually be merged into farms as
the people came to understand his purpose; and as farms need
fewer people to work them than a collection of crofts, the men
and women so released would either work in the town, find
employment locally as fishermen or labourers, specialise on the
weaving of tweed, or break in new land from the moor to enlarge
the arable part of the township's farms.

Just as he had taken great pains with the design of his new
houses in Stornoway, so he proposed a new type of country
cottage to replace the black-house:

These houses will be self-contained, one storey high, and will contain
a living-room, three bedrooms, scullery, pantry and bathroom. The

scullery and larder will have concrete floors, the living and bedrooms boarded floors. There will be a nice porch to keep the wind from blowing in at the doorway. The roof will be boarded, felted, and covered with corrugated iron sheeting, and will be painted a nice warm red. All the rooms would be boarded inside.[98]

These houses would be built by the people themselves, under the direction of an instructor, whose services would be available free of charge. The people might form themselves into clubs, of say a dozen members, who could combine to erect one another's houses. Leverhulme himself would provide the materials. Eighty per cent of the cost would be loaned to them on a long-term arrangement for repayment, provided that they paid at once the remaining twenty per cent, which might amount to £50 a house. The rent would be only nominal, one shilling a year. He put up a specimen of his nice cottage outside Stornoway, the outside walls of which were built of peat around a timber framework, but any applicant could choose to build his own walls of stone or concrete. (The *peat-pisé* walls were a failure, although he repeated the experiment in Harris. They were too porous to resist the damp climate unless faced with stone, as the builders of the black-houses had discovered long before.) Then came the rub. The tenants of such cottages would have only a quarter-acre allotment each, instead of the five or six acres of a normal croft. If they wanted more land, they could reclaim it from the common grazings, but he hoped that the offer would be taken up by men who wished to break with their crofting past.

Several examples of Leverhulme's cottages can be seen today at Tong farm, three miles north of Stornoway. They are hideous. It is quite clear, though incomprehensible, that in the matter of rural housing, aesthetics meant as little to him as they did to the inhabitants. 'Every house must have a garden,' he said on another occasion. 'Not rows and rows of houses, cheek by jowl, like sardines or kippers. We want the island dotted over with what I might call Villas—every man with his own home and garden, not a croft.'[99] The idea did not catch on. Leverhulme received many letters of enquiry, but almost every one ended with the request for 'a few acres of croft.' His patience by that time was wearing thin. The letters are scored with exasperated comments: 'Will they *never* understand?' 'No, no, no.' 'My whole object is that it *shouldn't* be a croft.'

When he turned his attention to the agricultural methods of

Lewismen, he found that long custom and dislike of innovation had prevented the introduction of the most rudimentary aids to good farming. Even within the hampering framework of a croft there was a complete lack of system. Rotation of crops was unknown, or at least unpractised: a field would simply be left fallow for a year or two. The cattle were left to feed on the croft-lands during winter, so that the cultivation of winter-crops was impossible: winter oats, winter rye and winter vetches were never seen in Lewis. The only cereals grown were oats and barley; almost the only vegetables, the potato. Carrots, turnips, cabbages, leeks and onions could easily have been grown but never were.[100] A flower-garden was an undreamed of luxury: so was fruit. Chickens roosted with the cattle, often inside the black-house, but until quite recently the eggs were little eaten by the people, 'for the egg passes as a coin of the realm, and may be seen handed over the counter in exchange for a newspaper or postage stamp.'[101] In 1919 the cattle were so cross-bred and starved of proper feed that they were almost the poorest in Britain. No pigs were kept; no goats. The staples of the country-people's diet were barley-bread, oatmeal, potatoes, fish, milk and the occasional egg. Meat was very rare. But even this diet was an improvement on forty years before, judging by the evidence given to the Crofters Commission in 1883:

Q   What is your principle food in this township?
A   Meal and water.

Q   Are you scarce of milk?
A   Milk is not to be had at all.

Q   What food do you give the children?
A   Porridge.

Q   What do you give them instead of milk?
A   Sugar and treacle, and mussels from the shore when we have no other food.[102]

The astonishingly low standard of diet which still existed in Leverhulme's day was explained to him as due to a number of causes, all of which could easily be remedied. The soil was suitable for many types of fruit and vegetable: cranberry, blue-berry, currants, raspberries, strawberries, gooseberries, apples; carrots, parsnips, early potatoes, Jerusalem artichokes. The stock of cattle, sheep and chickens could be improved by importing fresh breeds from the mainland. The people should be persuaded to give up their system of 'lazy-bed' cultivation (long mattresses of soil thrown up from deep ditches on either side) which merely wasted the land and accumulated weeds. They should be taught the use of fertilisers and rotation, and to fence their fields against the cattle in winter-time. Above all, they should rediscover the technique of reclaiming the peat-lands of the open moor.

These recommendations, and many others, were put to Leverhulme by Dr M. E. Hardy in a long report which he made in November 1919 after spending three months in the island.[103] His assistant was Arthur Geddes. Hardy's main concern was to advise Leverhulme on the possible uses of the peat-lands, both for reclamation and other purposes. But his report, which was the most valuable that Leverhulme ever received, went deep into the problem of crofting, and endorsed many of the conclusions that Leverhulme had already reached. After examining the effect of the Crofters Acts, Hardy went on:

A remedial policy based on extension of land for crofters is clearly no solution, since at best it only affects seven per cent of the sufferers. It merely carries on and extends the evils of the Crofters Acts, and of the unprofitable and amphibious mode of living and working. It is purely negative. It postpones the issue: nay, it obscures it. The universal opinion asserts that the double trade of fishing and crofting is imposed by the fact that the land does not pay. The whole evidence gathered in this survey goes to show that the land does not pay because of the double trade. No land, used as land is used in Lewis, would pay. . . . The conclusion is: Specialise, and separate the crofter and the fisherman. Either calling can be made profitable if well understood. Both lead to double failure when combined.

It should at once be noted that Hardy did not condemn the croft as uncompromisingly as Leverhulme had done. They agreed that a man who followed the sea as his calling should be mainly a fisherman, with a small allotment, perhaps, at which he could work in his leisure hours. But while Leverhulme assumed that no man could ever make a living from a croft, Hardy argued that it was possible to do so, if, like the fisherman, he devoted the whole of his time to the task, and adopted modern methods of cultivation. Hardy attacked bad crofting: Leverhulme attacked the croft itself.

Hardy advocated a policy of 'the development of crofting into skilled small-holding.'[104] The soil was too poor, and transport too expensive and erratic, for the island to live by exporting its produce to the mainland. But there was no reason why the local market should not be more fully developed. It was quite illogical that a peasant population should import so much of their milk and vegetables, and should scarcely eat meat at all. Even more absurd was the import of wool for tweed-making to an island where sheep did well and almost all the political troubles of the past had arisen from their multiplication. Only the lack of winter-feed prevented a vigorous development of sheep-rearing by the crofters themselves, for there was plenty of grazing in the summer. The climate was well adapted to sheep and cattle. This was where the agricultural future of Lewis lay: the crofts must become intensively cultivated allotments; the moors must become ranches for the production of wool and the tenderest mutton to be found anywhere in Britain.

But the moors were of great potential value for two other purposes: peat and reclamation. The islanders used peat as fuel: why could it not be exploited on a commercial basis? Lewis contained about 710 million tons of peat, in places twenty feet deep. There were no minerals of commercial value in the island, but 'peat would be the Lewis ore', argued Hardy. Five-hundred acres of peat would produce fuel equivalent to 280,000 tons of soft coal. In Canada, the United States, Scandinavia, Russia and elsewhere, peat had been cut, dried, reduced to powder and used successfully to generate heat in stationary engines and locomotives. There were also important by-products, chiefly nitrates and ammonia, and the Swedish Government had recently granted patents for the extraction of motor-oil and alcohol from peat. To these possibilities Hardy added tar, paraffin, asphalt, paper and cardboard, antiseptic dressings, stock food, and even articles of clothing.

'So far,' he continued, 'following tradition and inertia, un-consciously moved by the contemplation of the repulsive stretches of barren moors and of the misery hemmed in between the 'muck' and the sea, the common attitude has been to dismiss Lewis as a peat-bog and leave it at that.' It seemed to have been forgotten that every piece of land in Lewis, except the sandy stretches of coastal plain known as the *machars*, had once been part of the peat-bog. Almost every acre of the crofts had been reclaimed from it by the ancestors of the present tenants. Some-times it was done by skinning the land of peat, and stoning and treating the boulder clay that lay underneath; but more often the peat itself was made fertile by laying on seaweed and shell-sand. The farmlands, which now appeared to the people as so much more desirable than any other part of the island, were originally won from the moor in exactly the same way. *Peat cultivation is an economically sound proposition*, insisted Hardy with heavy underlinings. It has succeeded all over the world, including Scotland, including Lewis itself. 'A very large proportion of the now fertile areas of Inverness, Cromarty and Aberdeenshire has been cleared of that covering. . . . Caithness, once a continuous peat-bog, has been partially reclaimed by Sir John Sinclair.' In Holland and Germany, Denmark and Norway, Canada and the United States, vast areas had been reclaimed. All that was needed, Hardy concluded, was to choose areas where the peat was thin and sloping, construct strong underground drains, plough the surface, disk, harrow and roll it, and add fertilisers, either the natural sea-ware and shell-sand, or preferably in concentrated form. 'One acre treated thus will feed three times as many cattle as two acres of the present Lewis pastures.'

Hardy's report was a remarkable document. It was written with excitement, determination, and even anger. It so exactly matched Leverhulme's own mood at the time when he received it, that he failed to notice that Hardy did not condemn the crofting-system as such. It reached him comparatively late in the development of his ideas (November 1919), when he was already engaged in his struggle with the Scottish Office over the land question and was committed to his large-scale plans for the fishing industry. So it did not influence him to the same extent as it undoubtedly would have done had Hardy come to Lewis in 1918. There is no record that Leverhulme seriously considered the commercial exploitation of peat as a fuel or source of chemicals, and his experiments in reclamation were (for him) half-hearted. One of his difficulties was that he had no right as proprietor to appropriate any part of the common grazings, even for reclamation, without the crofters' consent, which they were most reluctant to give. He embarked on two pilot schemes, one of thirty-five acres on Tong Farm, and a second of six acres on the Arnish moor. He estimated that complete reclamation would cost up to £50 an acre, and would take twelve or fourteen years before satisfactory results could be achieved.[105] In terms both of investment and time, the project did not seem to him worthwhile. No crofter could pay an economic rent for land reclaimed at such expense. Nor did the experiment appear to have the support of the people. His fencing on Arnish moor was broken down: the apples of the small orchard which he planted there were stolen: his example was not followed by the crofters themselves.

Was Hardy's optimism justified? Technically, perhaps; but not in the circumstances which prevailed. Quick results were needed to prove to the people what they disbelieved, that peat was a soil no poorer than many another which had been successfully cultivated in several parts of the world. Like Leverhulme, he was incensed by waste. Exactly a hundred years before, a visitor to Lewis had written:

Let the speculator who admires the industry of the small tenants, turn his eye from the little rocky croft of the laborious farmer, to the wide, undrained, unenclosed and unproductive moor, and there he will find nature languishing for want of that attention which bestowed on worse subjects supports the crowded population of this country. He will then perhaps exclaim against the want of industry which suffers to lie waste tracts of land capable of yielding great resources and of maintaining a great increase of the present population.[106]

Hardy implicitly echoed those words. In the century that had elapsed since they were written, the land had remained the same, the people's character the same. His assistant, Arthur Geddes, commented that 'in failing to make reclamation an integral part of his plans . . . Leverhulme allowed peace to be wrecked'.[107] The discussion of the reasons why Leverhulme failed must be reserved till later: but let it be said now that this was not one of them. Doubts have been expressed by high authorities[108] whether pure peat overlying Archaean gneiss could ever be turned into good agricultural land. The partially unsuccessful experiments of the Canadian T. B. Macaulay on Arnish moor from 1928 onwards seem to confirm this view. But even if it were possible to reclaim the Lewis peat on a large scale, the time, the cost, the people's indifference, and often their hostility, to the idea were obstacles which even Leverhulme could not overcome.

He concentrated instead on forestry and fruit-growing, industries to which Hardy also devoted much attention. In August 1918, Leverhulme wrote:

I have here Mr T. H. Mawson, one of our best experts in England on afforestation and fruit culture. I am driving him over the island, taking a different route each day. Mr Mawson has already found one industry that will thrive here better possibly than in any other part of the world, namely the growing of willow. Covent Garden imports three million willow baskets a year grown in Holland. They should be grown in Lewis. . . . Many other parts of the island are eminently suited for growing raspberries, strawberries, black currants, gooseberries and similar fruits.[109]

In five years time, he said, he would have enough fruit to supply a jam factory. He also started an experimental patch for flax-growing, a nursery for raising spruce-seedlings, a herb-garden and a shrubbery. All these would lead to the establishment of new rural industries, including basket-making, timber production, the distilling of mint and camomile, and the manufacture of linen. It would bring about as great a revolution in the rural economy of Lewis as his fishing schemes would transform Stornoway. Many traditions would be swept aside:

In two or three years companies must be formed for ranching, poultry and dairies. . . . I have under consideration using the sporting lodges for housing managers of afforestation and willow-planting schemes. Of course it would be impossible to develop Lewis commercially, put railways through the island, construct docks and harbours, place herring canneries, and at the same time maintain the sporting attractions of the island, but my instincts lean towards men and women and not to salmon or grouse or deer, and if the interests of the two clash, the salmon and grouse and deer must go.[110]

Finally there was one industry, already established in the Outer Isles, which Leverhulme put second only to fishing. The manufacture of tweed for sale had started during the 19th century, when the women of Harris found that there was a luxury market for the cloth which they wove for the simple needs of their own families. The Dunmores, proprietors of South Harris, were the first to adopt the tweed for their own use, and they were soon followed by the English sporting visitors, who liked the tweed for its hard-wearing qualities and the pleasant subdued colour-schemes produced by the vegetable dyes used in its manufacture. The steady demand for Harris tweed before the first war developed into a boom soon after 1918. Lewis, where there had been few weavers in the early part of the century, took up the industry energetically, and was soon overtaking its neighbour-island in the production of what was still known universally but loosely as Harris tweed.

Traditionally, every operation was carried out in the crofters' own homes and on the simplest wooden machinery. Before the war, the wool came from the backs of their own sheep. It was dyed with the natural dyes available around the croft and on the rocks and moors—seaweed, lichen, dandelion, heather, bog-myrtle and many others—and it was fixed with soot mixed with ammonia. It was then carded (the wool drawn out into flossy lengths), spun on the old-fashioned spinning-wheels from a distaff, woven on wooden hand-looms, and finally 'waulked' by wetting and thumping the cloth to draw the threads closer together. By 1919 all these operations except carding were still carried out in the homes of the Harris crofters; but in Lewis much of the wool was dyed and spun as well as carded by machinery in two mills at Stornoway. The mills sent out the yarn and received back the cloth.

It occurred at once to Leverhulme that this was the only industry in which the Outer Hebrides had a natural monopoly. Harris tweed was already well-known throughout the world. But the demand for it depended largely on its reputation as durable cloth woven in the crofters' own homes. This was not solely an appeal to sentiment: there was a distinction, which even a non-expert could tell at a glance, between the genuine Harris tweed and imitations of it produced by machinery at Galashiels and elsewhere on the mainland of Scotland and even in Yorkshire. The question was (and still is) whether the advantage of maintaining the quality and sentimental associations of home-made tweed outweighed the obvious disadvantages of dispersing its manufacture to innumerable small sheds through the islands, when the work could be done more economically and efficiently with power-looms under a central factory roof.

Leverhulme was in no doubt that the existing system should, in its essentials, be preserved. He saw that the rural tradition of the industry, long since outmoded in Lancashire, was its main asset in the Hebrides. To this extent, at any rate, he refused to play the role of a Samuel Crompton. If the tweed was to sell widely in the United States and other luxury markets, he must be able to advertise it by illustrations of its manufacture in typically Hebridean settings. Besides, dispersal provided remunerative work in the furthest corners of the island. 'In Uig we are wholly dependent on the tweeds,' a crofter wrote to him, 'as there is no fishing, and no work to be got except for the few who can leave their homes to work in Stornoway.' Once a single weaving factory was established, the tweeds produced in it would lower the quality and undercut the price of every tweed produced at home: the crofters of Uig and other isolated districts would be deprived of their sole remaining means of livelihood.

Leverhulme did not agree, however, that the importance of maintaining tradition should extend to home-spinning. For many years much of the wool woven in Lewis crofts had been sent out from the Stornoway mills; and even in Harris, where tradition died harder, the people had been prepared to compromise with wool carded in a small factory at Tarbert, founded in 1900 by Sir Samuel Scott for the crofters' benefit. Leverhulme hoped to make this compromise universal. His wool would be machine-dyed, machine-carded, machine-spun: only the weaving and the finishing would be carried out in the people's homes. He was advised that the machine-spun yarn was indistinguishable from the yarn produced by the spinning-wheel, and to spin it by the old-fashioned method was a waste of the crofters' time. As much as £4 a week could be earned by a good weaver, but only 12/- a week by a good spinner. Therefore, he argued,

all the labour available in Lewis and Harris can be concentrated on hand-loom weaving, undiluted by time spent on the starvation earnings to be made by hand-spinning. My intention is to erect at convenient centres in Lewis and Harris small power-driven dyeing, carding and spinning industries to prepare the crofters' wool for the handloom weaver to work into cloth in or near their homes.[111]

There was a special significance in his use of the words 'in or near'. He saw no reason why the weaving should be done on the croft itself, where the loom was usually housed in a draughty and leaking shed. He proposed to erect or convert suitable huts in each township to hold four or six looms apiece, and heat them with small peat-stoves. ('The smoke from the peat must go up the chimney,' he wrote to James Simpson, 'but it wouldn't be a bad thing if a little of the smoke is allowed to escape into the shed for advertising purposes.') Such sheds were fitted up in the Ness, Barvas and Carloway districts, and equipped with modern automatic looms, which Leverhulme loaned free of charge to the crofters, on condition that they sold their tweed exclusively to Kenneth Mackenzie's, the Stornoway firm which would supply them with their yarn. These new steel looms, which came from Keighley in Yorkshire, were not strictly speaking hand-looms, for they were worked by the feet and the mechanism automatically threw the shuttle to and fro across the web. In the older wooden type of loom, the shuttles were thrown across by one hand and returned by the other. The steel loom was originally introduced to the Hebrides to assist disabled ex-servicemen who had lost the use of either hand, but they have since become universal, the wooden loom surviving as a museum piece. There is no recognisable difference in the tweed produced by the two forms of loom, but it must be admitted that by grouping these 'automatic' looms in township sheds, Leverhulme was stretching rather far the definition of Harris tweed as 'hand-woven in the crofters' own homes.' The sheds have since been dismantled, and weaving is again a genuine cottage-industry.

Leverhulme's personal interest in the industry did not stop short there. He acquired a controlling interest in Kenneth Mackenzie's mill at Stornoway. This enterprising firm, which until Leverhulme's purchase was known as Lewis Wool Mills Co, and had been established in 1904, was about to double its output of yarn to 6,000 lbs a week by installing two additional 300-spindle mules, run by a private electricity plant. In March 1919 Leverhulme bought two-thirds of the firm's Ordinary shares, and acquired the remainder four years later. Kenneth Mackenzie remained as managing-director, with his son to assist him. They distributed yarn widely in Harris as well as in Lewis, and undertook the marketing of the tweed in many parts of the world, particularly in Canada and the United States, where a mail-order trade, aided by Leverhulme's wide-spread connections and reputation, was quickly established.

It is not clear why Leverhulme decided to add to his already huge properties and undertakings in Lewis the islands of Harris and St Kilda. Certainly it cannot have been because he feared failure in Lewis, for he visited the southern island as early as August 1918, when his enthusiasm was at its height, and he was already in negotiation for its sale by the end of the year. It has been suggested that he needed Harris for the full development of his fishing schemes, but this is hindsight: Stornoway and the other island harbours had more than the necessary capacity for his purposes. His son says only that Leverhulme's 'attachment to the eerie beauty of the Hebrides and his confidence in the ultimate success of his undertakings was to be further evidenced by his acquiring the island of Harris.'[112] Attachment there surely was: but by that time there was also a certain love of acquisition for its own sake. Harris would round off a complete island, for whatever history or local government boundaries might show to the contrary, Leverhulme saw the Lewis-Harris land-mass as a single unit, in which the people and their problems were indivisible. He would develop both islands by the same methods, in conjunction with each other and not in rivalry.

Harris was divided into two parts by the isthmus of Tarbert, each belonging to a separate proprietor, and he acquired them both by stages. He completed the purchase of South Harris and St Kilda from the Earl of Dunmore in May 1919, with entry into possession as from January 1919. The price was £36,000. At first, one or two parts of the island were excepted from the sale, such as Borve Lodge, which Lord Dunmore continued to hold on a ninety-nine year lease, and several islands in East and West Lochs Tarbert, but within a few years Leverhulme's possession of South Harris was complete. The northern part of the island was purchased from Sir Samuel Scott in June 1919[113] for £20,000, Sir Samuel retaining a fifteen-year lease of the main residence, Amhuinnsuidh Castle, at a nominal rent of £1 a year. The island was actually transferred in October 1919, and in that month Samuel Scott issued to his tenants a printed notice in English and Gaelic, explaining his reasons for the sale:

Owing to the increase in taxation and great rise in all expenses caused by the war, I find that it would be impossible for me to continue in Harris as in former days. Till recently it had never entered my head that I should not remain your Proprietor during my life, and it was only with the greatest reluctance that I came to the conclusion that it was in the best interests of all that I should accept Lord Leverhulme's offer. . . . After long talks with Lord Leverhulme I was convinced that in him you would have a proprietor who would further your interests and do all in his power, far more than I could ever do, to help you. At my death the estate would have had to be sold, and I believed it best for you all that the estate should be sold to a man who will be a good and generous landlord than that it should be sold after my death to some unknown person who might not have had your interests at heart.

North and South Harris together were 146 square miles in area, with a population in 1921 of 4,750. Lewis and Harris combined totalled 570,000 acres. Leverhulme thus became the biggest private landowner in the kingdom.

# Chapter Six

# THE RAIDS

THE BUILDING OF the Stornoway factories and housing estates began in earnest during the early months of 1919, and the roads were started in the spring. Leverhulme was constantly travelling up and down to the Hebrides—he made eight separate visits during the year, none longer than three weeks, some as short as five days—to deal with the affairs of the various fishing, canning and tweed companies which he had formed, and to entertain his guests who flowed in and out of the castle and shooting-lodges throughout the summer.

In addition to his unceasing responsibility for Lever Brothers, and the work entailed in launching Mac Fisheries, he became Mayor of his native town of Bolton for 1919, a duty which he took extremely seriously, providing the people with a mayoral year such as they never witnessed before or since: in August, for example, he entertained all the ex-servicemen of the town and their wives, 28,000 people, at a stupendous reception in Queen's Park. He also went constantly in search of new ideas and information about the fishing industry to Aberdeen, Fleetwood, Newcastle, Grimsby, Great Yarmouth and Billingsgate fish-market in London. In September he was in Norway with Angus Watson, to look at housing-schemes and fish-curing methods; and in November he embarked on a two-months voyage to the United States, Canada and Japan, mainly on Lever Brothers business, but never missing an opportunity to pick up ideas useful to Lewis and Harris. The flow of suggestions, enquiries and instructions to his agents in the two islands continued across half the world.

1918 had been a year of self-introduction and planning; 1919 was to be the year for building; 1920 the year of development; 1921 the year of consolidation. This schedule was upset by a single unforeseen difficulty: the attitude of the Lewis ex-servicemen to the land, and the support given to them, despite Leverhulme's protests, by the Scottish Secretary, Robert Munro. The controversy between the two men came to dominate and eventually halt all Leverhulme's schemes for Lewis. It became a national issue, involving not only the future of the islands, but great principles of government which in our own day, in different contexts and different territories, are still matters of ardent debate.

The main questions which arose can be stated quite simply. Are the people of a backward country the best judges of their own interests? Even if it is assumed that they are not, should 'improvement' be forced upon them? To what extent should the views of a minority who resist change be allowed to prevail over the majority who desire it? Those were the questions of principle. The application of them to Lewis between 1918 and 1923 raised another set of questions. Was Leverhulme justified in thinking that his schemes would solve the problems of Lewis, and by example, the problems of the Highlands and Islands in general? Were his schemes incompatible, as he himself believed, with the maintenance of the crofting system? Was the clash between him and the Government unavoidable? These two sets of questions summarise the central subject of this narrative: the confrontation between a twentieth-century millionaire industrialist and the most primitive community to be found anywhere in the British Isles; and the conflict between a Government department and an intensely practical individualist.

Leverhulme's attitude to the crofting-system has already been stated. He thought it a wholly impossible life for a man because it divided his energies and did not produce a living income. It meant a life-sentence of hard-labour for the crofter, and exile for his son. Although there appeared to be more than enough land in Lewis to support three times the population, this was an illusion, for the moor could only be won for intensive farming by slow and expensive methods which would oblige the proprietor to charge for the resulting crofts a rent well beyond the average crofter's means. If nothing were done to relieve the coastal strips of their overburden of crofters, cottars and squatters, the land, and consequently the crops and stock, would deteriorate further, and as the population grew, so the crofts would be divided into smaller and smaller patches, until they became little larger than allotments. Leverhulme saw no end to the misery which surrender to mere habit would impose on the people. But if even a proportion of them could be induced to work as fishermen or in factories, and others were assisted to concentrate on tweed-making, then the crofts which they no longer needed would be added to neighbouring crofts to form holdings of a size which would be agriculturally and economically sound.

In his analysis of the problem, Leverhulme insisted that mischief-makers had misrepresented him in two important respects: he did not intend to industrialise Lewis in the same sense as the Midlands had been industrialised in the nineteenth century; and he did not wish to deny a croft to any man who preferred it to the way-of-living that he offered as an alternative.

In the earliest days of his proprietorship Leverhulme had certainly drawn a parallel between the poverty of eighteenth-century Lancashire and twentieth-century Lewis, and had given his hearers every reason to believe that he intended to adopt in one place much the same methods that had brought prosperity to the other. He realised, of course, that island temperament and the different sources of wealth in Lewis made the comparison inexact. It was also exceedingly unpopular. In talking to people in trains and on the island-ship,

I have found that the picture they have in their minds is one of huge iron-works, huge cotton-factories, machine-shops and so on. There is not a single word in any of my speeches to justify that idea. I do not think you could make a success of exotic industry in Lewis any more than you could grow bananas or coconuts in Lewis. If we are to succeed, we must have industries native to Lewis, chiefly fishing—and to carry on the life of the fisherman under modern conditions is one of the most remunerative of occupations.[114]

The last observation was certainly true: even in 1913, the crews of drifters were taking home an average weekly earning of £6 a man, compared to the few shillings at which Leverhulme valued the produce of a croft, and since 1913 the difference was even more greatly marked. But to suggest that his proposed industrialisation of Lewis was little more than the modernisation of fishing methods was to err on the opposite extreme. There were to be canning factories, spinning mills and weaving sheds in many parts of the island, and a railway system linking them, with (as a start) twenty-four trains a day. The permanent population was to be at least doubled; and sometimes he spoke of multiplying it ten or a hundred-fold. Electric power was to be widespread. Stornoway was to become the chief town and harbour of the north-west of Scotland, and now Harris was also to be involved. None of this could come about without a complete transformation of the economy. There was no disguising his belief, as he expressed it privately to his solicitor, that 'if the island were organised on broad lines such as in Lanarkshire, Lancashire, Yorkshire and elsewhere, but with more agreeable surroundings than industrialism is carried on in those places, then it would seem to me that a new era had dawned for Lewis.'[115]

Secondly, he insisted that any Lewisman who wanted to work on a croft would not be prevented by him from doing so. He could understand better than any industrialist of his age the significance of a house and garden of one's own and the leisure to enjoy it. Had that not been his motive in creating Port Sunlight, in transforming Thornton Manor, The Hill at Hampstead and Rivington for his own delight? Nor was he in the least unaware of the spiritual values attached to a croft. He admired the Lewismen's island patriotism and attitude to life; he found fault only with their attitude to work and their indifference to comfort, a word that he found difficult to disassociate from decency. But let them choose. Most, he predicted, would choose to break with the past: in that case, there would be more than enough crofts to spare for those who chose not to. For the former, it would not mean a complete divorce from the soil. The country would still be within easy walking distance of every part of Stornoway, and the houses that he proposed to build ten to an acre would have gardens attached to them in which they could grow, under guidance, more and better vegetables than they had ever grown before.

How, then, could any of the crofters suspect his motives when he put so reasonable a choice before them? Some of them did so, and carried their objection to the point of criminal defiance, because they saw in Leverhulme's proposals an attempt to deny them what they regarded as their birthright to land. While they acknowledged his promise not to evict any man from his croft, they asked what was to be done for those who were landless, or who were squatting unwanted and almost destitute on a corner of a neighbour's or parent's croft? It might take years before his schemes matured and sufficient houses were built in Stornoway and elsewhere to release the crofts he promised them. How could he be certain that the people would co-operate sufficiently for his plan to work at all? The Lewisman, they argued, generalising from their own prejudices, did not want to live in a town side by side with other families. Least of all did he want a town-house which would not be truly his own, and from which he could be instantly ejected by a proprietor who was also his employer. Rumours, which were not baseless, had reached them from Port Sunlight that a tenant held his house only so long as his conduct at work and in his leisure hours was found satisfactory, and that he was subject to all kinds of restrictions on the animals he might keep, the washing he might hang out, and the use to which he could put his garden. This was something quite different from a croft, which was a home as well as a house, 'a real centre for the loyalty of the members of the family, whether they are living or working there or are domiciled in a strange land sending back remittances and looking forward for the day of return.'[116] The point was well made by a correspondent to the local paper:

They can scarcely believe that in ten years time crofts will go a-begging—the reason being that a residence in the town, however attractive, lacks many of the advantages of the humble crofter's home. How often have we heard the expression *cha' neil ac' ach a rum mal* ('all they would have is one rented room'), and how familiar is the Lewisman's antipathy to such a dwelling. The crofter feels that whatever may happen to him, his family have a home, and any scheme which is to allure him to the town should provide for like fixity of tenure.[117]

The strong feeling that a croft was something to fall back on in times when all else failed, and to which a man had a right of occupation by long custom and (since 1886) by law, was shared by many who did not resort to violence or openly oppose Leverhulme. Some of them were specialist fisherman or specialist crofters, already devoting the greater part of their time to the sea or the land, and to them Leverhulme's argument that the fisherman had no need of a croft, nor the crofter of a boat, made little appeal. Each was a form of insurance should the fishing or the crops fail, not an additional occupation. That they would be deprived of the opportunity to turn from one to the other, and instead be obliged to chance their whole future on another man's business-gamble which even he admitted to be hazardous, losing at the same time the home in which many generations of the same family might have been born and died, assumed in their minds an even greater importance than their desire for independence from any employer.

Having little real confidence in Leverhulme's proposals, and immune to the personal impact which he had made on the island during his first summer, soldiers and sailors who trickled back to Lewis during 1919 thought foremost of the land to which they considered themselves entitled. They demanded crofts. The land had been wickedly taken from their grandfathers fifty years before. They had risked their lives for their country—the words 'land' and 'country' acquired a simple synonymy—and the Government had promised it to them. Where was the land to come from? Not from the open moor, which was wearyingly difficult to break in, and which was in any case part of the common grazings, another inalienable right. The new crofts could come only from the farms. So the Government must honour their pledge by breaking up the farms.

The farmland, the 'green land of their forefathers', through which the ruins of the old crofts still show like stones under a baize cloth, was desirable for four reasons. First, it was the symbol of the evictions, a wrong now to be righted. Secondly, it was thought to be the best land in the island. Thirdly, it was held by men who were not regarded as true Lewismen. And fourthly, it was the very land to which the Government's pre-war and war-time promises had referred.

Of the first claim, enough has previously been said: in the main, it was certainly true that the land was once in the occupation of the crofters who were dispossessed by sheep, and all opinion, including Leverhulme's, agreed that the evictions of the nineteenth century had been scandalous. The second claim was justified only in so far as some of the farms lay on the rich *machar* land but they 'possessed little or no initial superiority over neighbouring crofting settlements. . . . As Hardy wrote in his report, "the chief superiority of the farms resulted from levelling, drainage and enclosure," by landlord and farmer, sixty or seventy years before'[118] Since then, they had been more scientifically farmed than the crofts, and their contrasting appearance, seen over the rough stone dykes of the township, made them appear infinitely desirable.

That the tenants were 'foreigners' was to some extent true of the two farms which became the subjects of acutest controversy. Coll was farmed by a second-generation Lewisman, Charles

Hunter, whose father came from the south of Scotland; and
Gress by Peter Liddle, an Ayrshire man whose uncle had preceded him. Nothing was imputed personally by the crofters
against either man, but their non-Lewis ancestry reawakened
memories of the tacksmen planted in their island a century before;
and the farmers had always lived a life apart from the crofters,
helping them with advice or the loan of a bull when they could,
but inhabiting a larger house and farming the land on entirely
different principles. It was also said of the tenants that instead of
fighting for their country, they had grown fat on wartime profits.
By the time this accusation was made, passions were so inflamed
that there is no vouching for its accuracy.

The fourth claim on the farms was that the Government had
proposed, even before the war, that they should be broken up
for crofts. This was true of four of them. The 1911 Act had given
the Scottish Secretary power to divide farmland compulsorily for
the enlargment of existing crofts or the formation of new ones,
provided that they exceeded 150 acres in size or £80 in rental.
Home-farms were excluded from this arrangement, and any
farm 'if its appropriation would seriously impair the use of the
remainder as a deer-forest.' Compensation was to be paid both to
the landlord and tenant. Application had been made to Major
Duncan Matheson in 1913 to divide four of the Lewis farms.
They were: Galson, to form fifty-six new crofts; Gress, forty new
crofts; Carnish and Ardroil (run as one farm), twenty new crofts
and seventeen enlargements of existing crofts; and Orinsay-with-
Stimervay, fourteen new crofts. Coll was not among those
scheduled, for its rent fell below the limit that permitted compulsory division.

Major Matheson had opposed the Government's intention to
divide these farms on the grounds that they were not suitable for
crofting land, that he would lose in rents more than he gained in
compensation, and that the proposed total of a hundred and
thirty new crofts would go very little way to relieve congestion.[119]
The outbreak of war prevented further negotiation on the
complicated subject of compensation, but immediately after the
Armistice the Government's intention was remembered and the
crofters' claims renewed.

Leverhulme strongly resisted the proposal to divide up any
farms, particularly those, like Gress, which lay near Stornoway.
He put forward two main arguments against it. His first was

Major Matheson's third, that the division of the farms would do almost nothing to relieve congestion; the second, that the farms were essential for supplying Stornoway with milk. As the whole ensuing controversy was to turn on these two points, they must be further elucidated.

There were only seven farms in the island over 150 acres in size, and fifteen others between 30 and 150 acres. If all these farms were divided, they would supply no more than about three hundred and fifty new crofts. If the Government took only the farms which the law entitled them to divide compulsorily, they would form a hundred and forty-three new crofts of six acres each. The demand for crofts was more than ten times that number. Every squatter wanted a croft of his own, and there were 1,600 squatters in Lewis. In addition, there were the returning ex-servicemen, who had priority for any croft which fell vacant. The total required, Leverhulme estimated, was between two and three thousand new crofts, if a crofting policy were accepted; and it was on this estimate that he based his own decision to build 3,000 houses in the town and elsewhere. Let nobody be deceived, he said, by the number who had formally applied for a croft. They amounted to no more than eight hundred.[120] The others had not registered their claim only because they realised that the position was so hopeless. It was therefore quite absurd to imagine that the problem could be solved by splitting up the farms. This policy would merely whet an appetite that could never be satisfied. As soon as the Government's proposal was mooted, Leverhulme wrote to his Chamberlain:

It is as well to be candid and outspoken from the very beginning. I am strongly in favour of anything and everything that will improve the conditions of the people of this island. I am not, however, in favour that the proprietor should always be the stalking horse for immature schemes of Government. . . . I am not convinced that the proposals of the Scottish Office are other than a makeshift dealing with the matter, and that in twenty years from now, when all the farms have been absorbed, they will then be up against the proposition in as an acute a stage as it is in today.[121]

As proprietor, he considered that he held the land in trust for the people. It was as much his duty to defend them against a government department, and against the short-sightedness of a few hot-heads amongst the crofting population, as it was to protect the interests of the part of the estate that remained in his own hands. Had he been in Major Matheson's position in 1913, he might have considered assuaging the more clamant demands for land by splitting up some of the outlying farms. But circumstances in 1919 were quite different. The number of applicants for crofts was greatly increased; and his plans would make crofts redundant. Give him a fair chance, and he would soon replace the eight hundred applications for crofts which did not exist by eight hundred crofts for which there were no applicants. But for the plan to succeed, the farms were essential. He needed them to provide milk for the growing population of Stornoway.

To this argument Leverhulme returned again and again. It was quite illogical that an island like Lewis, with its vast grazings, should be obliged to import fifty gallons of milk a day from Aberdeenshire. With the curtailment of the steamer service to thrice weekly, the milk was at best thirty-six hours old on arrival, seventy-two hours old on alternate days, and as much as ninety-six hours old at week-ends. The extra transport-charge made it the most expensive milk in the country. The people could not afford to buy it at 2/8d a gallon, and the children's health was suffering. As soon as the new housing schemes were completed, there would be a milk famine. Lewis must become self-sufficient in milk. The crofters' cattle must be improved and proper feeding-stuffs imported (this was arranged by Lever Brothers), but the crofters themselves could not supply the milk for the town. The only solution was for the farms around Stornoway to be converted into proper dairy farms. He set an example by importing a superior breed of cow for the Manor farm, and instructed James Simpson to prepare plans for erecting steadings for dairy cows at Gress, from where the milk would be brought by road transport to Stornoway. This was the most important of the farms which the Scottish Office now intended to split up into crofts.

Leverhulme allowed the milk question to dominate all his thinking on farm policy. He was right to assume that the crofters could not themselves supply milk to Stornoway, for their surplus was too small to be worth collecting, and the conditions in which their cattle lived and were milked would have created a danger to public health: in November 1920 there was an outbreak of typhoid in Stornoway due to this cause. But the horror with which Leverhulme regarded the import of milk from Aberdeenshire was much exaggerated. The milk cost the consumer only a penny a quart more in Stornoway than in Aberdeen; and because it was sterilised and refrigerated, it arrived in better condition than much of the milk produced in the island itself.[122] Right though Leverhulme was to consider the organisation of dairy farms, his threatened milk-famine was a bogey. It never occurred except in a limited degree at the beginning of 1919, and need never have occurred again, for the excellent alternative source of supply from the mainland was already in operation. The almost hysterical tones in which Leverhulme conducted this part of his argument ('Will you let the children of the town die, or grow up as weak saplings?') suggests an untypical lapse in his sense of proportion. The farms were important, but not so important that their retention against the Government's policy was worth the sacrifice of all else. He dwelled on the milk-supply as if it were a matter of great principle, when it was nothing more than a matter for administration and compromise.

The Scottish Office opened negotiations with Leverhulme for the break-up of some of the Lewis farms in the summer of 1918, only a few months after he had assumed his proprietorship. Having compulsory powers under the Small Landholders Acts, they had no need to ask his approval, but they naturally preferred to take action with his co-operation than without it. Leverhulme's Edinburgh solicitor was shown a plan of the intended small-holdings in Lewis as early as 6 August 1918. It allowed for the creation of 131 new crofts and seventeen enlargements. Lever-hulme himself was shown the plan in mid-September, when Thomas Wilson, the Board of Agriculture's sub-commissioner for the Hebrides, called on him at Lews Castle. 'Mr Wilson took up rather an aggressive attitude,' Leverhulme reported.[123] A month later he first discussed the matter with the Scottish Secretary himself. Leverhulme's account of the interview was that nothing was decided: Mr Munro had merely asked to see the plans of the proposed harbour-works and railway-system, which were supplied to him. But the annual report of the Board of Agriculture gives a rather clearer indication of the trend of these discussions, and makes it obvious that the attitudes taken up by each side were already hardening:

Towards the close of the year (1918), the Board approached the new proprietor, Lord Leverhulme, with a view to securing his co-operation in putting the schemes [for the division of the farms] into operation. Lord Leverhulme, however, intimated that he had in view the projection of other schemes for the development of the industries and the improvement of transport facilities in the island, and considered that these would be more effective in solving the economic difficulties of Lewis than the constitution of small-holdings under the Small Land-holders (Scotland) Acts.

The Board represented to him that his proposals and their schemes did not conflict with each other, but could be carried out concurrently with mutual advantage, and that *the people of Lewis, accustomed as they are to crofter tenure, would not readily accept any other, but would on the contrary be likely to press for completion of the Board's proposals whatever other steps might be taken to ameliorate existing conditions.*[124]

The italicised sentence expressed the Board's consistently held belief. Robert Munro adopted much the same attitude, though he was anxious not to break with Leverhulme. Himself a Highlander, the son of a Free Church Minister from the eastern part of Ross-shire, he knew how passionate was the crofter's attachment to the land. His point of view was shared by all political parties. The Government was committed to it by many past statements and by the very passage of the Acts which permitted division of the farms, and it would have been difficult for the Scottish Secretary to withdraw at the very moment when the men were beginning to return to their homes and political pressure was mounting.

The General Election of December 1918 came at an unfortunate time for Leverhulme. It was the first election at which the Western Isles were given separate representation, and the division of the Lewis farms became the major issue in the constituency, overshadowing even the economic revolution which Leverhulme proposed. The strong Liberal vote was split between two candidates, Dr Donald Murray, a native of Stornoway and Medical Officer of Health for Lewis; and William Mitchell Cotts, a London shipowner of lowland origins, standing as the Lloyd George (Coalition) candidate. The Labour candidate was Hugh M'Cowan from Oban, who also stood under the banner of the Highland Land League.

All three, with varying degrees of emphasis, pledged themselves to support a policy of dividing up the farms:

*Murray*: There is no room for large farms in these islands. In many places the people have been driven from the good land and placed among the rocks. The process must be reversed. All the land which can be cultivated by crofters must be divided among the people.[125]

*Cotts*:      Q Would you be in favour of doing away with the deer-
              forests?
             A I would.

             Q Are you in favour of breaking up the large farms in
              Lewis?
             A Where the land is available, certainly.[126]

*M'Cowan*:  I assert the restoration of the land to the people, and
            their right to fish in the seas, lochs and rivers.[127]

Whenever Leverhulme's schemes were mentioned by either of
the Liberal candidates, it was always with politeness, more cordial
on Cotts' part than Murray's, but on the common assumption
that Leverhulme would wish to meet the evident desire of the
ex-servicemen for land, and that his plans were by no means
incompatible with the breaking up of the farms. This was the
general attitude at the time, for Leverhulme's growing dispute
with the Government was not yet public knowledge. Nowhere
was it more clearly illustrated than in a letter written from the
front by a Lewisman in the last weeks of the war:

Fritz is getting smashed on all fronts. . . . I see that the Lewis front
is as cheerful as our own at present, with Lord Leverhulme in command. He evidently means to do well for the island. Let us hope that
all the schemes will mature, and that in a few years time the place will
be a busy hive of industry in a network of electric railways. . . .

You ask for my opinion on the settlement of Lewismen on the land
after the war. . . . How can the majority of us be truly patriotic having
to fight for countless acres that by right should have been ours long
ago? We could do a day's work for a day's wage in any country and
under any flag. Let us have something of our very own to fight for in
the next war, and there need be no conscription. I think we can leave
it safely to Dr Murray.[128]

Enthusiastic support for Leverhulme could thus co-exist with
advocacy of the very policy to which he was utterly opposed. Dr
Murray at that moment read his constituents' minds correctly.
The only one of the three candidates to be born a Lewisman, the
longest in the field, and an attractive speaker, he was elected the
first Member for the Western Isles on 14 December 1918, in
spite of the split in the Liberal vote:

| | |
|---|---|
| Murray (Independent Liberal) | 3765 |
| Cotts (Coalition Liberal) | 3375 |
| M'Cowan (Labour and Highland League) | 809 |

Leverhulme, who had already seen in Dr Murray a potential antagonist, wrote to Cotts: 'Heartiest congratualtions on your magnificent fight. If you had had another fourteen days, you would have been returned, and I hope still to see you soon as Member for our Islands.'

During the first two months of 1919, there was little sign of impending trouble. The works progressed in Stornoway, and Mac Fisheries was gaily launched in London, while Leverhulme met the Scottish Secretary at intervals to press his case in private. In March the storm burst.

In the first week of that month a handful of men invaded the farm of Tong, three miles north of Stornoway, and began to peg out for themselves six-acre crofts. As it happened, Tong was one of the smallest and most ill-managed farms in the island. The raiders maintained that John Newall, the farmer, had no right to deny them the land which he neglected. They had chosen it for their demonstration because it was impossible to argue that Tong under crofts would be less productive than Tong as it was at present. But its very smallness introduced a further compli-cation. Newall appealed for protection to the Highland Land League, the crofters' powerful friend, on the grounds that Tong was little more than a large croft, and the League supported him to the extent of issuing a writ against Leverhulme for wrongful eviction when he deprived Newall of his land for building quarter-acre cottages on part of it. Meanwhile the raiders remained in occupation of about thirty acres.

The following week, on Saturday, 8 March 1919, their example was followed on a more serious scale. A party of ten men, shortly followed by thirty more, seized part of the land of Gress, drove off the farmer's sheep, drove on their own, and began frantically turning over the soil and planting potatoes. At Coll farm, between Gress and Tong, the raids were repeated. The raiders staked out their claims beside the river in a large field that had not been cultivated for nearly twenty years. As others joined them, soon the whole farm was covered with little knots of men busily tilling the soil while their women carried up seaweed from the shore to fertilise it. The farmer, Charles Hunter, stood aside, not daring to remonstrate for fear that they would set fire to his steadings. Next day, the crofters' animals were grazing over the land from which his own cattle had been driven out to the moor.

That was the beginning. Lawlessness spread rapidly to every part of the island. In April an attempt was made by the people of Shader to seize Galson Farm and mark out small-holdings for themselves; but when the posse arrived at the farm, they found themselves forestalled by the people of Borve, who had stolen a march on their neighbours and already divided up the best lands. An absurd situation developed on the ground, the Shader men demanding that the Borve men give them at least an equal right to trespass, and they came to an amicable arrangement to share the farm between them. In the Park district, worst hit by the evictions, half-a-dozen men seized Crobeg Farm. In the immediate neighbourhood of Stornoway there were raids on Melbost Farm and on Sandwick Hill Parks, which by June 1919 were overrun by a great number of horses, cows and sheep, belonging to upwards of a hundred different crofting families. By the end of the summer, sixteen Lewis farms out of a total of twenty-two had been occupied by force, wholly or in part.

In some cases the men remained, and began to erect the type of small hut that one associates with the gold-rushes of the past. On other farms there were merely token raids, the boundaries of the intended crofts being marked out with a plough, and the farmer left in occupation on the crofters' sufferance. Nowhere was actual physical injury done to any person or animal, for there was no resistance offered: the farmers could do little else than watch the raiders unharness the horses from the plough and dismantle the stone dykes which divided the farm from the neighbouring township.

Argument was unavailing. The men were determined. 'We fought for this land in France,' said one of them, 'and if necessary we will die for it in Lewis.' Others emphasised that the raids were not a demonstration against Leverhulme, but against the Government for their slowness.

Leverhulme's attitude was at first completely misunderstood. It was assumed that he would give the raiders his moral support. He found himself appealed to by the raiders of Gress to protect their growing crops from the animals of the farmer whose land they had stolen. He was asked to arbitrate between two rival townships who claimed prior rights to land that belonged to neither of them. Others, with the Highlander's natural courtesy, asked him to sanction their illegal acts:

Owing to difficulties of securing feeding-stuffs for our horses, we have acquired the park adjacent to Goathill Farm for grazing purposes during this year, and thereafter to be cultivated. We are quite prepared to pay a fair rent for the park. We trust therefore that your Lordship will grant us this request.[129]

Leverhulme immediately made it clear that he could not approve of raiding in any circumstances. To this letter he replied:

I would inform you at once that what you have done is an illegal act for which there can be no justification—and which leaves me with only one of two courses: either I must appeal to your practical common sense, or I must appeal to the strong arm of the law. . . . It amounts to just the same as if you had raided any of the shops or warehouses in Stornoway which sell food for horses. . . . Goathill Farm is essential to the development of Stornoway, both for the milk-supply and in providing sites for houses. The acts you are doing would make life in the island, if followed by all others, impossible. I am convinced that on consideration you will withdraw.

The men did so; but elsewhere Leverhulme's appeals were less successful. Three days after the raid on Gress, on 11 March 1919, he went to the township of Back, the local centre of the troubles, and spoke to the people in the schoolhouse. He repeated his main arguments for the schemes which he had undertaken in Lewis, and told them that at that very moment a large firm of contractors (Sir Robert MacAlpine's) were landing in Stornoway the materials for the first three hundred houses. He continued:

Do not think that I despise the croft. The man who wants a croft must have one, as far as the land will go. But I ask you to face the problem from the point of view of your children and grandchildren. All my life I have worked with people and not against them. I am not working against you now. . . . I ask you to give my schemes a ten-year trial—surely that is not unreasonable for a problem a hundred years old?

The speech was greeted with applause, and as his car left the schoolhouse, 'hearty cheers were raised for his Lordship.'

They were repeated the next day, less certainly, when he spoke to a gathering of people in the open air by the bridge at Gress itself. Colin Macdonald, the special envoy of the Board of Agriculture, who was himself present, has left an account of this speech and the replies which it evoked. It is so splendid a piece of reporting that its dramatisation and minor inaccuracies should not be reasons for omitting it from this account:

It was a sullen crowd, resentful of the situation which had developed. One wrong note might have precipitated serious trouble. But no wrong note was struck; and if Lord Leverhulme sensed any danger he certainly showed no sign. He walked right into the middle of the crowd, made a little ring for himself and his interpreter, mounted an upturned tub (in which the farmer was wont to brew a real knock-me-down brand of beer), raised high his hat, smiled genially all round and said:

'Good morning, everybody! Have you noticed that the sun is shining this morning?—and that this is the first time it has shone in Lewis for ten days?' (This was a fact!)

'I regard that as a good omen. This is going to be a great meeting. This is going to be a friendly meeting. This meeting will mark the beginning of a new era in the history of this loyal island of Lewis that you love above all places on earth, and that I too have learned to love. So great is my regard for Lewis and its people that I am prepared to adventure a big sum of money for the development of the resources of the island and of the fisheries. . . .

'Hitherto, more often than not, the return to port has been with light boats and heavy hearts. In future it will be with light hearts and heavy boats!' (*Loud cheers*). . . .

And just then, while the artist was still adding skilful detail, there was a dramatic interruption.

One of the ringleaders managed to rouse himself from the spell, and in an impassioned voice addressed the crowd in Gaelic, and this is what he said:

'*So so, fhiribh! Cha dean so gnothach! Bheireadh am bodach milbheulach sin chreidsinn oirnn gu'm bheil dubh geal's geal dubh! Ciod e dhuinn na bruadairean briagha aige, a thig no nach tig?* 'Se am fearann tha sinn ag iarraidh. Agus 'se tha mise a faighneachd* [turning to face Lord Leverhulme and pointing dramatically towards him]: *an toir thu dhuinn am fearann?*'

The effect was electrical. The crowd roared their approbation.

Lord Leverhulme looked bewildered at this, to him, torrent of unintelligible sounds, but when the frenzied cheering with which it was greeted died down, he spoke:

'I am sorry! It is my great misfortune that I do not understand the Gaelic language. But perhaps my interpreter will translate for me what has been said?'

Said the interpreter: 'I am afraid, Lord Leverhulme, that it will be impossible for me to convey to you in English what has been so forcefully said in the older tongue; but I will do my best'—and his best was a masterpiece, not only in words but in tone and gesture and general effect:

'Come, come, men! This will not do! This honey-mouthed man would have us believe that black is white and white is black. *We* are not concerned with his fancy dreams that may or may not come true! What we want is the *land*—and the question I put to him now is: *will you give us the land?*'

The translation evoked a further round of cheering. A voice was heard to say: 'Not so bad for a poor language like the English!'[130]

The debate ebbed to and fro, now Leverhulme in the ascendant, now one of his interrupters. They ended by cheering him, and he left with the impression that he had won the day. But as soon as he had gone, an eager crowd surged round Colin Macdonald, asking when the Government intended to divide the farms. He answered that they had allowed Leverhulme to believe that they no longer wanted the land, and had agreed to give his schemes a trial.

'Not at all', was the reply. 'And if he is under that impression you may tell him from us that he is greatly mistaken.'

'But why did you cheer him?' I enquired.

'Och! well: he made a very good speech and he is a very clever man, and we wanted to show our appreciation—but the land is another matter.'

Nearly a thousand men and women were present at that meeting by the bridge at Gress, and it was not easy then to assess where the majority feeling lay. It is even more difficult now. Throughout the controversy, resolutions in support of Leverhulme were passed by meetings of crofters and official bodies in the island, only to be contradicted a few days later by new outbreaks of raiding. The *Stornoway Gazette* backed Leverhulme strongly throughout, and its editor, William Grant, wrote an almost weekly article condemning the folly of raiding. Other contemporary sources, notably Leverhulme's own files of correspondence and reports in mainland newspapers, suggest that there were other strands of opinion.

The crofters' way of thinking, as Dr Geddes has pointed out, is 'the paradox of loyalty to one's fellows with loyalty to a lord, of stoutly equalitarian thinking bound up with fervid admiration for an aristocracy.'[131] Leverhulme's purchase of the island was therefore not resented in the same way as the lowlanders' tenure of the farms, because he was the Laird and the tenant-farmers were no more than intruding competitors. The Laird was credited with a certain majesty, whether he had Highland blood in him or not. If things went wrong, he was not to blame, but his stewards or circumstances (like the impoverishment of the Mathesons) beyond his control. Leverhulme was a type of laird that neither Lewis not any other part of Highland Scotland had ever seen before. The raiders and their associates viewed his schemes with scepticism more than dislike. If his plan succeeded, well and good; if it failed, they did not wish to find their lives irreparably divorced from the old life they knew.

Before the raids began, the people were amused by Leverhulme, and they admired his energy. His personality and plans were subjects for innumerable affectionate jokes; his visits great events for an island where life could be hard and dull. 'Give him a chance,' was a typical reaction: 'at least he can't harm the rocks and bogs.' There were many others, particularly in the town, whose attitude was more positively co-operative. But as soon as the strength of feeling of the returning ex-servicemen became apparent, fortified by political agitation and even by the *Ioalaire* disaster, which tragically emphasised the hideous wastefulness of the war and the claims and bonds of family, it was not easy for the people of an isolated village to denounce sons and neighbours who cried out for the land, with all its intensely emotional associations, and who seized it when it was denied to them.

Many of the raiders are still alive. In October 1959 I sat with one of them in his bungalow near the farm-house at Coll, and asked him to tell me whether he had had to face much opposition from the other people.

'No,' he answered. 'They understood us. They were our people. Most of us would have been willing to work in Lord Leverhulme's canning factory, but not yet. I had just come back from the war. I wanted to settle down with a secure home; and then, maybe, look around afterwards. I was living with my wife at the back of my mother-in-law's house. I was a burden on her. Although I had a share in a boat, the fishing failed, and I had no work. I wanted a croft and a home of my own.'

'But Lord Leverhulme offered you a home with a quarter-acre, and a good wage for a steady job?'

With great dignity he replied, 'We were not accustomed to living cheek-by-jowl.'

I asked him about the raids. Why had they seized the land which the Government had promised them? Why could they not have been patient a little longer?

'We had been promised so many things so often, and nothing had been done for us. We could not wait. Remember, we had been in the war. We were men, not boys. We could not live any longer on the charity of our parents.'

Another ex-raider now living on a croft carved from the old farmlands of Gress, confirmed to me this distrust of the Government. 'They hoped to fob us off; but we would not be hood-winked.' And then, looking round at his six weak acres won from the farm whose name had once been familiar to the whole nation, he added pertinently, 'Lord Leverhulme thought we were opposing him by taking the land. But he was wrong. We liked him, and wanted to help him. But before we could help him, we wanted a home we could return to.'

Neither of these men are by nature law-breakers. They have square fishermen's faces with level eyes. They raised no objection when I asked to take their photographs. They are proud of what they did. It is not the mean pride of criminals who have success-fully evaded the law, but of men who feel passionately that they were in the right. Theirs was a political gesture as much as an act of self-interest. If their methods were wrong, they considered, their motives were right; if they discouraged Lord Leverhulme, he was foolish to be discouraged, for nothing that he wanted to do for Lewis would be impeded by settling a few more Lewismen on the land where they belonged. Such, I believe, was the general attitude of the crofting population, until they realised that Leverhulme was adamant on the land-question. Then it changed to one of outright condemnation of the raiders. Mean-while, with typical Highland ambivalence and shrewdness, they refused to cut the ties which bound so prolific a brain and purse as Leverhulme's to the islands; but, at the same time, they refused to range themselves whole-heartedly against their own kin.

There were other lesser sources of opposition to Leverhulme which made themselves felt during the summer of 1919. They were best illustrated by a special correspondent of the *Scotsman* who spent many weeks in the island at the time. From his sympathetic reports it is clear that, at this moment, there were waverers:

The present atmosphere is, I am afraid, not too favourable [to the success of Leverhulme's schemes]. I have been surprised at the absence of goodwill which characterises the attitude of so many people here towards the proprietor's proposals. . . . There is a feeling that Lord Leverhulme is rushing things too quickly, 'He can't expect to graft a new civilisation right on top of the old one all at once,' these people say. These are the apostles of *laissez-faire*, a favourite policy in Lewis. . . .

But the attitude of the man in the street is also a trifle lukewarm. . . . The sympathies of the Free Church are undoubtedly with the crofters. In the disaffected regions the influence of the minister is being exerted to restrain them in the eyes of the law; but one Free Churchman told me he did not feel constrained to warn his flock against the seizing of the land.[132]

The reporter then went on to detail some of the causes of 'the unfortunate air of suspicion' that permeated Lewis. Leverhulme had tried to systematise the peat-cutting: the people concluded that he had designs on the common grazings for some ulterior motive. The castle policies, always open under the Mathesons, had now been closed to the public. The proprietors' right of pre-emption over any town-property which came into the market had not been exercised before: now it was, in the name of town-planning. The Minister of the Episcopal Free Church in Stornoway was required, for the first time, to pay rent for his house, because Leverhulme was not a member of his congregation. Leverhulme had stated that two hundred crofters had already sent in applications for his new houses: 'I should like to see their names and addresses,' was the cynical comment of Dr Murray, M.P. The merchants were grumbling, because Leverhulme's 'co-operative principles were little short of anathema' to them. The article ended:

Many people take the view that the only way in which Lord Leverhulme can hope to bridge over the present difficulty, and reduce the gap which has grown between him and the islanders, is by making some concession to the present demand for land.

That this report was based on searching enquiries is proved by Leverhulme's contemporary correspondence, which mentions all the detailed complaints listed above. He had answers, and good answers, to each of them: for instance, while it was true that he had closed the castle policies, he was building the Arnish road at his own expense to open up the west side of the harbour to the public; and his town-planning scheme gave every person whose house was to be demolished a better site in the new town. But if there was little substance in these small grievances, it cannot be ignored that they were steadily growing at a time when Leverhulme needed all possible support. There were two others, not mentioned by the *Scotsman*, but frequently referred to in the island today: the Church feared the coming of Sunday fishing in response to a demand for more efficiency in the industry; and the traders feared the competition of chain-stores which would be attracted to Stornoway by its development. The first suggestion was one that Leverhulme never put forward, publicly or privately. The second—although I have heard several crofters attribute Leverhulme's failure to this single cause—is an absurdity, for the proposed expansion of the town would mean a greater share of prosperity for everyone, whatever the competition, and the traders knew it.

These various criticisms, so muted that they never found their way into the pages of the *Stornoway Gazette*, only lowered the warmth of Leverhulme's popularity by one or two degrees. Neither then not at any later time, did they amount to an attitude of hostility towards him. Personally he was admired; financially his coming had already been a great benefit to the island, where the wage-bill on his public works alone averaged £2,500 a week throughout 1919. When he returned to Stornoway in August, for his sixth visit that year, he was welcomed by coloured rockets from the shore, and made his way to his motor through cheering crowds. A few days later he entertained three thousand island people at a fête in the castle grounds. The land-troubles were momentarily forgotten on both sides, and the good humour and astonishing versatility of this man were again recognised and acclaimed.

Outside the island, Leverhulme's reputation had suffered a setback from the publicity given to the raids on his farms. In the debate on the Scottish Estimates on 4 August 1919, Members of all parties, including his own, combined to criticise and even vilify him:

*J. L. Sturrock, Liberal (Montrose Burghs)*: Lord Leverhulme, at the very moment when we have emerged from the greatest war in history in the interests of liberty, is taking upon himself to tell these people ... that their future lives are to be guided along the lines laid down, not by themselves, not in accordance with the traditions of their ancestors, but *according to the dictates of a successful soap-boiler who happened to buy up that island.*[133]

The Conservatives took the view that although Sturrock's remark was 'not in the happiest of taste', it would be a pity if Leverhulme were to throw away his 'patriotic efforts' for Lewis by refusing to meet the people's wishes over the land-question. Dr Murray made a characteristically vigorous speech:

Lord Leverhulme cannot see that any other kind of life is worth living, except in a model town with nicely built cottages, curtained windows and a picture. . . . His Lordship thinks that the life of the people of Lewis is a very hard life, and a squalid life. It is nothing of the kind. It is as high a life as any in a city, say, like Liverpool.

Murray's views had great influence in the House, as they did in his constituency, for he was the most popular, hard-working and articulate of all the Highland Members, and knew his people intimately from long association with them as the Medical Officer for Lewis. He believed that the crofter-fisherman was a better man, physically, mentally and morally, than a factory employee, and although he was always careful to qualify his criticisms of Leverhulme's schemes, he was outspoken in advocating the division of the farms. In his maiden speech in March 1919, he had warned the Scottish Secretary that if he did not act quickly, 'he would light a fire in the Highlands and Islands that could not be put out.'

This speech was made in the very week of the first raids on Coll and Gress. It certainly was not calculated to deter the raiders. If Murray had reminded them that their actions were not only illegal but unnecessary, and that the importance of Leverhulme's schemes was greater even than the land-question, he might have brought about a compromise between them. He was the only man in the islands with sufficient standing to attempt it. But by the time Leverhulme's schemes were published, Murray was already committed by his strongly worded speeches in the early summer of 1918 to a policy of increasing the number of crofts. Laird and Member had come to see each other as a danger to the island's life. Leverhulme complained, rather unfairly, that Murray had never said a word in his support: Murray complained that Leverhulme worked for his political downfall. After his defeat by Sir William Mitchell Cotts in the General Election of November 1922, he made one of those bitter speeches that a politician never ceases to regret:

The cause of my defeat is known and read of all men. Lord Leverhulme from the beginning determined to get rid of me. He managed by innuendo and suggestion to make many people believe that I had something to do with the stoppage of his works. He demanded my political head on a charger. He has got it now. I hope he is happy.[134]

Murray died only six months later in London. When Leverhulme heard of his illness, he immediately went round from The Hill in a car loaded with fruit for his old antagonist. Murray was too ill to see him, but said to his wife, 'Send him a nice kind message, Janet.' Leverhulme replied a day later, with genuine grief at his death, 'He was a man universally respected by all who knew him.'

The political reaction to the controversy in Lewis caused Leverhulme much concern, and he began to feel that although he could not give way on the main question, he must make some conciliatory gesture both to public opinion and to the Government. In April 1919 he started making the road from Tolsta to Ness; and a few weeks later he offered to set aside for ex-service-men part of the farmlands near Stornoway for quarter-acre lots, provided that they did not interfere with the milk-production. To the objection that his houses would not be freehold but held on a tenancy which could be cancelled at a moment's notice, he replied in July by a long statement, issued through his Chamberlain's office, that he was willing to sell the houses at cost-price, advancing ninety per cent of the money: only if the occupier could not raise the ten per cent would Leverhulme become his landlord. If they wanted more land, they could reclaim it from the common grazings, and he would support their application to the Land Court for permission to do so, and to the Government for financial aid. In this way, they could solve their joint difficulties. Leverhulme would still have the larger part of his dairy-farms: the landless men would have a home of their own. 'So this is your choice,' he said to the people of Back in October. 'Either a quarter-acre allotment on part of the farms near Stornoway, or land reclaimed from peat. Two thousand men can get quarter-acre allotments on five hundred acres; but the ten-acre crofts which some of you are demanding, would take twenty thousand acres, which is clearly impossible.'

Few men took up either offer. The miserable half-dozen houses on Tong Farm are the only visible results of Leverhulme's suggested compromise. The raiders remained in possession of large areas of Coll and Gress. He refused to take legal action to evict them, and the police were powerless unless the proprietor made the first move to prosecute. Publicly he gave as his reason for this decision his unwillingness to treat ex-servicemen as criminals, when they were only misguided; privately he feared that a prosecution might not prevail against the strength of feeling in the disaffected areas and the political support which it had attracted from outside. ('It is just as if you put the administration of the licensing laws in the hands of licensed victuallers.')

With Robert Munro he could make no progress, nor Munro with him. Munro maintained his intention to break up the farms: Leverhulme asked for a ten-year trial of his schemes before the proposal was revived. Neither man would give way to the other, and Leverhulme began to speak in late August 1919 of stopping all his development work in Lewis unless the raiding ceased and the Scottish Office changed their policy.

For the moment, however, the work continued. In December 1919 a colossal programme was in hand. In Stornoway, the canning-factory had been erected to roof-level; the ice-factory and power-house were building; the gas-works were undergoing extensive renovation; two separate housing estates were rising in Matheson Road and on Goathill; the new town-dairy was ready; the internal reconstruction of the castle was approaching completion, and the making of the road to Arnish alone gave employment to 130 men. Outside the town, the Grimshader road was finished, the Tolsta-Ness road was advancing across the moor from both ends simultaneously, and other roads were being built or improved at Morsgail, Grimersta and Laxdale. Only the development of Stornoway harbour and the railways was temporarily postponed, but already rumours were reaching the town of Leverhulme's immense project for a new harbour in South Harris.

All this work had been undertaken at his personal expense. Before he left for his tour to America, Canada and Japan at the end of the year, he reaffirmed his faith and determination to carry out his promises to the two islands. Addressing the Philosophical Institute at Edinburgh on 4 November 1919, he referred to the effect of the land-troubles on his schemes:

What would your city think if in front of a burning house, the chief of the Edinburgh fire-brigade stopped in his work of rescue on the plea that he and his men understood the prejudices of his people to being aroused in their sleep?

He ended his long speech with this astonishing vision of the future:

The new Lewis and Harris must be full of thriving and prosperous cities, towns and harbours, and of happy, rich, contented men and women, ten, twenty or one hundred times in number that of the present population.

Ten days later he embarked for the New World, where his vision had already become a reality.

# Chapter Seven

# DISILLUSIONMENT

LEVERHULME'S OPTIMISM, and the Scottish Secretary's confidence that he had all-party backing for his policy, had hardened each man's attitude by the end of 1919. Leverhulme was determined that the splitting-up of the farms would make it impossible to carry out his schemes: Robert Munro believed that if the farms were not split up, there would be endless land-raids which no legal penalties could halt. Leverhulme waved aside the Government's past political commitments as irrelevant to the totally new situation created by his master-plan: Munro felt that the land-question was one apart from any other, and that there was no reason why his and Leverhulme's schemes should not proceed in step. There was room for compromise on both sides. Leverhulme could have given up all the farms that were not necessary for his milk supplies: Munro could have pronounced himself content with this, declared that no raider stood a chance of obtaining a croft on the land that Leverhulme released, and promised full Government backing for the fulfilment of his schemes. A move was made by both sides towards such a compromise during the next twelve months, but neither went sufficiently far to restore the complete confidence of the other.

The political weapons were shared equally between them. Pressure was put on Munro in Parliament to hasten the implementation of his policy, not to reverse it. He found himself having to explain to the House the financial and legal complexities which had made it impossible to create more than 282 new holdings throughout Scotland during 1919 in response to over three thousand applications. He was able to point to the co-operation that he had received everywhere except in Lewis from the owners of great estates, even in South Uist, where the proprietrix had voluntarily surrendered a farm for forming new crofts, and in Sutherland, where the Duke had given up the

Borgie estate for division among ex-servicemen. The 1919 Act which extended the Scottish Secretary's power to acquire land compulsorily for small-holdings had passed through both Houses with scarcely a murmur of disapproval. Munro also had the influential, if not wholly welcome, backing of the Highland Land League, the movement for Scottish Home Rule, and similar bodies, which supported the raiders of the Lewis farms with advice, money, and a stream of invective directed against Leverhulme personally.

On his side of the controversy, Leverhulme had formidable weapons for counter-attack. He could reiterate his argument that nobody had yet explained how the legal seizure of his farms by the Government could provide a solution any more permanent than their illegal seizure by the raiders. He complained that it was wholly unjust that a person whose property had been stolen should be required to initiate action to have it restored: the police refused to take steps to eject the raiders on the bare information that the raids had taken place, but insisted that the proprietor should first incur the odium of applying for an interdict against them and arraigning them before the Sheriff's court. In reserve he held the powerful threat to stop all his development schemes for Lewis. It was this threat that caused the Scottish Secretary to say:

It is true that I can take Lord Leverhulme's land under compulsory powers, but if I do that, the result will be that Lord Leverhulme's operations in the islands will not only be suspended, but permanently stopped. As at present advised, I do not feel disposed at the present moment to undertake that responsibility.[135]

But Leverhulme's strongest argument was the support that he had attracted in the island itself, and from Lewismen outside it. It has already been noted that there were one or two pockets of criticism in Lewis, but these were nothing to the resolutions that now reached him from every part of the island begging him to stand firm. It seemed to many islanders, as it did to Leverhulme himself, that the Scottish Office were applying to Lewis their policy for the Highlands as a whole, without regard to the island's very special circumstances. While Lewis had certainly provided more illustrations of the prevalent land-hunger than any other part of Scotland, it was also endowed with a greater opportunity, and the large majority of local people recognised it. Three

L

examples can be given from the most congested areas where raiding was either threatened or in progress. In October 1919 the men of Tolsta passed a resolution regretting their previous opposition to Leverhume and pledging their whole-hearted support in the future. A week later, at a meeting in Back, the storm-centre of the recent agitation, the people voted in hundreds for a resolution expressing 'their cordial support for his Lordship's policy in the island': the seventeen who voted against it had all taken part in the raids. At Port of Ness, on 14 October, there was not a single dissentient voice to the motion: 'That this meeting strongly repudiates the short-sighted action of a few fellow-crofters in raiding and breaking up the farms and thus jeopardising the bright future ahead.'

On the mainland of Scotland, Leverhulme received some strong backing. The *North British Agriculturalist* of 4 September 1919 wrote: 'Lord Leverhulme is very far from propounding any policy calculated to drive the Lewisman from his "lone shieling on the misty island", but what he is very anxious to do, while making the lone shieling a better place to live in, is to provide more elbow room for the younger generation within their own land. . . . It is inconceivable that they will let slip their present unique opportunity.' When Leverhulme addressed the Lewis and Harris Association of Glasgow on 7 November, his entrance was greeted by prolonged and enthusiastic clapping, and the pipers played *Lord Leverhulme's welcome to Lewis*, specially composed by Pipe-Major Peter Macleod. His faithful ally, the *Stornoway Gazette*, commented on these events: 'It must be gratifying to Lord Leverhulme that he has so completely won the hearts and co-operation of the people. The infinitesimal few who may still have their doubts may be regarded as the exception that proves the rule, although we think that even their opposition has now just about vanished.' It was with these acclamations sounding in his ears that Leverhulme left for America in November 1919. The next move, he considered, was the Scottish Secretary's.

In 1954 I found myself sitting next to Robert Munro (then Lord Alness) at a banquet in Bournemouth. It was my only meeting with him, for he died soon afterwards. He spoke freely to me about the Leverhulme incident, which he described as 'the most interesting and most difficult problem with which I ever had to deal.' I asked him if there ever came a moment when he felt that Leverhulme was right. 'Yes,' he said, 'in December 1919, when he was able to produce evidence that he had the mass of the Lewis people behind him.' 'Why then,' I went on, 'did you not withdraw your proposal to split up the farms?' 'I did so later,' he replied, 'but at that particular moment it was politically impossible. It was not only that the House of Commons was unanimously against any concession, but as soon as a new outbreak of raiding occurred, the people of Lewis seemed to forget their resolutions and return to their deeper family loyalties when they found their friends in trouble. If I had chosen that moment to reverse my policy I would have lost any confidence that the islanders still had in me, and my position in the House would have become impossible. I felt that basically Stornoway was for Leverhulme, but that the country people were uncommitted.'

Contemporary records reveal a similar difficulty in penetrating the islanders' minds. Within the space of a few weeks Leverhulme would receive contradictory advice from the same person, often the one best qualified to judge. Thus:

*Orrock to Leverhulme.* 3 Feb., 1920:
The agrarian trouble during the last few weeks has not improved, and I regret to say that it is growing worse. The people will not be guided by their best friends. They have simply got out of hand. Although not numerically strong, still every day is giving signs of support to their unlawful actions.

*Orrock to Leverhulme.* 26 Feb., 1920:
I am sorry to say there is no improvement in the situation. I think however that there are very few sympathisers with the raiders.

These reports were prompted by fresh raids on Coll and Gress at the time when the ground was being prepared for the spring sowing. The two farms, with Tong, were now directly under Leverhulme's control, the tenants having abandoned their tenancy in January, as they found it impossible to carry on under the threat of annual raiding. Now about thirty men from the Back district pegged out their claims on the land, as they had done the previous year, broke down hundreds of yards of walling, and began to erect rough shelters for their families. Leverhulme went up to Lewis to deal with the new crisis a few days after returning from America. He appealed in vain for police protection; the authorities again refused to take action against the raiders until he had secured an interdict against them. Such a course, he said, was 'repugnant to his instincts . . . because he had the fullest sympathy for the needs of the men who were wanting homes.' He only felt able to penalise them by denying them employment. He announced that he intended to abandon his schemes in the country districts of Lewis, and concentrate on Stornoway and Harris. Seventy men from Back and Coll were immediately dismissed by MacAlpine's on Leverhulme's instructions, and the two townships lost in consequence an income of £10,000 a year in wages for the sake of thirty crofts which the men themselves estimated to be worth no more than £50 a year apiece.

The move was unpopular and unwise, for it penalised the innocent with the guilty. There were four hundred ex-service-men in the Back district: only thirty of them had broken the law. The fishing had been a failure: how were the rest to support their families? The raiders, on the other hand, were delighted. 'That's Lord Leverhulme for you now,' said one of them. 'He has paid you off. We have the Government behind us, and we don't care if Lord Leverhulme never comes back.' Another said: 'We will defy him. We must have the land because we were promised the land and we fought for the land. We made a living before Lord Leverhulme came to the island, and we will make a living after he has gone. He is afraid of us: if he were not, he would have put the law in force against us.'[136]

Eventually Leverhulme was persuaded to do so. Colonel Walter Lindsay, who was now his permanent representative in the island, met the raiders on 6 March 1920 and made a last appeal to them to withdraw. They refused. On 13 March an interim interdict was granted against thirty-two of the raiders. On the 15th it was served on them at Coll and Gress by a Messenger-at-Arms from Glasgow, and on the next day he served another on the men who had simultaneously raided Orinsay Farm in the Park district. The latter respected the interdict and left the farm, but none of the raiders of Coll or Gress put in an appearance at the Sheriff's Court in Stornoway when their case was called on 23 March. In their absence, the interdict on them was made perpetual.

Leverhulme now had the legal power to call on the police to evict the raiders. A warrant for the arrest of twenty-two of them was actually issued at Stornoway on 1 April 1920, to become

effective on 12th April, in order to give them yet another chance
to withdraw peacefully. Again they refused. Colonel Lindsay
spoke to them on the 3rd, and Mr Weatherill, the chief-secretary
of the Board of Agriculture, on the 10th. The Gress men refused
even to discuss the matter, but at Coll they told the Colonel that
they had been loyal to each other until now, and would see the
matter through one way or the other. 'The men were most
respectful in their demeanour', a reporter noted, 'and when
Colonel Lindsay reluctantly gave up his efforts, they cheered
him as he left.' To Weatherill they said that they would withdraw
only if they were given a firm promise that they would receive
land the following spring. He replied that so long as they remained
in illegal occupation of it, the Board could do nothing for them.

Everyone expected that Leverhulme, who was then on his way
back from a visit to South Africa, would enforce the order. He
received a petition signed by nine thousand Lewismen asking
him to do so. He was left in no doubt that the islanders would
have supported a strong move to put an end to the raiding once
and for all. It was therefore with astonishment that his Edinburgh
solicitor, H. H. Macgregor, received this cable from Madeira
on 24 April: 'Have definitely decided not to press for conviction
or imprisonment raiders. Please stop all proceedings.' Repeating
the message to Orrock on the same day, Leverhulme added, 'I
know this is contrary to your views, but I feel I have no other
course open to me at present.' To James Simpson he telegraphed,
'Lewis position become impossible since March. Ship no more
material Stornoway.' Thus it was in Madeira, where Sir Herbert
Morgan met him on his return journey with a report of the latest
position, that the fate of Lewis was temporarily decided.

The reason for this sudden change of mind became public
knowledge only three years later, when Leverhulme, in his fare-
well speech to Lewis, gave this explanation:

In an interview with Mr Munro, Sir Herbert Morgan was requested
to inform me that whilst I had the power to get the raiders committed
to prison for contempt of court in disregarding the interdict, the
Scottish Secretary had the power to release them the same day. I
personally asked the Scottish Secretary with reference to this, and his
reply was that it was merely an expression of the power he had, but
it did not necessarily mean that he would exercise it. I felt this was
altogether too doubtful a position for me to act upon, and therefore I
never proceeded with any further steps under the interdict. It is the

fact that in every part of Scotland where the proprietor has proceeded to have raiders committed to prison, the Scottish Secretary has released them.[137]

His son adds: 'This possible result [that the men would be released by the Scottish Secretary the day after their imprisonment] would have reduced to a farce his attempt to enforce the law. His only judicious and reasonable course of action, therefore, was the complete closing down of his developments, and this course he took.'[138]

Robert Munro's chance remark to Morgan was a turning-point in the long controversy. The Scottish Secretary never denied making it, although he claimed that constitutionally he could not give the assurance desired. He later affirmed, 'I have never, in any case, ordered the release of persons imprisoned for breach of interdict.'[139] Indeed, to Leverhulme's own knowledge, convicted raiders of farms in Harris and Uist served their full term of imprisonment. In retrospect, it seems unlikely that Munro would have used his power of release on behalf of the Lewis raiders, for public opinion was then at least neutral, and he was as anxious as Leverhulme for a cessation of raiding in the island, which only made it more difficult for him to apply his policy and negotiate with the proprietor. Leverhulme pressed the point beyond the limits justified by the facts. On the other hand, there is evidence that Munro asked him not to enforce the interdict. In August 1920, Macgregor wrote to Leverhulme, 'It was at the specific request of Mr Munro himself that you did not enforce the interdict, at the same time as he reminded your advisers that should the raiders be imprisoned he had the power to liberate them immediately.'[140] Leverhulme replied that this was indeed the case, but he did not wish to contradict publicly Munro's statement in the House of Commons that the proprietor 'had not seen fit to enforce the interdict,' because he still hoped to win him round.

Whatever were the precise terms of the advice that Munro gave to him through Sir Herbert Morgan, its effect was to infuriate Leverhulme and delight the raiders. They were left in un-challenged possession of the farms, and other reckless men were encouraged to believe that they could sieze land throughout the island with impunity: the farms of Reef, Ardroil and Tong were immediately raided or re-raided.

It had the even more serious result of putting a stop to all Leverhulme's development works in Lewis. He had begun the year in a mood of great optimism. 'I feel that 1920 must be a banner year for Stornoway development in every direction,' he had written in January to his chief engineer at Port Sunlight: and as late as 23 February he told Duncan Maciver that 'there will be many thousands of tons of cargo to carry this year and next to overtake arrears of building of cottages and to complete the harbour. These will involve many years work.' Now everything was to stop. The Provost was informed early in May 1920 that the road-works, house-building and harbour development would cease at once. The men working on the Tolsta-Skegirsta road were paid off on 12 May, a dozen men only being retained to complete the Garry bridge. The two hundred men working on the Arnish road were dismissed at the end of the month. Work on the Goathill and Matheson Road houses was suspended as soon as the uncompleted buildings had been waterproofed. £61,000 worth of materials for the canning factory lay ready on the quay, but these too were left unused, and MacAlpines were informed on 17 June, 'I am closing down this work. Messrs. MacAlpine will be withdrawing entirely.'

There was consternation in the island. Leverhulme was exonerated from all blame, which was divided between the raiders and the Scottish Secretary, the former for defying the almost unanimous pledges given to Leverhulme at the village meetings in the previous autumn, the latter for his intransigent attitude to Leverhulme and his refusal to condemn raiding with sufficient force. Without revealing Munro's discussion with Morgan, Leverhulme cleverly managed to give the impression that it was the Scottish Secretary's implicit encouragement of the raiders which had made it impossible for him to continue with his schemes.

A new series of meetings was held throughout the island during the spring and early summer of 1920 in an attempt to avert the catastrophe of a permanent closure of the works. The leading men in Stornoway identified themselves whole-heartedly with Leverhulme's arguments. Councillor John Morrison's words at a meeting in Stornoway in May can stand for many similar views expressed at the time:

It cannot be said of Lord Leverhulme what could be said in former days, that he is reserving the land for deer and game, that he refuses to give land or help the people to build comfortable homes. . . . The present situation has been brought about by the Board of Agriculture, who seem to take up the position that because they adopted a certain policy in 1912, they must adhere to it now, although circumstances in the interval have entirely changed.[141]

This remark, and Provost Roderick Smith's comment that, 'if the Government persists in a policy which would involve the cessation of the development schemes, they will be injuring Lewis for political reasons,' were greeted with loud applause. During the following weeks they were echoed at meeting after meeting:

11 *May* 1920. 'That this mass meeting of the men of North Tolsta heartily approves of the schemes of Lord Leverhulme for the development of Lewis, and strongly disapproves of the attitude of the raiders of Coll and Gress farms.'

11 *May* 1920. 'That this meeting of the men of Ness regrets that the Government did not consider the island of Lewis as a whole instead of a small portion of it.'

14 *May* 1920. Provost Smith at Stornoway: 'Twenty years ago at the beginning of the summer herring-fishing there would be 800-1000 fishing boats in Stornoway: now there are not more than a score of boats, probably less. If Lord Leverhulme is allowed to go ahead, there will soon be hundreds of modern fishing boats in Stornoway, Portnaguran, Carloway, etc. The question is whether a dozen or two dozen men are to be allowed to baulk the rest of the population of the realisation of these bright prospects.'

14 *May* 1920. Donald Macdonald, crofter of Ness: 'A croft is just like a deep ditch to swallow up all you put into it. . . . It is better for the Government to break their promises than to ruin the island. It would have been better for King Herod to have broken his promise to Herodias than to have beheaded John the Baptist.' (*Laughter and loud applause.*)

21 *May* 1920. Leading article in the *Stornoway Gazette*: 'It is almost inconceivable that any Government department will place the interests of a handful of men before the interests of the vast majority of the population.'

By June feeling in the island was running so high that Dr Murray's supporters implored him to come north immediately, and put all possible pressure on the Scottish Secretary to restrain him from hindering the development of Leverhulme's schemes. Otherwise they could not answer for the safety of his seat at the next Election. This advice was most unwelcome to Murray. He ignored it, admitting to the House of Commons with a light laugh that 'I have not been to my constituency for a year. I act on the principle enunciated by Dickens, who when he began to grow a beard, said that he did so because the less his friends saw of him, the more they liked him.'[142] In such desperate circumstances, the joke was in poor taste and foolishly timed. In extenuation of Murray's conduct at this period, it must be said that the expense of the journey from London to the Hebrides for a man without private means and before MPs were granted free travel warrants, made it very difficult for him to visit his constituency frequently, and that he was assiduous in his attention to his duties at Westminster. Nevertheless, his failure to understand the strength of feeling in Lewis and his blind adherence to the views that he had earlier expressed on the land question, made the loss of his seat almost inevitable. How completely he was out of touch with opinion in the island is illustrated by a supplementary question that he once put to the Scottish Secretary:

*Dr Murray.* Is it not a fact, practically speaking, that it is only where men take possession of land, that the Board of Agriculture take action in the Highlands?

*Mr Munro.* That is a gross misrepresentation of the facts.[143]

Leverhulme's stock in the island was as high as it ever became. When he returned to Stornoway in June 1920, he was welcomed by the most remarkable demonstration seen in Lewis since the visit of Edward VII. Cheering thousands lined the quay and South Beach as the *Sheila* drew in, and a band of twenty pipers and drummers marched in front of his car as far as the entrance to the castle.

Leverhulme exploited his strong position with the utmost skill. He informed Munro that he would resume his schemes as soon as the raiders left the farms, 'and I am left in peaceful possession of the same.' At the same time he was willing to make certain of the farms on the west coast of Lewis available to the Government for the creation of small-holdings. Munro, in reporting Leverhulme's proposal to the Stornoway Parish Council, evaded the main point at issue:

The Parish Council is under a misapprehension in supposing that the suspension of Lord Leverhulme's schemes is due to any disinclination on the part of the Government to effect a compromise on lines acceptable to Lord Leverhulme. He has made it perfectly clear to me that the suspension of the development schemes is due to the raiding of farms and not to any action, or inaction, on the part of the Government.[144]

While the raids had certainly been the immediate cause of the stoppage, the Scottish Secretary was deceiving himself. Leverhulme's two conditions, that the raiders left the farms, and that he should thereafter be allowed 'peaceful possession' of them, clearly meant that the Government were not to step in when the raiders stepped out. His offer of the west-coast farms was his gesture of compromise, an alternative, not an addition, to the breaking up of the farms around Broad Bay. It is difficult to avoid the conclusion that Munro was at this stage making the same tactical error as Murray: he was putting a policy pre-conceived at Westminster before the urgent appeals of the islanders that he should abandon it. He was publicly assuming that the raids were the only cause of trouble, when he must have known that the raiding was only a symptom of the deeper divergence between his concept of the island's future and Lever-hulme's. It could only be settled by a forthright declaration that Leverhulme would be left in undisputed possession of the land.

Robert Munro announced his intention of visiting Lewis in person during the summer parliamentary recess of 1920. This announcement temporarily stilled criticism in the island, but it was made quite clear to him that if he did not succeed in per-suading the raiders to leave the land, there would be violence. A meeting of Lewis ex-servicemen in September sent him a warning that if raiding did not cease within a reasonable time after his visit, they would consider action to eject the raiders. The chief speaker at the meeting declared:

The people of Lewis have reason to go down on their knees and thank God that Lord Leverhulme had come to Lewis when he did. (*Loud applause.*) We are determined to see this thing through. (*Loud applause.*) The spirit which enabled many of you to face hell on Hill 60 will see to it that if red tape stands between us and our oppor-tunity to earn food for ourselves and our families, then we will cut red tape and damn the consequences. (*Loud applause.*)[145]

Munro was obliged to postpone his visit owing to the death of his wife. In his place he sent the Lord Advocate, T. B. Morison, a Minister who was even more deeply committed than the Scottish Secretary to a policy of extending the crofting system, for it was he who had declared in October 1917, in his speech at Inverness, 'Everyone is agreed that the people of the Highlands must be placed in possession of the soil.' There was a certain apprehension in Lewis that he would arrive with his mind made up, that he would give more encouragement to the raiders (for their motives, if not their actions) than to Leverhulme, and that he was not powerful enough to decide on a reversal of policy, even if he concluded from his visit that it was desirable.

He arrived in Stornoway in the fishery cruiser *Minna* on 1 October 1920, accompanied by Sir Robert Greig, Sir Arthur Rose and Thomas Wilson from the Board of Agriculture. As soon as they landed, they went directly to Back, where they met the raiders in the school-house. This meeting, which lasted two hours, was held in private, but a statement was issued afterwards explaining that 'the Lord Advocate suggested that the men should vacate the land, and after that was done, the Board of Agriculture would then have the opportunity to consider the whole problem of land-settlement throughout the island.' The raiders, negotiating, as it were, on equal terms with the Lord Advocate for Scotland, said that they would let the Scottish Secretary have their reply within ten days. The meeting had been friendly, perhaps too friendly, for the raiders were left with the impression that Morison had made them a definite promise of crofts if they withdrew from the farms. Five months later they gave the Scottish Secretary this account of the interview:

At the Lord Advocate's meeting with us here on 1 October, we were clearly led to believe that if we quitted the land we then occupied on Coll and Gress farms and complied with the interdict of the Board of Agriculture whose representatives accompanied the Lord Advocate and spoke to us, they would proceed with our settlement on holdings. ... The King's Advocate had come to us and promised to help us. We shook hands with him over it and we removed from the farms.[146]

That this impression was not merely hind-sight is shown by a letter which the raiders addressed to the Lord Advocate before they withdrew, assuring him that they were doing so on the understanding that their withdrawal would make it easier for

the Board 'to arrive at a solution that will be to our advantage.'
Nothing that Morison wrote to them or said publicly justified
this assumption: he had merely promised to review the whole
question once the raiders withdrew. But that the raiders' letter,
with its significant gloss on the Lord Advocate's promise, was not
immediately contradicted, led all three sides to the controversy
into deeper trouble later.

On returning from Back to Stornoway, the Lord Advocate
received two deputations, one from the ex-servicemen, and the
second from the representatives of the public bodies. The two
meetings were held in public, and from the full press-reports it is
clear that Morison had quite misjudged the situation. He
renewed the argument that the division of the farms was not
incompatible with Leverhulme's schemes; in fact, by this time
the two policies were incompatible, not for sound economic
reasons, but owing to Leverhulme's firmly rooted belief that his
schemes would not succeed if the farms near Stornoway were
divided—and as it was Leverhulme who was putting up the
money, he could also lay down the conditions. Secondly, the
Lord Advocate repeated to both delegations, although he was
immediately corrected by the first, that there was a conflict
between Stornoway and the country districts, as if he were
unaware that the recent resolutions in Leverhulme's support
had come from every part of the island. His third error is
revealed in this curious interchange between him and the
Provost of Stornoway at the second meeting:

The Provost said that it should be clearly understood that what they,
as representing the public bodies, deprecated was the extension of the
crofting system to the detriment of the whole island; and they asked
that a fair trial, for a period of ten years, be given to Lord Leverhulme's
schemes to see if they would not bring the island benefit far greater
than the perpetuation of the crofting system.

The Lord Advocate replied that he was glad to find that they took
very much the same view of the situation as he did himself.

This could have been the sort of soothing remark that a man
makes at the end of a long day in order to bring an interview to an
agreeable close. But the evidence shows the opposite. Morison
came to Lewis with the idea that the aspiration for land dominated
all other thoughts in the minds of the great majority of the
population. He saw the problem in nineteenth-century terms,

and himself as the defender of the people's rights against the ambitions of a landlord who was denying to the islanders what they demanded and what the Government had promised. He could not conceive it to be possible that they should now agree with Leverhulme's views on the crofting system, and wish to turn their backs on their past. He was not ungenerous to Leverhulme in his remarks: he even promised that the Government would do all in their power to assist him. But he cared more for the crofter: 'I should be sorry to think that the crofter's time was dead,' he told the ex-servicemen, when their delegation came fresh to him from a meeting at which the loudest cheers had gone to the speaker who said, 'We want work, not crofts. We have had enough of crofts.'

Sympathy for the raiders had begun to decline when it was strongly rumoured that they were encouraged and advised by political organisations on the mainland whose views were on the extreme left-wing, even Communist. Cheques made out to individual raiders by the Highland Land League were cashed at Stornoway banks. In the League's report for 1919, it was openly stated that 'the outstanding event of the the year has been the land revolution in the islands. In Lewis members of the League took forcible possession of holdings.' On 21 August 1920, the League held its annual meeting in Glasgow (having just moved its headquarters from London!), and the speakers included one John Maclean, a recent visitor to Lewis, who openly advocated Communism. He told the meeting that he had found the Lewis people afraid to open their mouths: 'Cowardice has come to the Highlands. I do not blame the people. It is the state of their dependence on Lord Leverhulme that makes them cowards. The same servile spirit that has characterised Highland gamekeepers and policemen is at work in Stornoway.'

To a similar source must be attributed a letter addressed personally to Leverhulme by the raiders of Coll and Gress on 8 June 1920, in reply to his appeal to them to withdraw:

To you law and order evidently mean liberty to starve our wives and children by withholding from us the land created not by yourself, but by a greater Lord for the use of His people. . . . We have at least as much right to the use of the land at a fair rent as you had to the use of labour and the products of labour at a price which enabled you to pocket the millions which you are today credited with possessing. . . . Your stubborn attitude is as silly as it is heartless.[147]

When this letter was published, it aroused as much pity as anger. What Lewis crofter was capable of so flowery an English style, or of such discourtesy? The raiders were dupes of political forces that they did not comprehend. The Lord Advocate was shown this letter, and reminded of the political affiliations of the Highland Land League to whose arguments the Government was apparently ready to pay more heed than to the wishes of the people themselves. It made little impression on him.

The Government could claim a minor success in persuading the raiders of Coll and Gress to withdraw, even if, as later emerged, the terms of their withdrawal had been misunderstood. *The Times* commented that the Scottish Office 'must be rather a sleepy retreat' to have delayed their intervention so long and allowed tension to mount to breaking point.[148] But the way was now open for Leverhulme to resume his works in the island. He publicly pledged himself to start again in the spring of 1921, provided that the raiders withdrew as they promised and that the Scottish Secretary would assure him that the farms would not be requisitioned by the Government for a period of ten years. On his side, Leverhulme agreed to allow the farms on the west coast of Lewis to be cut up for crofts. These pledges and conditions were contained in a letter which Leverhulme wrote to Munro on 11 November 1920, just before he set out on yet another visit to the United States. The key paragraph of the letter read:

All I ask before I recommence development work is that all illegal raiding of farms shall cease, and the raiders withdraw from illegal occupation of the raided farms, and that I be given to December 1930 —say ten years—in which the success or failure of my schemes for development may be tested before any farm-lands are scheduled for taking for crofts.

Munro sent a copy of Leverhulme's letter to the Provost of Stornoway, asking for his comments, as only the people of Lewis could give the promise to abandon raiding. Provost Smith pointed out in reply that Leverhulme also asked for another pledge, which only the Scottish Secretary could give. In the hope that the Scottish Secretary would fulfil his side of the bargain, the Town Council and Lewis District Committee would collaborate in obtaining from the people the pledge to which Munro referred. They immediately began to organise meetings throughout the island.

Thus began the third and most striking demonstration of the islanders' confidence in Leverhulme. Immediately before and after Christmas 1920, his schemes were put to the popular vote in every township in turn, and a resolution promising total abstention from raiding for ten years was proposed at the close of each meeting. In every part of Lewis except one, the unanimous approval of the people was almost a foregone conclusion. The exception was Back. The meeting there was held on 21 December, and it was packed to the doors. The case for the raiders was forcibly put by Murdo Graham, who said that if they had an assurance that the Government would grant them crofts, they would give their guarantee not to raid the farms again: 'But if the Government does not give us that assurance, it is as certain as anything can be that we will start raiding again.' He was asked if he were willing to accept a croft in another part of the island. He replied that he would go nowhere except Coll or Gress, not even to the village of Back. This obstinacy and unreasonableness created a very poor impression. When the usual resolution was put to the meeting, only nine hands were held up against it. The only other district where there was any opposition was Park, where one or two landless men refused to give the pledge. The majority for Leverhulme throughout the island was clearly higher than ninety-nine per cent.

In face of this evidence, Munro at last gave way. On 22 January 1921 he wrote to Leverhulme:

From the numerous resolutions which have reached me from meetings held throughout the islands, I think that I am entitled to assume that your policy is endorsed by a very large section of the community, and I gather that you only now wait the guarantee from the Government in order to arrange for the resumption of your schemes.

I have considered the position with very great care in consultation with my colleagues in the Government, and I have come to the conclusion that it is in the interests of the community as a whole that the assurances which you seek should be given. Accordingly . . . I am prepared on behalf of the Government, to undertake that the compulsory powers of taking your land for small-holdings shall not, while your schemes go on, be put into operation. . . . Should your development schemes for any reason not proceed, the hands of the Government will of course be free.

Each party to the dispute had now made one major concession. The raiders had withdrawn from Coll and Gress; the Scottish Secretary had agreed not to divide the dairy-farms near Stornoway; and Leverhulme had placed six farms on the west cost of the island at the disposal of the Board of Agriculture.* The work-schemes were due to start again in April. The only obstacle that remained was the threat of the raiders to resume raiding in the spring, unless by that time they had been provided with crofts on Coll or Gress, a possibility quite excluded by the agreement with Leverhulme. But for the moment the barometer was set fair.

It therefore created consternation when news reached the island in January 1921 that Leverhulme had given orders to close down all his private work that had been allowed to continue since the general stoppage in May. The reconstruction of the kitchen-garden at the castle was to be abandoned, the staff of gardeners, foresters and game-keepers drastically reduced, and the men working on the weather-proofing of the Goathill cottages were mostly to be laid off. The wage-bill for these various undertakings had totalled £56,000 in the last six months of July, and now, at the very moment when Leverhulme appeared to have triumphed, he was imposing a further penalty on the people who had supported him so resolutely. His chief engineer, B. P. Wall, reported to him from Lewis that William Grant, editor of the *Stornoway Gazette*, had told him that the dismissals

have practically undone the we of the holgood work among the people of Lewis which your Lordship's friends and well-wishers had striven to do during these critical times. He desired me to convey the opinion that practically every farm will be raided for the Spring sowings, and that your beneficial intentions to start the harbour and other works will be frustrated. He wanted to know what had occurred to induce your Lordship to make these reductions, but I said I had no information.[149]

The reason was that Leverhulme was passing through the severest financial crisis of his career. The glow of happiness that irradiated his face while he was in the islands concealed a gnawing cancer, the threat of bankruptcy.

* The farms were Reef, Croir, Mealista, Timisgarry, Dalebeg and Carnish-with-Ardroil.

12. Gress Farm, Lewis. Foreground, bridge where Leverhulme met the raiders; left centre, original farm-buildings of Gress; beyond, crofts formed by the break-up of the farm

13. Leverhulme's uncompleted road from Tolsta to Skegirsta in 1960, with the bridge over the River Garry

14. A former raider on his croft at Gress in 1959

It is not necessary to enter deeply into the reasons for the critical situation that faced Lever Brothers at the beginning of 1921, for it has been fully and frankly described in the official history of Unilever.[150] It need only be said that it had its origins a year earlier in the purchase of the shares of the Niger Company for £8 million. By this purchase, Lever Brothers acquired a further source of oils and fats needed for their soap and margarine factories. Leverhulme was in America at the time of the purchase, but approved the action of his Board of directors by cable. He did not then know that by an unbelievable oversight there had been no proper investigation of the accounts of the Niger Company, and that an undetected £2 million overdraft stood against it, for which Lever Brothers now became liable. In normal times the Company could have stood this shock, but it came at the very moment when the slump of the spring of 1920 hit the business world. Their stocks of unsold soap were growing at the same moment as the value of the raw-materials, of which Lever Brothers had acquired huge amounts with the purchase of the Niger Company, fell drastically. At the height of this blizzard Leverhulme was obliged to raise the £8 million purchase price and repay the £2 million overdraft. His underwriter refused to float the new issue to raise the £8 million, and the banks refused to help with the £2 million. On the day in June 1920 when he received an overwhelming ovation on his arrival at Stornoway, Leverhulme 'was never nearer disaster and the sacrifice of all his plans for the future.'[151] Only by desperate measures did he manage to raise the purchase money, and stall on the overdraft.

At the end of the year the demand for its repayment was again pressing. Leverhulme's accountant, F. D'Arcy Cooper, reported to him in November 1920 that the banks would not be prepared to renew the overdraft in January 'unless they had some undertaking from the Company that further developments by the acquisition of new businesses would cease. . . . They have asked for full details of the present financial position of the Company and of any capital commitments for 1921 and future years.' This was straight talking of a type that Lever Brothers had never experienced before. Leverhulme was in personal difficulties as well. The Inland Revenue were pressing him for payment of arrears of super-tax, and his offer to pay £25,000 on account was rejected as 'inadequate and cannot be accepted.' On the

M

very morning of 12 January 1921 when he instructed Wall to dismiss the gardeners at Lews Castle, he had received this letter from a leading bank:

The whole position has changed in a few months, and we must simply not be asked for more. We have in fact gone materially beyond the point which, as a matter of banking policy, we ought to go.

Leverhulme replied:

What I suggest is that you allow me an overdraft [for his Lewis and Harris schemes] until June 20th next up to £100,000. Mr Cooper informs me that my estate shows a surplus of £5,000,000 after payment of all liabilities. . . . Candidly I don't consider that you are using an old client of over thirty-four years connection with that consideration he ought to receive.

But it was no good:

Dear Lord Leverhulme,
    You will forgive me if I say that you do not appear to attach any weight to the considerations which I put forward in my letter to you. The whole position is entirely changed since, as a matter of course, we let you have in your private account whatever you wanted from time to time. . . . If I hurt your feelings, I can only say that I am sorry. Kindly let me hear from you.

    Of course Leverhulme survived. Even the goose of his Niger Company eventually became a splendid swan. But he only managed to stave off disaster by putting himself in the hands of the banks. In February 1921 the bankers 'were willing to delay no longer. Unless they were given satisfaction on their own terms, the Niger Company's bankers threatened to issue a writ. Liquidation would be the inevitable consequence.'[152] From this ghastly position Leverhulme was rescued by D'Arcy Cooper, who negotiated with Barclays Bank a loan against the issue of Debenture stock, nearly all of which was held by the bank itself. This meant, in effect, that Leverhulme, for the first time in his life, was not his own master. He must run his business in such a way as to satisfy his Debenture holders, who would be unlikely to view with great favour an adventurous policy at a time of slump, whether the adventures were African or Hebridean. To the annual meeting of the Company in April 1921, Leverhulme admitted, 'Until our Debentures are greatly reduced, your directors would not feel justified in entering upon any new undertakings requiring cash capital.'

Lewis and Harris were not part of the business of Lever Brothers, but it was difficult to disentangle the Chairman's personal affairs from those of the Company, as he was the holder of all its Ordinary shares. The fortunes of one had their effect upon the other. Since November 1919 his enterprises in the two islands had been placed under the Lewis and Harris Welfare and Development Company (Lahwad) in which Leverhulme was the sole shareholder except one allotted to his son, and one to Sir Herbert Morgan. In practical terms it made little difference to his schemes, though emotionally it detracted from his status as Laird, as the people preferred to be governed by a person rather than a Company. He gave as his reason for the change that he could not live for ever, and that it would not be to the islands' advantage if all depended on him alone. In one of those vivid images of which he was still capable, he said 'If you want to drive a mill, how can you drive it with water from a barrel?' By transferring the islands to Lahwad it would be easier for him to raise the necessary capital, and on his death, his shares would pass to his son who would carry on his work. On the other hand, since the beginning of 1920, Lahwad held 4,610,820 20 per cent preferred ordinary shares in Lever Brothers, which amounted to about half Leverhulme's personal fortune: in 31 March 1921, when the financial crisis caused him to enquire how much he was worth, he was told that including the Lahwad shares and his great art collections and house-properties, his total assets were £9,486,954. Seldom can a millionaire have known so precisely the extent of his fortune!

No more need be said to indicate that when Lever Brothers passed through a period of stress, so did Lewis and Harris. It was assumed in the islands that Leverhulme's purse was bottomless, and nobody there read with close attention the published accounts of his great Company. So when Leverhulme ordered stringent economy in the first few months of 1921, even his closest collaborators never guessed the truth. It was thought strange that Leverhulme did not intend to resume his operations until the spring, after both his conditions had been satisfied in January and unemployment in the island was now acute (3,500 men in Lewis were drawing relief in mid-February); but this delay was put down to the necessity to plan carefully before making a new spurt. It was not until the autumn of 1921 that Leverhulme was obliged to admit publicly that the world slump obliged him to curtail his plans. Only in confidence would he hint at the crisis through which he was passing. For instance, he told Duncan Maciver on 18 April 1921, 'To commence canning herring in Lewis at the present moment would only be to make a very serious loss.' He intended to postpone his fishing projects 'until conditions of trade become normal.'

Meanwhile attention was focussed on the probability that raiding of the farms would be resumed in the spring of 1921, since the raiders had given notice that unless they obtained crofts on either Coll or Gress, they would seize them for the third year in succession. Munro's undertaking to Leverhulme made compulsory division impossible; and Leverhulme's firm condition that the resumption of his works was dependent on the total cessation of raiding, recreated the uneasy situation of the previous autumn. Three of the four parties to the dispute (the proprietor, the Scottish Secretary and the mass of the population) had struck a bargain; the fourth party, the raiders, would not conform, and unless some further compromise could be reached with them, the efforts of the other three would be unavailing.

One obvious solution, that the raiders should be given the chance of a croft on one of the farms on the west coast that Leverhulme had agreed to split up, was not acceptable either to him or to the raiders. He regarded it as utterly unjust that the men who had broken the law should be placed on an equal footing with the great majority of landless men who had not. The raiders themselves maintained that only a croft on Coll or Gress would satisfy them, for the remotest farms in the Uig district were as far as sixty miles away from their homes ('as it might be,' one of them said, 'in another country'), and by this time their pride was stubbornly linked with the two farms that they had raided annually. Nor were they to be persuaded by Leverhulme's further offer to put at their disposal part of the farm at Tolsta for creating quarter-acre allotments, and gradually to enlarge them by bringing under cultivation sections of the surrounding moor. Indeed, this latter suggestion aroused the opposition of the majority of the crofting population who supported Leverhulme in every other respect: illogically, but with a firmness that could not be ignored, they refused to surrender any part of their common grazings for this purpose, because it would reduce the area, small enough already, for the township *soumings*. In giving Leverhulme the pledge that he required, almost every township made a specific exception of this part of his plan.

There was a third possible compromise, which was suggested to Munro in February 1921 by Donald Shaw, the solicitor who was advising the raiders on behalf of the Highland Land League. Let Leverhulme keep Gress, but surrender Coll. Coll, argued Shaw, was of minor importance for dairy-farming. The men, he said, 'are suffering so severely from want of land and proper dwellings that it is useless to expect them to give up their claims to these lands unless we are in a position to make a reasonable alternative offer.'[153] Thomas Wilson, the local representative of the Board of Agriculture, added his own recommendation that Leverhulme should be advised to make some further gesture of this sort in order to forestall new outbreaks of raiding.[154] Leverhulme was adamant. He would give up neither Coll nor Gress. If the men were suffering hardship, which he did not deny, he could give them work as soon as his schemes were resumed in April at a wage much greater than the income they could ever make from a croft. The raiders repeated that they were only interested in the land. The Lord Advocate had implicitly promised it to them. They wrote to Munro, 'We hope to hear from you that the undertaking (*sic*) given to us will now be honourably implemented.'[155]

The deadlock was unresolved when Leverhulme re-opened his public work-schemes on 2 April 1921. They were on a smaller scale than before, ostensibly because the threat of raiding was not yet removed, but privately because the banks were still putting pressure on him. Work on the Tolsta-Ness road was begun only at the Tolsta end, where huts were erected for the workmen near the site to save them the long daily walk to and fro; while at Stornoway harbour, the work was confined to laying the approaches for a light railway to bring construction materials to the sea-wall. Thus only 140 men in all were re-employed, but to abate possible criticism, Leverhulme announced that many more would be taken on as the work progressed. This explanation did not convince the men of Ness, who could see no reason why the road to Tolsta could not be re-started at their end to relieve the acute unemployment in the district, and rumours at last began to circulate, strongly denied by the ever-loyal *Stornoway Gazette*, that Leverhulme was in financial difficulties. His trump-card was the proof he could adduce that he had more vacancies for workmen on the Tolsta end of the road than applications for them, and even at the harbour the gangs were not up to strength.[156]

Less than a month after the work began, the raids, as everyone expected, began again. On 28 April 1921, twenty men called on the manager of Coll Farm and told him that he need not trouble himself with the farm any further, as they intended to take it over themselves. On 3 May, they enforced their threat by removing the farmer's horses from the plough and leading them back to the stables. A day or two later they occupied the land. At the same time the farm of Orinsay in the parish of Lochs was also re-raided.

Thomas Wilson's private report on these raids survives in the records of the Scottish Office. It well illustrates his sympathy for the raiders, which undoubtedly influenced the attitude of the entire Scottish Office, from the Scottish Secretary downwards:

I confess that it is not unnatural that those ex-raiders should feel they are not receiving the consideration being given to other ex-servicemen in Lewis. Last October they gave an attentive hearing to the Lord Advocate, and listening to his appeal to them, obeyed the law, withdrew from the raided farms and patiently awaited the consideration of the Government.

They are only ordinary human beings—having the same feelings as other mortals—and it is not possible for them without a heartache to see everywhere in Lewis something being done to meet the requirements of other ex-servicemen, but nothing being done for them. At other places in Lewis they see small-holdings being constituted or enlargements of holdings granted; homestead lots or house and garden sites given off; or division of skinned lands made for reclamation; but in Coll and Back they stand exactly where they stood last November after they obeyed the law and withdrew from the raided farms. They are living under deplorable housing conditions, which cannot continue. It is hopeless to expect them to exercise patience indefinitely. Unless a solution is had, they will certainly break the law. . . . Assuredly, were I situated as they were, I would not hesitate about breaking the law, but would do so and accept the punishment with pleasure, rather than go on to the end of my life in the wretched hovels they reside in.[157]

This report was not fair to Leverhulme. It was misleading to suggest that nothing had been done for the raiders of Coll and

Gress. They had been offered work on the Tolsta road or in Stornoway and huts had been provided on the site: they had refused to take it up. They had been offered quarter-acre lots and a house at Tong or Tolsta, and help had been promised with the reclamation of the moor: neither suggestion appealed to them. But Wilson's report was more than misleading: it reveals a strong sympathy with the law-breakers that must have been very evident in his discussions with them. (They say today, 'We knew we had the Board of Agriculture with us.') It is true that he agreed that further raiding must be countered by legal action, but he spoke only of the one occasion when they obeyed the law, not of the many other occasions when they broke it. Nor did he even mention in his report the two overriding factors in the whole controversy: that the great majority of the population of Lewis had by this time explicitly or implicitly condemned the raiders and supported Leverhulme, and that further raids would mean the permanent cessation of all his schemes, to the great disadvantage of the whole island. This was the man of whom Dr Murray said that 'the Board has made more progress in settling ex-servicemen in the Western Isles than perhaps in any other constituency in Scotland . . . largely due to the fact that one official of the Board of Agriculture is thoroughly well acquainted with my constituency'.[158]

Wilson suggested that crofts should be provided on the outrun (the semi-fertile land between the arable and the moor) of Coll and Gress. Munro repeated the suggestion to Leverhulme, urging on him that his dairy-farms required the arable parts of the farms only.[159] Such a scheme would provide for twenty to twenty-five holdings on Gress, and twenty-five to thirty on Coll. Leverhulme refused, on the grounds that the mere suggestion was a breach of the Scottish Secretary's promise not to raise for ten years the question of splitting up the farms. Munro's proposal could provide at most fifty-five crofts for 1,200 to 2,000 applicants. Besides, the raiders were the last to deserve crofts: to grant them would be most unjust to the law-abiding. 'For these and other reasons,' he concluded, 'I sincerely regret that it is impossible for me to accede to the suggestions contained in your letter.'[160]

Every possible form of compromise had now been discussed. There remained two alternative methods of proceeding, and the initiative lay in both cases with Leverhulme. Either he could apply for a new interdict against the raiders, and enforce it, or he could close down his works, this time permanently.

Leverhulme was unwilling to adopt the first method so long as Munro reminded him of his power to release the convicted men immediately. This prerogative of the Scottish Secretary had again been mentioned at an interview given by Munro to Morgan and Sanders (representing Leverhulme during his absence abroad) on 4 May 1921. Leverhulme's second-hand account of this interview contained the words, 'You repeated the reservation that you could give no guarantee that if I did take such proceedings as resulted in the raiders' imprisonment you would not order their release; it is quite obvious that, although the obligation of taking proceedings devolves upon the proprietor, under the circumstances it would be quite futile for the proprietor to commence proceedings, and I do not intend to do so.'[161] It is difficult to understand why Munro could not give a more categorical assurance that he would not order the release of the men if he had no intention of doing so. Although he was bound by the constitutional doctrine that a Minister cannot give a ruling in advance of the event, and affirmed that Leverhulme 'would receive the ordinary protection to which law-abiding citizens are entitled', there would have been no object in reminding Morgan and Sanders of his powers unless he intended at least to hold them in reserve. He knew the importance which Leverhulme attached to this point. Why did he therefore not do everything to reassure him that the raiders, if convicted, would pay their penalty? A possible explanation lies in the strength of public feeling on the mainland of Scotland, where the men would have to serve their sentence, there being no gaol in Stornoway large enough to hold them. In August of 1921, an incident occurred at Inverness which illustrates the possibility that there would be as much local trouble if the Lewis raiders were sent to prison as if they were not. Six ex-servicemen who had forcibly taken land in North Uist and had refused to pay the fine imposed on them, were taken from the Outer Hebrides to Inverness for sixty days imprisonment. A large crowd gathered at the railway station to welcome them. Cheers were raised for the raiders when a sympathiser mounted a rostrum and said with great fervour, 'It is a disgrace to the Government that Irish Fenians should be released, and Highland men who have served their country and are unable to get land, should be sent to prison.'[162] Munro's difficulty was that opinion outside Lewis was frequently quite different from opinion in the island itself. Lewismen would not have resented the arrest of the raiders: in the rest of Scotland and England, he feared that it might arouse some opposition. Accordingly the Scottish Secretary did not feel able to commit himself.

There remained only the alternative course, and Leverhulme took it. On 9 May he again ordered the complete closure of his development works. He let it be known that if the raiders were to withdraw again, and satisfy him that raiding would be abandoned for ever, he might reconsider his attitude. Meanwhile he intended to concentrate on Harris. As if to underline his disillusionment, he had the fire-engine, which he had recently presented to Stornoway and emblazoned with its arms, dragged by six horses over the mountains to Harris. He cancelled the invitations to all his guests who were to have visited Lewis that summer, and leased the shooting-lodges to strangers. He announced that he would not visit the island himself:

It is a great disappointment to my sisters and myself and all our guests that we are not able to visit Lewis this year, but under the present circumstances, my sisters and myself do not feel that we should get either benefit in health or pleasure from a visit, and we feel unable to make one. I hope however that better counsels will prevail with the raiders, and that in succeeding years we shall be in the happy position of being able to come.[163]

In June work was at a complete standstill. No action was taken against the raiders of Coll and Orinsay, and in consequence there was further raiding at Galson Farm on the Barvas coast and on outlying fields of the Manor Farm, just outside the gates of Lews Castle. In July, Colonel Lindsay, Leverhulme's permanent representative, left the island and did not return. Lewis was in disgrace with its proprietor, and the islanders responded with a mixture of contrition, resentment against the raiders and the Scottish Office, and the hope that in spite of all that had passed, someone would change his mind sufficiently to make possible a resumption of the works.

Optimism grew when it became known that Leverhulme intended, after all, to pay a brief visit to Lewis in August 1921. It was his only visit of the year. He appeared to be at the top of his form when he addressed his first public meeting at the Stornoway Agricultural Show, making one of his few references to his deafness:

I am under the disadvantage of not having heard what the Provost said in introducing me, but this also has its compensations; for whatever may have been said against me I do not have to answer; and whatever may have been said in my praise I do not have to contradict. (*Loud laughter.*) It reminds me of the story of the ladies at a tea-party who disagreed about something, and one of them said, 'Well, it would not do for all of us to be of the same opinion, for if we were, you would all have wanted my husband.' (*Laughter.*) 'Oh no,' replied another, 'if all of us had been of my opinion, none of us would have wanted him.' (*Loud laughter.*)

Enjoyable as this was, his audience were waiting for the passage of his speech in which he was to announce his future intentions. When it came, it was a great disappointment. He suggested that they should keep goats and sell heather. The latter intention he immediately carried out. The children of the island were instructed to bring sack-loads of heather to the now completed but unused canning factory, from where it was sent in boxes to Mac Fisheries shops throughout the country. The experiment was a flop. The canning factory was soon filled to the roof with unsaleable heather, and Sir Herbert Morgan wired to Leverhulme begging him to stop any further supply. Reluctantly Leverhulme agreed. The heather still stored in Lewis was used as bedding for horses. It was the last attempt that Leverhulme made to capitalise the natural resources of his island.

On 31 August 1921, the day before he left Lewis, he announced the indefinite suspension of all his projects. In a speech at the Stornoway Highland Games, he said:

Three years ago it was mutually accepted that our relations would be strictly on a business basis—that there should be no odious taint of philanthropy to lower ourselves in each other's esteem. No one regrets more than myself that the canning factory, the fish products and the ice companies cannot be opened for work. But the conditions of supply and demand in these industries make it impossible to do so. These businesses could only make heavy losses if they operated at present, and we must wait patiently for world markets to be cleared of surplus stocks before prices will adjust themselves to the costs of production.

Similarly with resumption of harbour making and road construction. Owing to the high cost of all such work today, neither of these can proceed at present, and must be suspended until normal costs are restored. . . . There must be a complete change in present conditions before any of this work can be resumed.[164]

For the first time since he came to Lewis, a speech by Leverhulme went uncheered. He was formally thanked for his presence and for distributing the prizes. The speech was made on Thursday, 31 August 1921. It was fully reported in the *Scotsman* on 2 September, and a leading article commented, 'A serious view of the new position in Lewis is taken by the authorities in London.' Indeed it was. On Sunday, 3 September, Munro drafted a letter to Leverhulme which was delivered to him by hand at The Hill on 6 September. It read *in toto* as follows:

Dear Lord Leverhulme,

I have read in the *Scotsman* of 2nd September the report of a statement made by you at a gathering in Stornoway on the previous day (*sic*) on the subject of your development schemes in Lewis, and in writing to you now, I do so on the assumption that the report accurately defines your position.

I appreciate the considerations that have led you to take the decision now announced by you. I recognise that circumstances over which you have no control have compelled you to suspend indefinitely, but not, I trust, permanently, the various enterprises for the benefit of the island which you had in hand and in contemplation. I am well aware that you must deplore this necessity, and I share the regret which you express that commercial conditions are such as to leave you no option in the matter.

I am confident that you on your part will just as fully appreciate the important influence which the new situation must have on my attitude and future action.

The undertaking which I gave you on behalf of the Government was that compulsory powers of taking your land for small-holdings should not be put into operation while your development schemes went on, but that if for any reason these schemes did not proceed, the hands of the Government should be free.

In my view the latter contingency has, through no fault of yours, now arisen, and I am bound to reconsider the situation—freed from the undertaking above mentioned.

In the circumstances as they are now, I feel that I would not be justified in refraining any longer from putting into operation a generous measure of land settlement.

I should much prefer to do so with your co-operation and assistance, and I trust that I am not too sanguine when I hope that I may count upon your good offices in the matter. I am sure that the knowledge that the alternative policy of land-settlement was proceeding with your assent would have a considerable effect in assuaging the keen disappointment which must be felt by the many persons who looked to your schemes with hope, and would also secure for you the hearty goodwill of the people generally.

If, as I trust you will be, you are prepared to meet me on these lines, I shall give immediate instructions to the Board of Agriculture for Scotland to get into touch with your representatives in order that the necessary action may be taken without delay.

Yours sincerely,

Robert Munro[165]

Leverhulme was deeply hurt by this letter. He replied to Munro that he would regard the compulsory splitting-up of his farms 'as a breach of the spirit of the understanding between us, as raiding still continues. . . . It would of course make it impossible for all time for either myself or others to develop the island on the lines I had proposed. You cannot build up a healthy community on crofting, nor healthy towns without adjacent farms.'[166] But by the end of October, realising that further struggle was useless, and having lost much local sympathy by abandoning his schemes, Leverhulme gave in. Acknowledging that Munro was 'technically relieved' of his undertaking, he wrote to him:

Sooner than have to submit to these two farms being taken piecemeal, I have decided not to oppose your taking the whole of the farms of Coll and Gress subject to satisfactory terms being arranged.[167]

For good measure, he threw in Orinsay and North Tolsta farms as well. Coll, Gress, Tolsta, and Orinsay were taken over by the Board of Agriculture at the beginning of 1922 for subdivision into 120 new crofts and 81 enlargements of existing crofts.[168]

As Leverhulme acknowledged defeat on the point of principle, there remained only one question. All agreed that priority should be given to ex-servicemen, and that the choice of tenants for the new crofts should be decided by ballot. Where the raiders to be eligible to ballot? Munro had at last announced, in December 1921, that 'in future land-raiding is to operate as an absolute bar to land-settlement,' but if he excluded the Lewis raiders from the chance of a croft, these men would certainly raid other farms and the trouble would start again. Leverhulme was equally determined that the inclusion of the raiders in the ballot-lists would violate every principle of justice. With a degree of indignation unusual in their coldly polite correspondence, he scrawled at the foot of one of his last letters to Munro, in which he asked that late applicants should be considered:

I cannot consent to any croft being allotted to Raiders. I gave intimation of this in my speeches during the last three years. No raider's
name can therefore be included amongst those to be balloted for.*[169]

Even on this point, Leverhulme was obliged to give way. His
Chamberlain, Captain A. M. Fletcher, who had succeeded
Charles Orrock in 1920, had the unhappy duty of informing him
that 'the majority of the raiders have been successful in securing
holdings'. There were eight raiders on the Coll list, eighteen on
the Gress list, and an unspecified number who obtained crofts
on Orinsay. The controversy died away with this final restate-
ment of their points-of-view by Leverhulme and Munro:

I am more than ever convinced that the crofting policy is a mistaken
one. I see its evil effects on all sides and I regret that you should be
continuing it to the lasting detriment of the welfare of the island. . . .
There is only one sound policy for Lewis, which is the development of
native industries, natural to the island, which can give employment for
the population who can never exist solely on the cultivation of the
land. This was my hope and intention, and I regret it should have
been made impossible.[170]

Munro replied:

While agreeing with you as to the desirability of the fullest possible
development of all native industries, I adhere to the view which I have
expressed to you before, that there does not appear to be any essential
reason why such development should conflict with the policy of small-
holdings. In my view the two policies are complementary, and it is
possible, I think, for each to go on to the benefit of the other.[171]

What went wrong?
It must be reserved for a final summing-up to decide whether
Leverhulme's ambitious schemes for the Hebrides could ever
have succeeded, for this can only be judged in the light of his
experience in Harris. But the personal controversy between
Leverhulme, Robert Munro and the raiders, which has occupied
the greater part of these two chapters, should be seen as the core
of the story, if not the core of the problem.
There was much truth in Munro's claim that the Government's
policy of providing crofts for landless men was not incompatible
with Leverhulme's schemes. Leverhulme's fear was that the

* See fascimile facing p. 180.

creation of new crofts would encourage the perpetuation of a
system that he considered dangerously out of date, and that it
would divert attention from the revolutionary nature of his
schemes. He believed that the great emphasis placed by the
Government on settling a few men on small patches of land
would merely induce others to demand land that would never
become available in their life-time. He did not so much fear the
competition of the croft as the competition of the crofting idea.
If the men were led to imagine that there was something splendid
in their traditional way of life, they would never exchange it for
a better one.

On the other hand, he had already had proof that the great
majority of the islanders accepted, and most of them welcomed,
his schemes for their future welfare. Most previous accounts of
these events have assumed that the crofting population resisted
to a man the introduction of Leverhulme's modern methods,
and that the incident should be seen as one of conflict between
the old and the new, between a rich and insensitive old man and
a noble peasant tradition extending back hundreds of years.
This view is quite fallacious. Leverhulme showed great tact and
skill in dealing with a people almost as remote from his own way
of thinking as the peasants of the Ukraine. He won them over.
But when he was confronted with a handful of men who would
not be won over, he adopted an attitude towards them that was
inconsistent with his previous determination to lead and not to
force.

He could and should have given up the farms. Munro was
justified in his observation that 'it does seem a pity that the
whole future of the islands for years to come should be jeopard-
ised, and indeed wrecked, on account of a difference of policy
regarding two small farms'.[172] It was of no real consequence that
barely a tenth of the demand for crofts could be met by breaking
up the farms. The clamour for land would have been satisfied,
if not the need, once all the available land was seen to have been
handed over. The surplus of landless men for whom no land,
except the common grazings, would then have been available
would have been attracted all the more willingly into Leverhulme's factories and fishing fleets. Justice, as they conceived it,
would have been done, and no alternative occupation would have
remained to them except emigration, which they were anxious to
avoid.

By that time, however, Leverhulme's pride was involved. He had come near to saying on more than one occasion that his purpose was to destroy the crofting system. How then could he be a party to its extension? Realising, perhaps, that he was on weak ground, he adduced his second main argument: that the farms were essential for supplying the town with milk. The hollowness of that claim has already been examined. Dairy-farms were desirable; but they were not essential: the milk for Stornoway could be obtained from the mainland, and the country districts were already self-sufficient. Even before the raids began, his mind was made up that he would not give way on the farm question, and that if the Government used their compulsory powers to acquire the farms, he would abandon his schemes, partly in disappointment, and partly because he had persuaded himself that one policy was incompatible with the other.

It is sometimes said that in his later years Leverhulme was a victim of megalomania. If this means that he believed himself capable of succeeding in any project to which he put his hand, it is true and not to his discredit. But if it means that he had so inflated an idea of his own importance that he rode roughshod over any opposition, it is not true. On the contrary, he was pathetically anxious to be liked. He adopted his stubborn line on the farm question because he thought he would win, and he thought he would win because he had the people on his side. His mistake lay in his failure to recognize that if he faltered he could not win, because he was dealing with a Government that had compulsory powers and the overwhelming support of the British population, who misunderstood the attitude of the islanders themselves.

Then came the raids. Leverhulme could find some sympathy in his heart for men who wanted land, but none for men who seized it. Then he made his second mistake. He should immediately have interdicted every raider, and pressed the interdict to the point of imprisonment. Nine thousand islanders had petitioned him to take this course. He refused, partly for fear that he would incur increased unpopularity on the mainland, and partly because he convinced himself that the Secretary for Scotland would release the prisoners. There would certainly have been an outcry from the Highland League, and perhaps demonstrations when the raiders were brought to gaol. He could have endured this without flinching, for the Lewis people would still have supported him, and public opinion generally, after a few affectionate gibes at the old soap-boiler, would have agreed that law-breakers should pay the penalty. It now seems improbable that Munro would have taken any other view. He knew well that to release these men could have earned him more contempt than popularity, and would have led to new outbreaks of raiding all over the Highlands and islands.

Did Leverhulme seize upon the raids and the ambivalent attitude of the Scottish Secretary as pretexts for abandoning schemes which he could no longer afford? To his detractors this has proved an attractive theory, for which the publication of the details of his financial troubles in the official history of Unilever has provided additional support. Undoubtedly Leverhulme concealed the extent of his embarrassments even from his closest associates in the island, as he had every right and reason to do. But when he announced the indefinite postponement of his schemes in August 1921, he gave at least half the real reason. He could not say that Lever Brothers was in difficulties without irreparably shaking the credit of the Company: but he did honestly admit that his decision was due to the general state of trade throughout the world. Earlier, he had not been so open. He appalled his friends in the island by closing down all his works in January at the very moment when Munro had agreed to allow him the ten-year trial for which he asked, and left them to explain it as best they could. When he resumed his projects in April 1921, they were on a much reduced scale, and the assurance that the work would grow rapidly in volume as it advanced was not wholly convincing. Yet even at the worst moment of the crisis Leverhulme saw his way ahead: the dividend on Lever Brothers' shares was not reduced at any stage. By 1922 the Company had completely recovered. In February of that year, D'Arcy Cooper wrote to him: 'The soap business of Levers is probably in a better position than it has ever been. The leaks in the ship have practically all been stopped, with the exception of the Niger Company, and Levers are in a position to face any losses in that connection which they have made or are likely to make.'[173]

It can therefore be assumed that Leverhulme would have gone ahead with his projects in Lewis, as he did in Harris, even if temporarily on a smaller scale, had it not been for the other difficulties that he encountered. His emotions, his pride, his convictions, were too deeply bound up in the two islands for him

The Rt.Hon. Robert Munro, P.C.,K.C.,M.P.                    Page 2

advised that any action which would shut out these men from their
chance in the ballot would raise the gravest dissatisfaction in
the Island.    This I know you are as anxious to avoid as I am, and
I hope that you may find a way of getting over the point which has
arisen.

Yours sincerely,

*Leverhulme*

*I cannot consent to any croft being allotted to Raiders I gave intimation of this in my speeches during the last 3 years no Raider's name can therefore be included amongst those to be balloted for*

15. Page of a letter from Leverhulme to the Scottish Secretary,
31 March 1922. See p. 177

16. At the opening of the town bowling-green in Stornoway, July 1922. Left to right, Sir Harry Lauder, Leverhulme, Provost Roderick Smith, Captain A. M. Fletcher (facing, in cap)

to abandon them without a cause that seemed to him overwhelming. He did not abandon Harris. He abandoned Lewis because he faced defeat on an issue which he considered to be crucial, though in retrospect it appears merely incidental. He had lost his normally keen sense of proportion.

On his side of the controversy, Robert Munro must share the responsibility for the collapse of Leverhulme's grand design. Forced temporarily to give way by the pressure of public opinion in the island, he made no secret of his belief that the ex-servicemen were entitled to the land they claimed, and he seized with alacrity on the first opportunity that Leverhulme presented to escape from his pledge. He was ill-advised. Thomas Wilson was so deeply sympathetic to the raiders' cause that his counsel should have been suspected. Dr Murray MP, to whom must go a large share of the blame for misleading parliamentary opinion, failed to understand the change of attitude in his constituency because he did not visit it for a year. The Lord Advocate, as we have seen, arrived in Lewis with the notion that there was a conflict between Stornoway and the country districts, and left the island no wiser, giving the raiders, indeed, the impression that they had his moral, if not his legal, support.

Confronted by all this misleading advice, constantly reminded in Parliament and outside of his Government's past pledges to settle the men on the land, and armed with special powers to do so, Munro saw no sound reason for making an exception of Lewis. He was not unsympathetic to Leverhulme, and delayed using his powers to divide the farms long enough to provoke public criticism. He hoped, not unreasonably, that either Leverhulme or the raiders would give way. When neither did so, he was faced with the choice of putting his authority behind the claims of one or the other. At first he chose Leverhulme, and gave him his ten-year pledge; but he did so in such a way as to suggest that his sympathies lay with the landless men. Not until it was too late did he make the vital statement that no raider would qualify for a croft; and he gave Leverhulme reason to believe he was likely to release the raiders once they were condemned to imprisonment. He was ungenerous in his haste to cancel his agreement with Leverhulme at the first public sign of the latter's financial difficulties. He could have asked the proprietor how long a postponement of his plans he envisaged. Instead, he presented him with a decision which was bound to put an end to Leverhulme's plans for ever.

N

Perhaps Munro regarded this move as a triumphant vindication of his policy. The new plan for Lewis had failed; the old plan must now be put into operation. But the new plan, as Leverhulme commented,[174] had not failed, because it had never been tried. The raiding was still the main reason why he did not feel able to continue; the setback in trade was merely an additional and temporary reason. So when Munro tore up their agreement 'with indecent haste', as Leverhulme put it, he was ignoring Leverhulme's promise to continue as soon as normal conditions returned. Leverhulme made a tactical error in his speech at the Stornoway games by referring only to the financial reason for the stoppage without reminding his audience of the underlying reason. Munro exploited this error with untypical cynicism.

Another course had been open to the Scottish Secretary from the very beginning of the dispute. Admittedly at the risk of severe criticism in the House of Commons, he could have stated that the situation at Lewis had been transformed by Leverhulme's projects and the fortune that he was prepared to spend there, and advised his colleagues that in view of the wide support which these schemes commanded in the island, he proposed to encourage the few Lewismen who still demanded land to abandon their claims in the interests of the island as a whole. Different views could be taken of Leverhulme's argument that the farms were essential, but as his were both the brain and the purse behind the schemes, some consideration should surely be paid to his desires, and even to his prejudices. Munro's reproach that it seemed a pity that the enterprise should be wrecked on account of two small farms, could be applied to his own policy as well as to Leverhulme's. Such a course must have occurred to Munro. It would probably have succeeded, and if it had, Lewis might be a very different place today.

Both men, therefore, attached disproportionate importance to the issue of the farms on which the whole scheme foundered. If only there had been in the island a man big enough to point out with enough cogency the folly of this controversy in comparison with the immensity of the prize involved; if only, one dark night, the ex-servicemen who backed Leverhulme could have taught the raiders their lesson; if only the accounts of the Niger Company had been properly inspected before its purchase by Lever Brothers. If only. . . . But history made up of conditionals, ceases to be history.

# Chapter Eight

# THE END IN LEWIS

FOR TWO YEARS after he had announced the end of all his plans for Lewis, Leverhulme continued to toy with the idea of reviving them. He was still proprietor of the island; but having yielded the power to develop it as he wanted, he temporarily lost the desire, and transferred his energy to Harris. It was a curious cat-and-mouse relationship that he henceforward maintained with the Lewismen. At one moment he was telling his Chamberlain not to plant up the garden at Lews Castle because there were unlikely to be any further visitors; a year later, he was giving minute instructions to his head-gardener for the sowing of seeds and the layout of the new paths, and installed in the ball-room an expensive 'stentorphone', which relayed recorded music at a volume that was deafening to everyone not already deaf. He could write to the Provost, 'I never had a visit to Stornoway that I enjoyed more than my last one. Each succeeding visit seems to be a greater stimulus and to give me greater enthusiasm for the people of the island and the opportunities there;'[175] but he made no move to reopen his works, referring to himself as 'a bird with one wing broken'. In July 1922, within a few weeks of writing so encouragingly to the Provost, he had said publicly in Stornoway:

I am sorry that my plans have been interfered with, but I think you will all agree that if a man is going to do a thing entirely at his own expense, it is not unreasonable that he should say on what conditions he is going to do it. . . . It causes me great distress that I have had to abandon my schemes for the development of the island, but the past has gone and I have no power to revive it.

In his private dealings with the shareholders in the island companies his attitude was equally ambiguous. At one time he told them individually that the companies were all to be wound up except for the offal factory, which was the only one in operation, and offered to buy back all their shares at par, so that they would suffer no loss, an offer of which most of the shareholders took advantage; a month later he was writing privately to Morgan, 'We would like to see the canning factory in Stornoway commenced ... I am quite prepared to take considerable risks in the matter;'[176] and at a meeting of the Specialities Company in October 1922, he spoke of increasing the canning factory to ten times its size, adding, 'We are going, I think, to have every prospect of making an excellent start in Lewis.' As late as April 1923 he was hinting that the rebuilding of Stornoway would continue and that the utilisation of his now completed but empty factories would shortly begin ('we have all those buildings, and it would be a pity if we could not use them'). But the only work that actually continued was the making of the road along the west side of the harbour to Arnish, which was an amenity to the castle policies but in no sense an addition to the island's economic assets.

Leverhulme's alternating optimism and resignation did not please the islanders. They saw in it an attempt to maintain his popularity by raising false hopes. They viewed the contemporary development of his Harris schemes with mixed feelings: on the one hand it was proof that Leverhulme was not financially crippled and had not lost his affection for the Hebrides; on the other, Lewis had been his first foundling, and his excuse for abandoning it now began to appear thin. If he was in a position to spend all that money, he should have spent a large part of it on Lewis, where the people had backed him so resolutely. Lewis had gained almost nothing of permanent value, and had been made to look foolish. So when Leverhulme held out guarded hopes of reviving his projects, they were received with some scepticism. When they were not realised, scepticism began to turn into indifference. The medical officer for Lewis, Dr Harley Williams, watching one of his later arrivals in the island, observed that 'a respectful crowd thronged the wharf, but I remember that there was no cheering, no enthusiasm, and the thickset, grey-combed figure move up the gangway, and drove away between silent throngs'.[177]

The relationship between Leverhulme and the islanders had moved into its penultimate phase. In the space of four years he had encountered first, curiosity; secondly, excitement; third, enthusiastic support; fourth, disillusionment; and now, indifference tinged in some quarters by contempt. These transient emotions had varied in intensity from one part of the island to another, according to the benefits conferred by Leverhulme on a particular district, the scale of raiding, or the presence of an influential critic or supporter of his schemes. The Lewisman, as this record has shown, was capable of facing both ways: expressing great enthusiasm, but at a deeper level desiring no change, and even hoping that Leverhulme's enterprises would fail. Leverhulme was himself unaware of these hidden reservations among even his most enthusiastic audiences, for the Gael is a great flatterer, whether out of politeness or self-interest, and he will say to a man's face the opposite of what he says behind his back. Dr Harley Williams recalls one incident that can be taken as typical of many. One day, when Leverhulme was visiting a remote township, an old woman at the door of a black-house looked at him and muttered, *An e sin bodach an t-shiabainn?*—'Is that the old soap-man?' Always alert to know what people were thinking, Leverhulme enquired from his entourage what she had said, and one of the sycophants, standing near, dexterously translated: 'She is asking, "Is that the soap-king?", my Lord.'

These deceptive compliments became more infrequent once it was almost certain that Leverhulme had washed his hands of Lewis, for now there was no longer anything to be gained by them. The few men who still worked for him on the Arnish road and the estate farms became contemptuously idle, and the Stornoway branch of the Transport Workers Union gave him endless trouble with their exorbitant wage-claims for the most trivial services. Poaching became a serious abuse, and Leverhulme's head gamekeeper advised him not to prosecute the poachers, 'considering the simmering discontent in the locality . . . and the spirit of retaliation which prosecution would provoke.'[178] More serious were the renewed outbreaks of raiding, particularly in the Park district, where the raiders cut their names defiantly in the turf. The tenant of Eishken, Mrs Platt, appealed in vain to Leverhulme to prosecute them. The stage had been reached where neither firmness nor leniency could completely restore Leverhulme's prestige. He continued to visit the island, and even staged a ball at the castle in October 1922, when Prince George, serving as a midshipman on HMS *Mackay*, visited Stornoway with his flotilla. On another occasion he persuaded Sir Harry Lauder to open the new bowling-green in the town. But in spite of his exuberance at these functions, Leverhulme's star was setting in Lewis as it rose in Harris. He had allowed himself to be defeated, and his defeat had brought destitution to thousands.

There was great distress in the northern island during the winter of 1921–22. Throughout Great Britain it was a period of acute unemployment, and Lewis suffered as much as any other part of the country, its people bearing an additional hardship as crofters, who did not qualify for unemployment relief since they were counted as self-employed. Their normal sources of income had vanished. The potato crop was a complete failure; the sale of tweed had slumped disastrously; the fishing was unremunerative both in the Minch and on the east coasts of Scotland and England. So low had the island's fortunes fallen that it became necessary to import fresh fish to Stornoway from the mainland, and the crofters were obliged to sell at bottom-prices their sheep and cows, almost their only capital, to raise enough money to see their families through the winter. An official medical report of July 1922 recorded that forty-two out of the ninety-two children of a particular Lewis township (North Tolsta) were 'seriously under-weight . . . some looking like famine orphans.' Inevitably, much of the indignation aroused by these conditions was directed at the proprietor. Leverhulme had let them down, and the whole recent history of the dispute, including their own acclamations for him, was obliterated in the crofters' minds by the stark contrast between his apparent affluence and the penury of his countless tenants.

They turned, instead, to the Government. Pressed by demands for state aid from every direction, the Scottish Secretary felt a particular responsibility for Lewis, since he had antagonised Leverhulme by his actions. He promised a £35,000 grant for road-making in the island, omitting, however, to spend any of this sum on the Tolsta-Ness road, although the distress in these two districts was severe. The following summer, in August 1922, Munro paid his first visit to the island that had caused him such anxiety. If he expected to be welcomed as a liberator, he was immediately undeceived:

The Secretary for Scotland's visit to Lewis last week excited practically no interest in the island. How different would have been the case had he been able to come when the break-up of Coll and Gress farms hung in the balance against Lord Leverhulme's industrial development schemes. . . . The present apathy is engendered by tragic disappointment.[179]

Munro arrived at Stornoway in the fishery cruiser *Minna*, accompanied by Sir Robert Greig, chairman of the Board of Agriculture, and went at once to inspect the new crofts at Coll and Gress, where even the ex-raiders scarcely spared him a glance. The official party then drove to Balallan to see the new road leading to the villages on Loch Erisort, and finally visited some of the west-coast farms. They left the island almost unnoticed the following afternoon. A few months later Munro relinquished his office, and after an interval, was succeeded as Scottish Secretary by Lord Novar.

The hopeless prospect in Lewis drove many of the young islanders to their traditional remedy. By the end of 1921 hundreds of applications had been received from Lewismen anxious to emigrate, and the Dominions were glad to have them. In April 1923 the first batch of three hundred left Stornoway in the Canadian Pacific liner *Metegama*. Twenty of them were girls, the remainder young men of an average age of twenty-two, and all went to Ontario, where each was offered 160 acres of virgin ground and a hut for shelter. In spite of this promise of an acreage princely by Lewis standards, the crowd at the quayside as the young men and women embarked was full of foreboding. It was a repetition of the Lewismen's endless quest for security somehow, somewhere, and a symbol of the final failure of Leverhulme's schemes. He himself, though absent from Lewis at the time, felt it deeply. He had a mass of flowers sent from the castle gardens to the ship—more a wreath than a bouquet—adding to his note of instructions to Fletcher, 'I would like to have done more, but it would have looked as if the emigration solution had my support, which it has not.'

Leverhulme had by then not only suffered personal disappointment in Lewis, and lost what most men would regard as a fortune, but he was exposed from a fresh direction to a new outburst of anger and ridicule. The controversy over the title he chose when he was created a Viscount attracted at the time such publicity that it has since been quoted as a major cause of his failure. Chronologically the controversy followed over a year after his decision to cease work in Lewis; humanly, it had little effect on his relations with the islanders. But the incident provides an important illustration of the antagonism shown towards him by Gaels outside the Hebrides, who from the start had felt a smouldering resentment at his intervention in their affairs.

Leverhulme's elevation to a Viscountcy was announced on 11 November 1922, and he was re-introduced to the House of Lords a few days later, with Viscounts Haldane and Devonport as his sponsors. He was already Baron Leverhulme of Bolton-le-Moors in Lancashire. Now he announced that he intended to style himself 'Viscount Leverhulme of the Western Isles in the counties of Inverness and Ross and Cromarty.'

There was an immediate outcry that the choice of this title was an affront to Highland sentiment. It was said to resemble so closely the historic designation 'Lord of the Isles', held originally by the head of the Clan Donald, and since the sixteenth century by the Prince of Wales, that Leverhulme, if he had any respect for Highland feeling, should immediately substitute for it another more suited to a Lancastrian upstart. The violence with which this view was expressed can be gauged from these sample quotations:

*The Duke of Atholl* (speaking at a banquet in London, attended by the Prince of Wales himself): The men of the north honour their Prince as 'Lord of the Isles', a title, or even its semblance, the right to which they yield to no other person. (*Cheers.*) If any meaner subject claims it, we resent it in Scotland. From 1503 the title has been absolutely associated with the Scottish Crown.[180]

The *Scotsman* (leading article): From the Lewis the blast of indignant protest against what is regarded as a specimen of gross Saxon presumption and invasion has spread to the neighbouring islands and the mainland.[181]

*A. G. Paisley* (in a specially revised preface to his book *Wanderings in the Western Highlands and Islands*): The sway of the vulgarian Sassenachs in Gaeldom is increasing. . . . As well might a crofter, having bought a tablet of Sunlight soap, term himself 'of Port Sunlight', as the chairman of the Company having bought one of our 300 islands in the Hebrides style himself 'of the Western Isles'.

Meetings were held in every main centre of Scotland to pass resolutions deploring Leverhulme's lack of taste. Research-workers were brought in to sustain the challenge on historical grounds, but they were soon obliged to admit that the last of the mediaeval lairds who assumed it had forfeited the title in circumstances so discreditable that the Clan Donald would be unwise to press their claims. Nevertheless the title had become part of Gaelic song and legend, and romantic qualities were attributed to the old robber-barons of the Minch which would

have astonished them and their followers. Leverhulme was
doubly guilty in the eyes of their descendants. He had appropriated a title forfeited to the Crown: and by assuming it on the
strength of his purchase of Lewis and Harris, he was implying
the superiority of his line over the Macleods of Lewis and
Harris, the Macneils of Barra and the Macdonalds of Clan
Ranald, each of whom had a far better claim to its use, were they
presumptuous enough to make it.[182]

Leverhulme rode this storm with equanimity. He was fortified
by messages of support from Lewis itself, including one from the
local Lodge of Freemasons and another from representatives of
all the public bodies in the island, who presented him with an
illuminated address expressing their pride that he should have
chosen to honour the Western Isles in this way. Fletcher told
him not to worry. The *Scotsman* article had been quite baseless:
'The title has given entire satisfaction to all in the Lews, and has
been taken as a compliment to the inhabitants of the island.'[183]
An old Lewis woman wrote to him: 'Dear Viscount, Don't give
up your title. May you long grace its beauty. We Lewis folk love
our proprietor to own it. Never mind that big Macdonald Uist.'
Leverhulme knew the island character well enough by this time to
realise that such language might as easily be pleasure at the
Macdonalds' discomfiture, as genuine delight at his choice. In
fact, most of the island people probably cared little one way or the
other, for the habits of the gentry were mysteries to them, and
their historical sense was not as keen as was often claimed on
their behalf. They let the incident pass with a shrug of the
shoulders.

But the Gaelic societies of the mainland refused to let it rest,
the Gaelic Society of Inverness taking the lead. Their Secretary's
correspondence with Leverhulme and the Prime Minister was
published several years after Leverhulme's death.[184] In an opening
letter to Bonar Law, the Society pointed out: 1. That Leverhulme
was not even the owner of Lewis and Harris, which belonged to
the Lewis and Harris Welfare and Development Company Ltd.
2. That even if he were the owner, he had no right to the title,
which belonged to the King. 3. That the Lyon King at Arms
(the chief heraldic authority in Scotland) had not been consulted
before the announcement was made. Of the first point little was
made. As for the second, the historical wranglings were continued
at deeper and darker levels. But the third point was awkward, for

the Lyon King had certainly not been consulted by his English colleague, the Garter King, who had written to Leverhulme, 'I do not think there will be any difficulty in your taking the title you desire, but the matter has of course to be placed before the King.'[185] The King had approved it on the recommendation of the College of Heralds. Lyon King was furious. In a statement to *The Times* he confirmed that the title 'Lord of the Isles' belonged to the Prince of Wales, and added that it was 'unfortunate that the style to be conferred on Lord Leverhulme was not submitted to the Scottish Court of Heraldry.'[186] There was little that Bonar Law could do. He replied to the Gaelic Society of Inverness that it was now too late to change the title, since letters patent had already been issued, but pointed out that the words 'of the Western Isles' was a descriptive designation, and not part of the title itself. Besides, there was surely a significant difference between 'Lord of the Isles' and '. . . of the Western Isles', which should allay any misgivings that the title had been filched.

The Society then appealed to Leverhulme himself. Thinking no doubt that he would understand better a commercial parallel, they wrote to him:

Your Lordship is employing what would, under the Merchandise Marks Act, be called a 'colourable imitation' of the words 'of the Isles'. . . . The 'Western Isles' has always been applied to the two groups comprising the Outer and Inner Hebrides*. . . . In any case, I think I am right in saying that the islands of Uist, Benbecula, Barra, etc., do not belong to your Lordship. Therefore you are not entitled to include them in your territorial designation, even though the term 'Western Isles' comprehended the Outer Hebrides only.

Leverhulme replied that the Duke of Argyll did not own the whole of Argyllshire. But he vested his claim on more solid grounds. A territorial title implied that the holder was in a position to render service to that part of the country. Nobody could deny the service he had rendered to Lewis and Harris, which together included the greater part of the 'Western Isles', as he understood the term. For his Barony he had taken the name of Bolton, though he did not own Bolton. For his Viscountcy he had adopted the name of the Western Isles, for

---

* Technically, this is correct. But the term 'Western Isles' is usually taken to be synonymous with the Outer Hebrides only, and they are so described in the title 'Western Isles' given to the parliamentary constituency which comprises Lewis, Harris, North and South Uist, Benbecula, and Barra.

precisely the same reason: 'I viewed Bolton in the position of a
mother, and I viewed the Western Isles in the position of a wife.'
This argument, replied the Secretary of the Society, in the tone
of voice of a man who was losing it, was quite irrelevant. The
only point at issue was Leverhulme's encroachment on an
ancient title. Leverhulme refused to give way, saying that if he
surrendered the title he would cause far more pain to the people
of Lewis and Harris than pleasure to the Gaelic Society. A further
appeal to the Prime Minister went unanswered. Leverhulme
won the battle, and his grandson today still bears the designation
'of the Western Isles', although the family have long ceased to
own any part of the islands.

The controversy neither added to Leverhulme's popularity in
Lewis nor detracted from it. He was left with a large island on his
hands and responsibility for the welfare of 30,000 people whose
future he could no longer guide in the direction that he had
intended. His attention was fully engaged in Harris. What was
he to do with Lewis? As he would never be content with the role
of absentee landlord, he began to consider ways of disposing of
the island. But he needed a better reason than his own failure.
He was determined to emerge with dignity from his long controversy with the Scottish Office, and if possible to win the last
round.

Lord Novar provided him with the pretext he wanted. After the
division of Gress, Coll, Tolsta and Orinsay, the Government
requisitioned the much-raided Galson Farm, and in June
1923 divided it into fifty-two small holdings. At the same time
they created new crofts on part of the common grazings of the
townships of Lionel and Knock. Leverhulme continued to object
to the multiplication of crofts, though he had now no substitute to
offer, and was objecting more out of habit than conviction. Then
Lord Novar hinted that he intended to use his powers to divide
every farm in the island except those immediately round
Stornoway. This hint was given during an interview held at the
Scottish Office on 14 June 1923 between Lord Novar and some
of his officials on the one side, and Sir Edgar Sanders, representing Leverhulme, on the other. After the division of Galson Farm
had been exhaustively discussed, Sir Robert Greig, chairman of
the Board of Agriculture, remarked that 'it might be necessary
to take all the remaining farms in Lewis, unless the demand for
crofts was sooner satisfied.'[187] Leverhulme pounced on this

remark when it was reported to him. In response to his enquiry whether this was indeed the official policy, the Under-Secretary for Scotland, John Lamb, replied that the remark was 'not a statement of policy, but merely an expression of Sir Robert's fear that so long as there was any land available in Lewis, there would be a demand for it and a danger of raiding'.[188] Later, in reply to further enquiries, Lamb added: 'It was neither said nor implied that the Government policy was to take all the remaining farms in Lewis. Time will show whether Sir Robert Greig's fear was well founded or not.'

Leverhulme now finally abandoned any intention to make use of his factories in Stornoway, or to proceed with his town-planning schemes, putting the whole of the blame on the Scottish Office. 'It would be madness for me,' he said, 'to disregard this clear intimation from the Scottish Office that under certain circumstances they might be compelled to take every farm in Lewis except the Manor Farm.' But his reaction was so quick and so final that it arouses the suspicion that he was seizing on these chance words of Sir Robert Greig as an excuse for a decision that he had already taken. The parallel with his earlier reaction to Robert Munro's hint that he might release the raiders if they were imprisoned is very close. On both occasions the remarks were made not to Leverhulme, but to his representatives, and were conveyed to him at second-hand. On the first occasion, Leverhulme was passing through a severe financial crisis; on the second, he was casting round for a reason finally to abandon Lewis. It could no longer affect his fishing policy if the re-maining farms were divided, for his Lewis policy was already in ruins. On the very morning when Sanders saw Lord Novar, and before he could possibly have heard the result of the interview, Leverhulme had written to Sir Herbert Morgan that he had decided to remove the ice-plant and power-plant from Stornoway to his new harbour in Harris, now named Leverburgh.[189] If he still believed that his Lewis schemes turned entirely on the question of the milk-supply to Stornoway, as he once more argued when giving his public explanation of these events, he would have abandoned the schemes as soon as the chief farms round Broad Bay had been taken. Instead, he had allowed hope to linger to the point where it was becoming an embarrassment. 'You and I,' he had said in his letter to Morgan, 'ought to con-centrate our efforts entirely on the Companies at Leverburgh.'

That was already his dominant thought when Greig made his casual remark in the Minister's presence, and Leverhulme saw his chance.

There remained only the question of how to dispose of Lewis. He could sell it for the trifling sum that it would raise. He would lose a lot of money; but more important, its sale would damage his pride and prestige. Now that Lever Brothers had recovered financially, he could afford to cut his losses in Lewis, but he attached more importance to the manner in which he wound up his association with the island. He wished to do something for the benefit of the islanders (for whom he still had a genuine regard, even if it was no longer so fully reciprocated), and at the same time to heap coals of fire on the heads of the Scottish Office, who had treated him, he believed, quite atrociously. The dramatic gesture that he planned during the summer of 1923 was inspired as much by political as humanitarian motives.

He decided to give Lewis to its people. The idea occurred to him in June 1923, a few days after the Novar-Sanders interview, when he asked Fletcher to send to Hampstead the one-inch Ordnance Survey sheets of Lewis, showing how the whole island was divided between moors, farms, crofts, town and forest. In July he acknowledged the receipt of the maps, 'which are very helpful to me in the matter I have under consideration at present'.[190] But nobody except his personal solicitor was taken into his confidence. Fletcher himself was not told of the proposal until a few hours before Leverhulme made it public.

On Monday, 3 September 1923 Leverhulme made one of the most startling speeches of his career. At his special request a meeting of the members of the Stornoway Town Council, the Lewis District Committee and the Stornoway Parish Council, was convened in the Town Council Chambers. Leverhulme's speech had been typed out in full, and a copy of it is preserved in the Council's archives.

He began:

I never had a more uncongenial burden laid upon myself than the one that devolves on me today, which is to explain fully and without reserve the position I find myself placed in with regard to my relationship with the Island of Lewis. As I explained to you at our first meeting, I was not attracted to Lewis by any love of sport, but entirely by the possibilities of doing something in a small way for the permanent benefit of its fine people.

He then gave an account of his long negotiations with the Scottish Office, the world-slump and the succession of farm-raids, which had caused him to modify and finally abandon his plans. He continued:

I am really now left without any object or motive for remaining here. For me merely to come each year as an ordinary visitor to the castle, and knowing that I could take no interest in fishing or sport, would be meaningless. I am, like Othello, with my occupation gone, and I could only be like the ghost of Hamlet's father haunting the place like a shadow. I should feel rather depressed than exhilarated.

Then came the details of his offer, which are set out below in tabulated form, incorporating the slight amendments which were made in subsequent weeks:

1 *The town of Stornoway.*

    i *Lews Castle.* The castle and its policies he offered as a free gift to the people; the former to be used as the Town Hall, public library, and the Provost's official residence, the latter to be renamed Lady Lever Park 'after my wife, who was with me on my first visit to Stornoway in 1884.' The gift of the castle was to exclude all the furnishings, which were unsuited to a municipal building and would be removed within twelve months.

    ii A *Stornoway Trust* was to be formed by the Town Council to manage the castle and other properties gifted to them.

    iii The *factories* erected by Leverhulme would remain the property of the Companies which he had promoted, with the exception of the Gas Company, the Fish Offal Company and the steam laundry (the only Companies that were operating), which he donated to the Stornoway Trustees in order to provide them with a sufficient income to maintain the castle and the Lady Lever Park.

    iv The *town-properties* that he had purchased for eventual demolition under his town-planning scheme, he offered to re-sell to their original owners at ten per cent less than the price he had paid for them.

2 *The Parish of Stornoway* (which extended northwards from Arnish moor as far as Tolsta).

    i All the *farms*, including the Manor Farm, and all the *sporting and fishing rights* in the parish, together with the sporting lodges, were offered as a free gift to the people, to be administered for their benefit by the Stornoway Trustees.

ii The freehold of all the *crofts*, except those occupied by ex-raiders, were offered as a gift to their present occupiers. Any croft of any man who chose to turn down this offer, and any croft occupied by an ex-raider, would be given to the Stornoway Trustees, together with the common grazings now in the hands of the proprietor.

3 *The remainder of the island* (Parishes of Barvas, Uig and Lochs) The *farms, lodges and sporting rights* were offered as a free gift to the Lewis District Committee, to be managed by a second body of Trustees, half of whom were to be nominated by the Committee, and the other half elected by the voters on the parliamentary list.

ii The *crofts* were offered to the crofters on the same terms as those outlined in 2–ii above.

4 From this offer, Leverhulme made only a few exceptions:

i *The Shiant Islands*, 'which are of the greatest interest to me and are occupied by a tenant living in Harris (Malcolm Mac-Sween), and really both they and the Flannan Islands can just as well be attached to Harris as to Lewis.' Valued at £150.

ii *The Flannan Islands*. Valued at £35.

iii *Seaforth Island* in Loch Seaforth, which lay half in Lewis and half in Harris. He proposed to attach it wholly to Harris. Valued at £15.

iv The islands of *Rona* and *Sula Sgeir*. Valued at £30.

v The *salmon-fishing in Loch Erisort*. Valued at £250.

Leverhulme asked for a reply to his various offers by 6 October 1923, as he was leaving for Australia shortly afterwards, and if his offer were to be rejected, he wished to have ample time to sell the island. If it were accepted, the transfer would take place in November 1924.

He ended his speech:

I am leaving Lewis with deep regrets, but carrying with me the happiest recollections of my five years residence among the people of Lewis, and my most profound gratitude for the full and generous welcome and support I have always received practically unanimously from all. . . . I hope you will receive my proposals as indicating my desire when leaving Lewis to do all in my power to secure the future welfare, prosperity and happiness of its people.

Provost Mackenzie replied in a single sentence that they all appreciated his princely offer, and would give him their reply within the stipulated time. Leverhulme then withdrew, so that he would not hamper their discussions, and as he left the room, all present, moved by a common impulse, rose to their feet. Leverhulme was much affected. 'I accompanied him to the ante-room,' Fletcher recalls, 'and helped him on with his overcoat. He was greatly distressed, and said to me that this was one of the two saddest days in his life, the other being the day he lost his dear wife'.[191] Soon after he returned to the castle, it was observed that the flag on the tower was pulled down.

He left Stornoway that night, and on reaching London, wrote to Fletcher:

I had an enjoyable sail across the Minch—in fact, the calmest sail I ever remember—and arrived here safely and well. . . . I will not trust myself to refer to the incidents of Monday, but as I mentioned then, I felt it very keenly, and still more so when our friends met me on the boat as I was leaving. I hope they did not misunderstand my making a lot of silly jokes, but whenever I feel any occasion deeply, I invariably try to joke upon it, on the principle of the boy who whistled whenever he had to go through a churchyard, but I am sure you would understand me.[192]

There is no mistaking the genuineness of his emotion. Yet so many-sided was his character, that referring to this same sad journey across the Minch, he wrote to MacBrayne's:

On my last journey from Stornoway to Kyle on the *Sheila*, I noticed that you had a Danish make of soap upon the boat. I cannot quite understand this. As far as my knowledge goes, soap cannot be produced in Denmark of equal value to that of English manufacturers.[193]

Leverhulme's offer of the island of Lewis to its people was very typical of the man. It was generous, imaginative, magnani-mous, and an implied rebuke to the Government which had thwarted him. His gesture was hailed with admiration by the same newspapers that had violently attacked him a few months earlier. The *Scotsman* wrote: 'He could not have been blamed if, in his disappointment, he had sold the estate and cut his losses. But Lord Leverhulme is clearly cast in a different mould.' The *Glasgow Herald* said: 'Cavilling at his motives should be finally stilled. . . . It places him in a unique position among the outstanding figures which the modern industrial system has produced.' From the

island itself the tributes flowed in. Almost every public organisation sent him a message of gratitude, and letters reached him
from crofters in every part of Lewis, of which the following,
obviously written with great difficulty, was typical of many:

I am seeing the island now as a ship without a rudder in the middle
of the ocean, but I sincerely hope and pray that our Lordship, and all
Lewis men will come together like one stick and that there enemies
get a joke. Please excuse my bad language. I cannot express my sorrys.

Leverhulme had won back much of the regard that he had
recently lost. It was not so much the generosity of the gift that
appealed to the islanders, as its magnificence. They had a great
respect for the heroic.

That Leverhulme also had a political motive for making his
offer was an aspect quite overlooked at the time, and it has never
been referred to in later printed comment. Yet even without
Leverhulme's contemporary private correspondence to guide
us, it must be quite obvious that his offer was not wholly dis-
interested. For five years he had been at loggerheads with the
Scottish Office over the disadvantages of perpetuating the
crofting-system, and with a few of the islanders over their demand
for land. By offering to make each crofter the owner as well as
the tenant of his croft, and by presenting the people with the
farms, Leverhulme was outflanking the Government's own
policy and satisfying the landless men beyond their dreams.
They wanted land: very well, let them take the entire island,
including the Laird's castle itself. The Government had set
themselves up as champions of the supposed wishes of the people:
let them deal with the people directly, without any intervening
proprietor to use as a whipping-post. Then they might discover
that the proprietor had his uses and his burdens. They would
discover, for instance, that the finances of a large Highland
estate meant a constant drain on the proprietor's purse, that the
rating system was inequitable, and that the Land Acts were so
grossly loaded on the side of the crofters, that it was impossible
to run an estate scientifically or even economically.

In his great speech of 3 September, Leverhulme had let fall
one hint of the political tit-for-tat which was at the back of his
mind. He said that the transference of the island from his ownership to that of the two bodies of Trustees and individual crofters
'would effect a very material change in the view of the Scottish

o

Office. . . . It would create an entirely different atmosphere and viewpoint.' Privately he went further. To a friend in Bolton he wrote: 'The industrial schemes I had are impossible side by side with crofting. I think there is nothing that will bring this home to the people better than owning the island themselves and seeing what they can do with the island without industrial employment.'[194] To his niece, Mrs Rossiter, he wrote: 'I have no disappointment with the people of Lewis. My disappointment centres firstly, lastly and all the time round the action of the Scottish Office.' Most significantly, a letter to Dr Donald Macdonald, a Lewisman who had married another niece, Miss Paul, included the phrase, 'I am confident that my only course is the one I am taking, so as to call attention to the inequalities and absurdities of the Scottish Land Act.'[195]

There was pique, and even a little malice, in his gesture. He watched with understandable amusement the consternation that it created both in the Scottish Office and in the island itself. The former maintained a dignified silence, saying that Leverhulme's action would have no effect on their plans for the island, but privately they must have wondered how the rates would be raised now that there was no proprietor to pay them, and what would be the reaction of the people to any further breaking-up of the farms if the farms passed into the hands of the people themselves. They experienced the embarrassment of a seducer who finds himself presented by a complaisant husband with the woman he has seduced.

In the island, three choices had to be made within a month of Leverhulme's statement. The Stornoway Town Council must decide whether to accept the castle, the neighbouring farms, and all that went with them. The Lewis District Committee must make the same decision in regard to the outlying parts of the island. And each crofter must decide for himself whether to accept the gift of his croft.

The Town Council decided unanimously to accept the offer. They believed that the revenue from the gas-works and the offal factory would by itself be sufficient to maintain the castle and its grounds. In addition, there was the revenue from the ten remaining farms that lay within Stornoway parish, from the sporting estates, and from the twenty-two town properties which Leverhulme added to his original gift.

At first an attempt was made to comply strictly with Leverhulme's wishes. The policies were named Lady Lever Park. The Provost took up his residence at the castle, and received £500 a year to cover his expenses. The Stornoway Trust was formed. But soon after Leverhulme's death the Trust found itself in financial difficulties. It was discovered to be uneconomic as well as inconvenient to site the Town Hall in a position relatively remote from the centre of the town. The Trust deed was varied to allow the castle to be let to sporting tenants, who occupied it year after year until the second World War, and later it was converted into the Lewis technical college, which it remains today. But although Leverhulme's proposal to the Town Council was not carried out in full, its main element survives. The Stornoway Trust owns an important part of the town and the immediately surrounding country, which it administers in the interests of the people. 'Not only building property, but essential sources of production on land and sea are in communal possession.'[196] How strange an outcome from the efforts of one of the most remarkable exponents of private enterprise that this century has known!

The Lewis District Committee, on the other hand, rejected Leverhulme's offer, because investigation of the accounts showed that the excess of expenditure over revenue would be about £1,365 a year. There was no way round this difficulty. The proposed Trust for the three country parishes outside Stornoway was not to be endowed so munificently as the Stornoway Trust. They would have the rents from the farms and the sporting estates, it was true; but most of the farms had been split up, and the remainder were threatened; and in a time of universal depression, there was no certainty that the annual sporting rights would find tenants. Meanwhile the Trust would become responsible for paying the rates and taxes, and maintaining the sporting part of the estate in a condition suitable for letting once better times returned. The Scottish Office were asked to give financial help for a few years, and appoint their own representatives to the Board of Trustees. Lord Novar hastily turned down both suggestions. He said that no public money could be used to prop up an indigent estate, and that his officials could not serve two masters, the Scottish Secretary and the Trust, when it was not inconceivable that the two might come into conflict. His refusal left the councillors of the three parishes in an embarrassing position. If they accepted the gift, they would soon become insolvent. If they refused it, they would become 'the laughing stock of the world,' as one of them remarked, their people having clamoured for land only to turn it down when it was offered to them as a free gift. Eventually, on 5 October 1923, twenty-four hours before Leverhulme's offer expired, the Committee voted on the following resolution:

That the Lewis District Committee tender their grateful thanks to Viscount Leverhulme for his generous offer, but after carefully considering the statements of income and expenditure furnished for the parishes of Barvas, Uig and Lochs by his Lordship's Chamberlain, and in view of Viscount Novar's decision not to meet the deficit on the working of the estate, they must regret that they cannot see their way to become the nucleus of the proposed Trust.

Six councillors voted in favour of the resolution, and three against. One abstained on account of his age and health.

Of the three groups to which Leverhulme made his offer, the crofters were faced by the most difficult decision, and they were required to make up their minds in a very short time on an unprecedented situation and with almost no legal advice.

The basic reason why the great majority declined the gift was that a crofter who owned his croft would be required to pay owner's rates as well as occupier's rates. At the moment, since they only paid rates on the agricultural value of their holdings, they were assessed at less than a quarter of the whole rental, the proprietor paying the remainder. For example, in the parish of Lochs, the rateable burden was distributed as follows:

|  |  | £ |
| --- | --- | --- |
| Rates paid by Leverhulme: | as proprietor | 2,109 |
|  | as occupier | 1,275 |
| Rates paid by all other ratepayers: | as proprietors | 249 |
|  | as occupiers | 656 |

If they became the owners of their crofts, the crofters would not only lose the benefit of partial de-rating, but they would become liable for the whole of the proprietor's share as well. One crofter put the problem very simply: 'The rent of my croft is £1 per annum. I pay 3/9 a year in rates. If I become my own proprietor, what is to hinder the Assessor putting a value of say, £20 on my house?' Thus they would lose the security of a fixed rateable value (since their rents were fixed), and simultaneously become liable for a scale of tax quite outside their means. It is true that they would have ceased to pay any rent, but what they gained by possessing the freehold of their crofts would have been far outbalanced by their increased liabilities for tax. That their fears were not baseless was shown by the additional burdens immediately imposed on the few who accepted the gift; their assessments were increased seven or eight fold, according to the type of house on the holding. If only the 2,000 cottars and squatters in Lewis were also assessable, the problem would have been solved: but this was impossible, since the cottars and squatters, having no legal rights, had no legal liabilities, and they were too poor to pay a rent to the crofters, in lieu of rates to the Trustees.

It was unfortunate that Leverhulme's offer happened to coincide with a period of great economic depression in Lewis. The potato crop had again failed, the tweed and fishing industries were at low ebb, and the weather had been so bad that even the peats would not dry out. Psychologically it was the worst moment to launch an experiment of this nature. 'The crofters all appreciate the offer,' said the *Stornoway Gazette*,

but they hesitate on one ground only—that possible failure to meet their obligations as owners may bring discredit on themselves and disappointment to Lord Leverhulme. Were every season normal in Lewis, with no crop or fishing failures, there would be little hesitation, but the smaller men have the fateful uncertainties staring them in the face.[197]

The rating difficulty was not the only reason for the crofters' hesitation. One of the great advantages already enjoyed by a crofter under the Land Act, was the right to compensation for his croft, and for any improvement made to it, whenever he gave it up. Leverhulme had often protested against the iniquity of this charge on the proprietor: a croft might be deserted by an emigrant, and whether a new tenant was found for it or not, the Estate was still liable to pay compensation. In a year of great exodus, the total sum might be enormous. Once a crofter obtained his freehold, he would lose this right: he would have to find a buyer on the open market, instead of automatically obtaining valuation from his landlord.[198]

Furthermore, the crofters were advised that they would lose the right to Government grants for the improvement of their holdings, and the protection of the Land Court. The Clerk to the Court told an enquirer that all the traditional rights of appeal against the decisions of a proprietor or his agent would be forfeited if the offer were accepted. The Land Court existed to protect crofters against their landlords, and as their own land-lords they could not be expected to do themselves an injury. The further legal difficulty that they might lose their rights to the common grazings, which caused many crofters to hesitate until it was too late, was overcome by the creation of a special Com-pany, Lewis Island Crofters and Squatters Ltd, to which were conveyed all the crofting lands exclusive of those held by the Stornoway Trust.

The financial and legal complexities created by Leverhulme's offer deterred men who were quite content with the rights they already held. Unlike the Irish peasants, the Lewismen had never asked for freehold. It had played no part in their agitation for land. The Crofters Acts had conferred on them security of tenure, the right to bequeath a croft to a near relation, a fair and fixed rent and the right to compensation if they left. That was all they asked. Leverhulme's suggestion would not create a single new right nor a single new croft. It would only take away some of their existing rights, and render them liable to heavier taxation. Besides, they would feel naked without a proprietor to guide them and a Chamberlain to nurse them. There would be nobody to criticise, nobody to appeal to, and nobody to take ultimate responsibility. A crofter candidly stated his fears in a letter to the local paper:

When the people get the land free, I don't think anybody will have the ruling. Therefore we would rather have someone to rule us, and to abide under the Crofters Act as crofters. My idea is that when every-body will be his own master, everybody will put his cattle where he likes and when he likes, and there will be no law or order in the place. What I want is law. . . . Any attempt to change the present system would be sure to lead to disputes and even bloodshed.[199]

Only once before had any group of crofters become their own masters, at Glendale in north-west Skye, and the experiment had not been a success. The crofts, the common grazings, the sheep-stock and the sporting rights, had all deteriorated owing to the lack of skilled supervision by a factor and the absence of any civic sense among crofters of equal status.[200] Nearly all the appre-hensions of the Lewis crofters had been borne out at Glendale.

So the Lewismen refused Leverhulme's offer. Only forty-one crofters out of over three thousand accepted his gift. The others chose to remain tenants, as they and their forefathers had always been, and patiently waited for Leverhulme to sell the freehold of their land to a new proprietor.

Leverhulme was disappointed by the poor response. He had only succeeded in giving away his castle, the farms around Stornoway and his properties in the town. The rest of the island was still his own, in an even more real sense than before, because he had been obliged to buy Lewis back from Lahwad for £40,000 in order to make his offer of a free gift legally possible. But having gone so far, he intended to dispose of Lewis by any means he could. He wrote to his Chamberlain after the dead-line for the acceptance of his offer had passed:

I am determined to divest myself entirely of any proprietorship in any property in Lewis. As the Lewis District Committee have not accepted my gift, in my opinion it would best serve the interests of the island that I should sell the sporting properties and so introduce, not tenants, but owners who will take a more personal interest in the future fishing and sporting amenities than a mere yearly tenant would do.[201]

But it was not easy to accomplish this. He gave the lodge at Uig to Dr and Mrs Macdonald, advising them not to take the Uig crofting townships with it, 'as you would receive begging letters at every time of stress merely because you were the proprietor and not because there was any claim upon you', and they would be liable for heavy compensation charges. Mrs Platt was allowed to remain as tenant of her old home at Eishken, under the nominal proprietorship of a specially formed Company, but the rest of the estate was put up for sale in March 1924. Bidding was so low that only one of the eight lots offered was actually sold. This was the 56,000 acre sporting estate of Galson on the Barvas coast, which went for £500 (just over 2d an acre) to Mr Edward Valpy, the only bidder, who gave his address as the Oxford and Cambridge Club. There were no bids for the Park deer forest, none for Morsgail, none for Soval, none for Aline, none for Barvas, none for Carloway. For the world-famous Grimersta salmon-fishing, £13,000 was offered but not accepted. The burden of the crofting townships attached to the huge acreages of moor made the properties virtually unsaleable at a time of economic slump. Later in the year a few of the properties were disposed of, among them Grimersta to a sporting syndicate and Soval to a Lewis businessman, but the bulk of the Lewis estate remained in Leverhulme's hands until his death.

Suggestions for its use reached him from all over the world. An American wrote to Leverhulme saying that he would be glad to accept Lewis as a gift, if nobody else wanted it, for conversion into an orphans' home. From Leipzig came the idea of settling poor German families there, provided that Leverhulme would pay their travelling expenses. An Australian suggested that the Outer Hebrides should be annexed by Northern Ireland, with which they had once had close links. More impressively, every able-bodied man in Uig petitioned Leverhulme to incorporate their parish in Harris, so that they might still enjoy the benefits of his schemes. Affectionately, but a little wearily, he replied that he had no power to alter county boundaries established by Act of Parliament.

He continued the sad process of dispersing his private and commercial properties in Lewis. In February 1924 forty-two cases of books and furniture were sent from Lews Castle to The Hill at Hampstead. Another ship-load, including the stentorphone, went to Borve Lodge, his home in Harris. The ball-room tapestries went to the Lady Lever Art Gallery at Port Sunlight, the chandeliers to Thornton Manor. Two bays of the canning factory, which had never produced a single can, were dismantled, and transported in sections to Leverburgh, where they joined the ice-factory, which had never produced a cube of ice. The shareholders in the Lewis companies received back their investments in full. Work on the Arnish road was halted just short of the Creed river. The unfinished Tolsta-Ness road began slowly to crumble away. The island entered its third successive winter of widespread unemployment and acute distress, while the great liners anchored off Stornoway harbour to embark further parties of young emigrants. At the beginning of this terrible winter of 1923–24, there was a General Election which returned another Liberal as Member for the Western Isles: his Unionist opponent, noted Fletcher, 'is a young barrister, a native of North Uist, a Captain Morrison, who is a brilliant speaker.'[202] Thus, in these dismal circumstances, did the future Speaker of the House of Commons and (as Lord Dunrossil) Governor-General of Australia make his debut on the political stage.

Leverhulme had intended never to revisit Lewis. As there was no direct steamer-service to Harris, he made elaborate arrangements to avoid Stornoway by driving from the ferry-head opposite Kyle of Lochalsh to Uig on the north-west of Skye, and thence by a fishing-boat direct to Leverburgh. But in fact he saw Stornoway twice more, once secretly, and once in a glare of publicity. At the end of October 1923 he motored up from Harris to work for a few hours in Lews Castle, and slipped silently away by night. Nearly a year later, on 5 September 1924, he delivered the oration at the unveiling of the Lewis War Memorial, in which he had shown a personal interest from the very start of his proprietorship. Standing in the open air at the foot of the great tower a mile outside Stornoway, he said to the huge crowd:

Not only have the people of these outer islands contributed overwhelmingly to the defences of Empire, but with equal magnificence, and again out of all proportion to their population, to the building of the British Empire overseas. In Canada, New Zealand, Australia, Africa, India and elsewhere these islands have provided a hardy race of pioneer adventurers and settlers, whose high standards of life have set a tone and influence that holds the Empire together by the abiding stability and solid worth given by high character and frugal industrious habits.

The people of these islands have accomplished this in spite of the fact that no people are so deeply attached to peace, the arts of peace and to their beloved native island. Lewis men love their home, their wife, their children, with a passionate ardour that few can realise who have not lived in these wind-and-storm swept isles.

Let me remind you of the words of the Canadian boat-song familiar to us all:

> 'From the lone shieling of the misty Island
> Mountains divide us and the waste of seas;
> Yet still the blood is strong, the heart is Highland,
> As we, in dreams, behold the Hebrides.'

That night, before the mail-boat sailed, Leverhulme called on Kenneth Maciver, son of the closest friend he had made in the islands, and asked Maciver to go with him to the canning-factory, which was then already half dismantled. The two men stood there in the dark, Leverhulme a little ahead of his companion. Maciver suddenly saw the outline of the great shoulders trembling with sobs. Neither said a word to the other. They walked back along the quay, and shook hands at the foot of the gangway. Leverhulme never saw the Hebrides again.

# Chapter Nine

# LEVERBURGH

IT WOULD BE wrong to think of Leverhulme's enterprises in Harris as an anticlimax to the events so far described. He was anxious to redeem his reputation by success in Harris, and by inference to show the Lewis people and the Government what they had missed. But Harris was not a *pis aller*. Within a few months of acquiring Lewis in 1918, Leverhulme had been negotiating for the purchase of Harris, and it is quite clear that he had intended to run both islands in common harness. When he decided to abandon Lewis, Harris benefited from a larger share of his money and attention, and far from giving way to general disillusionment with the Hebrides and its people, Leverhulme continued his Harris schemes with the same gusto as had marked the first phase in Lewis. Several times in each of the years 1923 and 1924 he made the difficult journey to Harris by way of Skye, and supervised his engineering and other works with a care for detail that astonished a new set of factors, architects, surveyors, local government officials and crofters. At the end of his life, he felt that he was in sight of the fulfilment of his dreams.

It has often been said that there was a difference in temperament between the men of Lewis and Harris, that accounts for the comparatively few disagreeable incidents that arose between Leverhulme and the Harris crofters. They were said to be milder, less quarrelsome, more adaptable. In 1796 the author of the *Old Statistical Account* had written of them:

They are sober, docile, sagacious and capable of industry, were a channel opened to them in which industry might be profitably exerted. They are kind and courteous to strangers, hospitable and charitable even to excess. They have the strongest attachment to their native country, and entertain the most ardent gratitude to benefactors.[203]

Much of this testimonial would be questioned by those who know
Harris well. It is an idealist's view of island men; it could have
been written by Captain Cook of the inhabitants of a South Seas
atoll. In truth, the Harris crofters display all the paradoxes evident
in the characters of their Lewis neighbours. They have a romantic
view of life, but drive hard bargains; they are proud, but apt to
be flatterers; they are capable of arduous labour, and of extreme
slothfulness; superficially friendly, their reserve and innate
suspicion make them difficult to know; anxious for a greater
share in the amenities of life, they are privately sceptical of
success in any new enterprise suggested to them. Certainly they
are less litigious than the Lewis people, who would rush to the
Land Court at the first indication that their rights were being
invaded. But to attribute Leverhulme's relative success in
Harris to a difference in the islanders' mentality would be to
ignore the more obvious reasons. These were: the different
economies of the two islands; and the experience which Leverhulme had gained of the Hebrides, and the Hebrides of him,
by the time he came seriously to consider the problems of
Harris.

Harris had no towns—Tarbert was little more than a large
village—and no middle-class. In 1920 there was not even a
resident doctor in the island, and the Ministers were only better-
educated crofters. There was no form of manufacture except
tweed-making, still a cottage-industry, and the only trade was
carried on in a few village stores. Communications with the
outside world were erratic, the internal road system a disgrace.
Harris had no centre like Stornoway for political agitation, no
newspaper of its own, no leaders to stir up trouble, and a long
tradition of dependence upon the lairds. Primitive though
their conditions were, the Harris crofters did not labour under a
sense of grievance. They were fatalistic, accustomed to accept
what few benefits came their way, resigned to the worst, endlessly
hopeful of the best, and prepared to continue generation after
generation the crofting-fishing life which was all that most of
them had ever known.

Here and there, voices were raised in tune with those of the
land-hungry men of Lewis. But in Harris there were fewer,
smaller and poorer farms, and the demand that they should be
split up for crofts was correspondingly less urgent. The major
grievance caused by the nineteenth-century evictions from the

sandy Atlantic coast to the unfertile Bays district of south-east Harris had already been remedied by the resettlement of some of the evicted families in new model-townships like those of Northton and on the island of Berneray.[204] Harris was consequently less overcrowded than parts of Lewis. Its total population in 1921 was only 4,750, little more than that of the town of Stornoway, and there was no equivalent to the congested Back district of Lewis where trouble could ferment.

In mid-1919, when Leverhulme came to grips with Harris, both he and the island people had learned the lesson of the Lewis incidents. Leverhulme now realised that something more than geniality and a display of good intent were required in dealing with so unpredictable a people; and the islanders had observed that Leverhulme was a man with prejudices that must be humoured, and that there was a limit beyond which his patience should not be tried. Harrismen, ever jealous of their neighbours, were too astute to miss this opportunity to score off the Lewismen by welcoming their disillusioned Laird. At the first news of his purchase of the island, there was some consternation in the Harris townships: it was rumoured, quite untruthfully, that he had begun to evict crofters. But when he came personally among them, the pattern of events during the first summer in Lewis was repeated. He was received politely, even obsequiously, and ballads were written in his honour:

> South Harris sons, and daughters too,
>   And children at their play
> Will all turn out, and so will you
>   To greet our Lord this day.
> For he has come among us here
>   A father here to be,
> To start great works, erect a pier,
>   And make his cottars free.
> His houses building everywhere
>   Around our mountains high;
> His factories, how they will glare
>   Beneath our Harris sky.
> Let us all now be united,
>   And let our bagpipes tune,
> Long live and may our blessing all
>   Attend Lord Leverhulme.*

* These dreadful verses were addressed to Leverhulme on 22 July 1919 by a crofter of Obbe on the occasion of his first visit to that township.

Leverhulme was no longer taken in by this kind of skin-deep adulation. He wished to make quite clear the terms on which he was prepared to give his ideas a new trial. Already threats had been made to the Harris farms, couched in the same language with which he was all too familiar. Even before his purchase of South Harris was complete, ten crofters of Northton had written to the Board of Agriculture, claiming the farm of Rodel as theirs by right:

The old excuse that the farmers held the land under lease is, we fear, not going to hold any longer. . . . We shall never submit tamely like our forefathers. We shall not be compelled to leave our native land without a struggle. If something is not done soon, I am afraid we shall be compelled to take possession in our own way. The following are those who wish to be given a small-holding on Rodel without delay.[205]

Then followed the list of signatories. The same threat was made verbally to Leverhulme when he visited South Harris in July 1919.

It was this threat, combined with his current difficulties in Lewis, where the conflict over Coll and Gress was approaching a climax, that caused Leverhulme to summon a special meeting of crofters at Obbe, on 15 August 1919. He told them that he intended to create a large fishing harbour in their township, but it would only be a waste of his money if he were later to run into opposition from the local people. So as a preliminary to starting the work, he required their agreement to five conditions:

1 They should work 'whole-heartedly with me and not against me.'
2 If it should become necessary to clear any crofts from the site of the future works, the crofters would accept alternative sites elsewhere, and Leverhulme would pay the entire cost of removal.
3 If part of the common grazings were needed for the same purpose, it would be replaced elsewhere.
4 All intention of raiding farms should be abandoned, and no claim should be made to the Board of Agriculture for dividing farms until a ten-year trial had been given to his schemes.
5 Any 'unforeseen points' that might arise would be dealt with in the same spirit of co-operation.

Leverhulme put these five points to the meeting three times over, and each time they were translated into Gaelic. The meeting assented to his conditions unanimously. Subsequently, a document was drawn up based upon them, and copies of it were signed by Leverhulme, his Harris factor, Norman Robertson, and the chairman of the meeting, John Morrison.

In reporting these events to Robert Munro, Leverhulme added:

The meeting was enthusiastic in favour of the scheme, and a pleasing incident occurred after the meeting. The crofters came up to the Estate office—so Mr Robertson reported to me—with a request that if a new fishing harbour was founded there, they might have it called 'Leverburgh'.[206]

Some of the older men of Leverburgh who were present at this meeting, agree today that Leverhulme's five conditions were unanimously endorsed, but they have a slightly different version of the origin of the name Leverburgh. Towards the end of his speech, they say, Leverhulme remarked that the word 'Obbe' appeared to him too blunt and monosyllabic to be worthy of the great harbour that was to rise on the Sound of Harris. Could they not call it after one of the old proprietors: 'Port Macleod', for instance; or 'Port Dunmore'? 'Call it after yourself!' said a voice. 'You are spending the money!' 'Very well,' replied Leverhume, 'if that is your wish, it shall be known as Leverburgh.' Whatever the exact circumstances of its origin, the petition to alter the name from Obbe to Leverburgh was made to the Postmaster-General by the crofters themselves, and the change was officially made on 1 December 1920. Today Obbe survives only in the name of its loch. There is no record that the alteration aroused public opposition or ridicule at the time, but its supposed arrogance and tastelessness were recalled when the controversy over the title 'of the Western Isles' was at its height two years later. The 'honourable name of Obbe, with associations deep in Harris history' (nobody particularised them), had been discarded for the profane monstrosity 'Leverburgh', as if it were a settlement carved out of the African jungle, from which, indeed, Leverville was then emerging. The Harris people accepted it as they accepted Leverhulme himself—with amused resignation.

By and large, the crofters of Harris kept their promises to Leverhulme. In subsequent years there were only two serious incidents that caused him to remind them of his threat to withdraw unless his conditions were observed. The first concerned the farm at Rodel, which had been named in the petition of the Northton crofters to the Board of Agriculture early in 1919. In spite of the pledge given at the Obbe meeting, six of the men renewed their demand for crofts. Robertson advised Leverhulme to resist it strongly. The part of the farm that they claimed (Lingerbay) was quite unsuited for crofts, and the local population were incensed against them. 'Quite truthfully,' reported Robertson, 'I can say that there is not one person in the Obbe, Strond, Rodel and Northton districts but who is prepared to carry out to the letter what was arranged at the meeting of 15 August, and a very strong feeling is now abroad against the six men.' The six then wrote to Lloyd George that it 'was not sweet' to hear from Leverhulme that they would never get any of his land, 'which we fought for on the bloodiest fields of history, on to the borders of Hades. . . . Every farm in this district is most suitable for small-holdings, and every farmer almost ripe for the hangman's rope'.

The Prime Minister and Leverhulme ignored these letters, and there was no actual raiding of Rodel until April 1921, when six other crofters from the Bays district (the original Northton men having given way to local feeling) seized Lingerbay and began to re-erect the ruins of the black-houses that they found there, while an old woman lay down in the furrow before the farmer's plough. Leverhulme refused to prosecute until the men started to demolish the fencing, which he considered an act of robbery instead of mere trespass. Then he allowed proceedings to be taken against them, and they were sentenced to forty days' imprisonment. In view of Leverhulme's contemporary reluctance to take any legal action against raiders in Lewis, and his suspicion that the Scottish Secretary would release convicted men, it should be noted that the Lingerbay raiders served their full sentence at Inverness prison (less three days for good conduct), and that on their return to Harris, according to Robertson's report to Leverhulme, there was no demonstration in their support, no welcoming committee, and the men went back to their former houses with their tails between their legs.

The sequel to this incident was even more significant. Eighteen months later, in December 1922, three men from the northern part of South Harris pegged out claims for themselves on Rodel farm and began to raise rough shelters for their families. When the news reached Leverburgh,

about 150 men marched to Rodel . . . and in an amiable and conciliatory manner urged on the raiders the consequences of what they
were doing. One of the raiders said that it was land he wanted, and
that 'it was the law that would put us out of here.' There were shouts
of, 'No, we will put you out, and we want your decision now.' Over-
awed by the throng around them, the raiders assented to clear out on
condition that they received an assurance of work. Mr Norman Robertson, the factor, was sent for, and confirmed his previous assurance of
work to the satisfaction of the raiders, who left.[207]

The two raids on Rodel, both of which were halted in time,
one by the police, the other by the people, were the only raids on
Harris farms. But there was one other incident of a similar kind,
when Leverhulme showed that by this time he too was capable
of judicious surrender. In the Sound of Harris there are innumerable small islands, some inhabited, some mere grazings for sheep,
some attached to North Uist, others to farms on the mainland of
Harris. One of the largest is Berneray, on which, twenty years
previously, the Board of Agriculture had settled two new
townships. An intense rivalry had grown up between them. In
May 1920, the sheep of one of the townships were placed
illegally on three small neighbouring islands attached to the farm
of Scaristavore. But as the islands were of little use to the farmer,
Leverhulme agreed to add them to the township's common
grazings, provided that the men first withdrew their sheep. They
did so, but immediately the rival Berneray township announced
that they would put their own sheep on the three islands. The
original raiders anticipated their action by re-occupying the islands
themselves, and seizing at the same time a further three islands
belonging to Rodel farm. The row dragged on for years, and was
still not cleared up at the date of Leverhulme's death. Telegrams
flew backwards and forwards between Leverhulme, his agents, the
Board of Agriculture and the spokesmen for the two rival Berneray
townships, while the flocks of sheep were ferried to and fro like
counters in a prolonged game of draughts.

At no time did the Scottish Secretary make use of his compulsory powers to settle the few Harris land-disputes, although
he once reminded Leverhulme that the powers existed. The
ten-year pledge which Munro gave to Leverhulme, and which
Lord Novar subsequently reaffirmed, was not withdrawn in the
case of any Harris farm, since the industrial schemes for Harris
were steadily progressing, and the demand for land was less. The

17. The whaling station at Bunaveneader, West Loch Tarbert.
Right, Clisham, the highest mountain in Harris

18. The 'Bays' district of South Harris today

19. The Sound of Harris, looking south-west over Leverburgh. Leverhulme's fishing piers lie in the centre of the mainland shore, with Obbe Loch on the near side. The dangerous approaches to the harbour are clearly illustrated

20. Approaching the Shiant Islands from Tarbert, 1959

conflict with the Scottish Office was confined to Lewis; but the minor troubles in Harris were dealt with in a manner that strongly suggests that a similar attitude to the Lewis land-question might have prevented the collapse of Leverhulme's projects there. Leverhulme used his powers firmly and reasonably, the Scottish Office withdrew to a discreet distance, the people themselves played the decisive role at the most critical moment, and from the very beginning Leverhulme came to a clear under-standing with the crofters that raiding would automatically mean a cessation of his works. The lack of friction in Harris was due to wisdom learned from experience.

Leverhulme's main purpose in Harris was the same as in Lewis. He intended to raise the people's standard of living by giving them immediate employment on public works, which would lead to a rapid transformation of the island economy from one based on crofting and small-boat fishing to a new economy based on large-scale developments in the tweed and fishing industries. 'My schemes are not very revolutionary,' he wrote, when the purchase of North and South Harris was complete. 'I want to develop the fishing industry and the handloom weaving.'[208] Many of his longer-term plans for Lewis did not re-appear in Harris. There was no talk of island railways (though he did much to improve the road system), little of land-reclamation, com-mercial exploitation of peat, forestry, fruit cultivation or additional cottage industries. From first to last his main interest was in Leverburgh, and his secondary interest in tweed.

He wanted to found an extensive fishing-harbour in Harris to provide local employment and to supply Mac Fisheries from an additional Hebridean source. Stornoway boats mainly fished the Minch. His Harris boats would concentrate on the Atlantic, particularly around St Kilda, where the matje herring was believed to shoal in its finest condition. These fishing-grounds were scarcely fished at all. If he could find the site for a harbour in Harris with equal access to the Minch and Atlantic, he would have a new base with unrivalled possibilities. His plan was to station his fleet within half a day's reach of these untapped fishing-grounds, so that they could return with their catch while the fish were still fresh. The herring deteriorated so rapidly on being taken from the water that a longer distance would mean salting

P

them on board, a process which reduced the quality from first to second grade. On shore there must be all the facilities for treating the herring for dispatch to market, and a fleet of carrier ships to transport them rapidly to the mainland. Fleetwood was again to be the main receiving and distributing depot, and Mac Fisheries the retailer.

Leverhulme did not search long for the site of his harbour. He found it at Obbe. It was a pity that he and his advisers did not give the matter further thought before embarking on the the engineering works, for Obbe was not the best possible site. Tarbert would have been preferable, for it had deep sheltered water, and it would not have been beyond Leverhulme's scope to dig a canal through the narrow isthmus linking the East and West Lochs Tarbert, and so provide his boats with access to the seas on both sides of the Hebrides. This proposal was urged on him at an early stage by Duncan Maciver; and his personal representative in Lewis, Colonel Walter Lindsay (who had apparently not heard of Maciver's idea), raised it again in October 1920. 'It struck me yesterday,' he wrote to Leverhulme, 'that it would be a great advantage if a canal could be cut at Tarbert, as there is extremely good anchorage in both lochs.'[209] But it was in that very month that work at Leverburgh began in earnest. Why Leverhulme discarded the obvious claims of a Tarbert canal is not clear. Perhaps he feared its proximity to Stornoway, or did not wish to harm the interests of the thriving community of fishermen on the isle of Scalpay at the entrance to the east loch. Or perhaps it was for the more personal reason that once the decision had been taken to rechristen Obbe 'Leverburgh', it became unthinkable to abandon it.

The great disadvantage of Obbe lay in the dangers of the Sound of Harris. One who knew it well wrote in 1923:

The Sound of Harris is considered very dangerous for the navigation of vessels. It is full of rocks, numbers of which are sunken at a short distance from the surface of the water; and again, the current is always so strong during a calm that there is great difficulty in keeping a vessel off those dreaded skerries.[210]

The engineers of the Scottish Fishery Board told Leverhulme that Obbe was quite unsuitable. So did the skippers of Mac-Brayne's steamers. So did the Northern Lighthouse Commissioners. Halliday Sutherland, who saw Leverhulme on the site in 1923, found him quite unrepentant, even after he had himself run aground at the entrance to the harbour on one of his journeys from Skye:

In vain the local sailors—and they are amongst the most fearless I ever knew—told him that the Sound of Harris with its thousand rocks could not be navigated at night in winter. The persistent old man replied, 'If the Harris men cannot sail my ships, I will get English sailors, and if necessary, I will put a light on every rock in the Sound of Harris.'[211]

Determined not to be thwarted by a mere accident of geography, Leverhulme blasted away some of the rocks and put gas-beacons on others. He saw only the gap in the long ridge of the Outer Hebrides that opened up between South Harris and North Uist, presenting him with his much-needed avenue from east to west, and attributed the experts' apprehensions to a want of vision. He was always complaining that they were incapable of thinking big. The rocks and small islands were a protection, not an obstacle:

I do not know why the pessimists should wail over the prospects of Leverburgh. I stood on the scaffolding at the end of the pier on Saturday, and you could not get a view of the open sea in any direction. Whichever way you looked there were intervening islands blocking the way. These islands produce a bay for Leverburgh, and I am confident that any vessel can ride out the storm there as well as in Stornoway harbour.[212]

Leverburgh was never tested as a fishing-harbour under winter conditions, but the distrust of its approaches among local and mainland skippers was one of the reasons for its abandonment on Leverhulme's death.

His staff-engineers from Port Sunlight were Wall and Bostock, who were more concerned with the quays and shore-installations than the harbour approaches. They were in no doubt from their preliminary surveys that a good harbour could be formed at Obbe if the approaches could be improved. When Leverhulme first saw it, there was nothing more than a straggling township on the road between Northton and Rodel, with a lagoon lying between the road and the sea. He proposed to thrust out a stone jetty from the shore far enough to provide a minimum depth of fifteen feet at the jetty-head. From it would project at right-angles two temporary wooden piers, the three quays combined providing enough room for fifty herring-drifters to lie alongside. In the second phase of development, the lagoon would be converted into an inner harbour to take a fleet of two hundred boats. A channel would be blasted between the lagoon and the open sea, and fitted with lock-gates to maintain a constant depth of twenty-five feet of water in the inner harbour. In the third phase breakwaters would be built as additional protection to the outer harbour, making use of existing rocks and islets as foundations.

To provide room for the sheds and curing-yards adjacent to the quays, Leverhulme removed a number of crofts and levelled a low hill. The resulting space measured 170 acres. On it he erected several buildings, mostly of temporary construction in order not to delay the start of fishing operations, intending to replace them by permanent structures later. They were of two kinds: buildings for accommodating the men and girls who would crew the boats and cure the fish; and industrial buildings for carrying out the various processes of curing and packing. For the former purpose, two women's barracks were put up, long, low, white buildings, each with twenty rooms, accommodating 240 women in all; and equivalent quarters for 180 men.[213] The industrial buildings included two large curing yards built of steel framing (part of the original canning-factory from Stornoway); a kippering house of twelve kilns; a two-storey net-store; a garage for twenty cars; a water-tower for providing fresh water to the quayside; a refrigerating plant (also removed from Stornoway); and various offices, workshops and store-sheds. The whole group of buildings was connected by a new road and bridge to the highway running through the old township of Obbe.

It was said that Leverhulme intended to found a complete town at Obbe, with an eventual population of 10,000 inhabitants.[214] There was no town-planning scheme on the magnificent scale of Stornoway's, no art gallery, avenues, nor railway station. But he began at once with the construction of permanent terraces of houses, some of which still survive to indicate the scope of his plan. As many crofters as possible were persuaded to erect their own houses under skilled supervision, and for the managers and other professional men whom he hoped to attract to Leverburgh, he built larger houses on the model of those in

Matheson Road at Stornoway. His first idea was to build workmen's houses of reinforced peat, like the cob-cottages of southern
England, but when the peat was found to be too porous and
vulnerable to wind and rain, he imported a few prefabricated
wooden houses from Norway, which blend well with the landscape and stand up to all weather conditions. At the same time
he offered to supply any man with £250 worth of building
materials and a quarter-acre site at a nominal ground rent of 1/-
a year, provided that the houses were built to one of six approved
designs. Over fifty crofters eventually took advantage of this
offer, and as soon as the first three houses were ready, a plate
was fixed to the palings round the garden of one of them with
the name 'Lady Lever Terrace'. Of the manager-type of
house, six were almost complete on Leverhulme's death, eight
half finished, and a further eight begun. Today they remain the
best houses in the island, apart from a few private properties
in Tarbert and Rodel and the lodges attached to the sporting
estates.

Of Leverhulme's public buildings at Leverburgh, only one
survives, the Hulme Hall. Now a school, it was intended as an
inn and recreation hall for the people, and was equipped with
a cinema-projector, but (on Leverhulme's express instructions)
no drinking license. He also planned to fill in a branch of the
Obbe Loch to provide a level building-site for a church and
town-hall. Eventually Leverburgh might have gained some
dignity. The site is a promising one, lying between the sea and
high hills at the junction of two glens. But there is a curious lack
of orderliness about Leverhulme's initial work which suggests
that he was devoting all his attention to the harbour and leaving
the town to grow spontaneously. The modern visitor to Leverburgh can see nothing there of the inspiration behind Port Sunlight. It is drenched in melancholy, the original black-houses
and tin shanties alternating with the shoddy architecture of
Leverhulme's £250 cottages and his four-square managers' houses
climbing the shoulder of the hill above the deserted quay. His
concrete water-tower is the dominant feature of the landscape,
rearing its club-foot against a sullen sky.

The harbour works were started in the autumn of 1920, as soon
as the necessary permit was obtained from the Board of Trade,
and within a few weeks three hundred men were at work on the
site with compressor drills, earth-moving machinery, and pile-

drivers. Later, two locomotives were imported to run on short stretches of track between the loch and the sea. The men came from all the surrounding townships within walking distance, Strond, Rodel, Northton and even Finsbay, but Leverhulme needed more labour than they could provide. He brought in manual workers from Uist and Lewis, and as soon as the fishing started, girls from Wick, Fraserburgh and Aberdeen. Among the office staff, Halliday Sutherland saw

half-a-dozen attractive English typists with bobbed hair, short skirts and silk stockings. These girls aroused the ire of one of the preachers on the island who denounced Lord Leverhulme and all his works: 'Oh my dear friends, it is something awful to see the harlots and the concubines of Lever running about the streets of Obbe.' Lord Leverhulme had antagonised the island.[215]

This was, of course, a gross over-statement. On each of his visits Leverhulme was greeted with coloured rockets and banners strung across the road. 'They seem to know here on which side their bread is buttered,' he once remarked with a glance in the direction of Lewis, taking these demonstrations of welcome at their face value. It was obvious that the men of Harris wished him to continue with his scheme, since it provided them with employment at a time when the Hebrides as a whole were suffering from acute distress. To encourage him, they would tell him anything that he wished to hear. When it seemed possible that his plans might fall through owing to general economic conditions and Lever Brothers' special difficulties, he called a meeting at Leverburgh and asked the people whether they thought that they could catch the fish if he provided the harbour. 'Yes, yes,' was the shouted answer, 'you can walk on fish between here and Skye.' 'But what fish?' said Leverhulme. There was an excited babble of voices. 'What do they say? What do they say?' Leverhulme asked D'Arcy Cooper, cupping a hand to his ear. 'They are naming every fish in the sea,' Cooper grimly replied.

Even at the worst period of his financial crisis, Leverhulme was most reluctant to reduce the rate of his expenditure at Leverburgh, fearing that unemployment in the district would lead immediately to outbreaks of raiding. The wage-bill was averaging over £500 a week, and the cost of the materials was proportionately high. The whole expense was borne by Leverhulme himself, for he had not even been through the useless formality of applying

for a Government grant, and although both North and South
Harris were on paper the property of the Lewis and Harris
Welfare and Development Company, Leverhulme, as a holder of
all the company's shares but two, was as deeply committed as if
he were paying the costs out of his personal banking-account.
But early in 1921 he found himself obliged to order a slow-down.
The labour-strength at Leverburgh was reduced from 260 to
120, and other works in Harris were temporarily closed. Something of the truth began to percolate through the rumours.
Malcolm MacSween wrote to him on behalf of the people of
Tarbert: 'We are in sympathy with any individual directly
responsible for such a large concern as your own at the present
juncture of the world trade depression. We are all passing through
a dark hour in history.'[216] This was the month of the first raid
on Rodel Farm, and it was only due to the influence of men like
MacSween that the trouble did not spread.

At only one other place in Harris did Leverhulme attempt to
exploit the riches of the surrounding seas. At Bunaveneader on
West Loch Tarbert a Norwegian company had established a
whaling station before the war, and resumed their operations
there in 1918. Leverhulme purchased it in 1922 on behalf of
Lever Brothers (it was the only Hebridean business acquired
directly by the Company), partly to provide employment, but
also because he suspected that the Norwegians were deliberately
contaminating the herring-ground with whale offal to drive the
herring to Norway. He put the station in repair, and in 1923
purchased three Norwegian vessels with which he began to
catch whales in the North Atlantic. From the very start the
venture was a financial failure. The Norwegian company had
been converting the whale-carcasses into guano. Leverhulme
had a better idea. He would extract the oil for Port Sunlight and
turn the meat into tinned sausages for African natives. 'As whale-
meat is rather tough, it will improve the possibilities of masti-
cation. . . . The native is not an epicure, so long as it is good
wholesome food.'[217] But he was disappointed. 'The meat was
hard and tough,' he told Sir Herbert Morgan a year later, after
some 6,000 tons of whale had been treated experimentally,
'and the watery juice was very unpleasant. I do not think it
would really pay to can it even for Africans.' He did not give up

hope of using it in some form, and one of the last installations to be added to Leverburgh before his death was a special building for *smoking* whale-meat, which he intended to export in this form to the Congo.

The whaling-station was one method of compensating the people of North Harris for the advantages that the southern part of the island enjoyed in the development of Leverburgh. More important was the stimulus that Leverhulme gave to the manufacture of tweed. During the immediate post-war boom, when the Lewis tweed industry was expanding rapidly, Leverhulme had determined that the original home of Harris tweed should share in the profits to be made. His initial difficulty lay in the reluctance of the Harris weavers to use machine-spun wool. Temporarily their prejudice was worn down, and by 1920 Kenneth Mackenzie was sending three times more yarn from his Stornoway mill to Harris than to Lewis. But in the remoter districts of Harris hand-spinning continued, and the women were carrying their wool great distances to be carded at Tarbert, where the only mill in the island was located. The sight of these unhappy women tramping twenty miles with their heavy loads made a deep impression on Leverhulme. He decided to build at his own expense a spinning and carding mill at Geocrab on the east coast of South Harris, and if the experiment succeeded, to transfer both the Tarbert and Geocrab mills to Kenneth Mackenzie Ltd. If it failed he would bear the loss himself. The mill, which cost with its machinery over £17,000, was ready in July 1922. It stood at the head of a remote inlet of the sea, a miniature factory worked by water-power from a loch two-hundred feet above, and included spacious rooms for the issue and reception of wool and finished tweeds, as well as the main spinning and carding rooms where Leverhulme installed a mule of three-hundred spindles and automatic looms for demonstration purposes. Alas, the spinning machinery never worked. The old prejudices returned. The people of the Bays district would not weave any other than home-spun wool, and made use of Geocrab solely for carding. They protested that the mills were driving out the old hand-spinners, and that tweed woven with mill-spun yarn was no longer 'the real article'. Leverhulme replied that hand-spinning was a waste of time. The wool spun on his machines would be indistinguishable from the hand-spun wool. But it was no good. The men-weavers supported the women-spinners. 'I went to very great expense to put a spinning mill at Geocrab,' wrote Leverhulme sadly to one of them, 'so that the crofters' own wool could be spun on the island and to ensure its quality, but I have never been asked for one single pound of wool to be spun.'[218]

It was the only occasion when Leverhulme found himself faced in the Hebrides by outspoken and unanimous resistance to an economic change. Even his old friend Malcolm MacSween would not support him. The Harris men felt that 'their' tweed had been pirated by the other islands, and that their only defence was to maintain its reputation as a cloth spun, dyed, woven and finished on the croft. Of course it was quicker and cheaper to spin the wool by machinery. That might be good enough for Lewis. But it would no longer be Harris tweed, and more than five-hundred women who had spun wool on the distaff all their lives would be thrown out of work if 'factory tweeds' were once allowed to creep into Harris. Meeting after meeting was held in Tarbert to thrash out the argument, the men talking, the women crowding the open door to contribute their choral assent to what they heard. The controversy was only brought to an end by a sudden slump in the whole industry, which rendered almost unsaleable the thousands of yards of finished tweed that had accumulated in the mills at Geocrab, Tarbert and Stornoway. Leverhulme was spared further argument and probable defeat by the virtual stoppage of all the island looms.

Unemployment mounted so alarmingly in the whole of Harris except in the immediate neighbourhood of Leverburgh that Leverhulme felt bound to provide alternative work. It was a moment when he might have reconsidered the project for a Tarbert canal; but, instead, his mind turned instinctively to road-making. He had already begun one road on the Harris-Lewis border, a two-mile diversion of the main road to ease the one-in-five gradient on the northern approaches to Clisham, the highest mountain in Harris. His object had been to improve communications between Stornoway and Leverburgh. When he decided to leave Lewis and export the Leverburgh catch entirely by sea, he handed over the completion of the Clisham diversion to contractors for the Government, and offered to share with the Scottish Office the cost of constructing three other roads in Harris. These were a six-mile stretch from Tarbert along the north shore of East Loch Tarbert to the township of Kyles

Scalpay; a road four miles long from near Amhuinnsuidh Castle to Hushinish opposite the island of Scarp on the north-west coast; and a further five miles from Leverburgh to Finsbay.

Each of these roads, combined with the 'Bays' road that the Government was making from the Grosebay district southwards to Finsbay, would relieve unemployment and provide outlying townships with long-needed communications. The hardship imposed on them was rapidly growing intolerable. The two hundred people of Scarp, for instance, were obliged to fetch all their food by boat from Tarbert, and when the weather was wild, they faced starvation. In the populous Bays district, the lack of a road held down the people's living standards to the level of mediaeval peasantry. There was nothing more than a footpath to link the townships. The materials and machinery for the Geocrab mill could only be delivered at some risk by sea, and when Leverhulme visited it, he was obliged to walk the last two miles. South of Geocrab, a rough cart-track ran north from Rodel to Finsbay, and there stopped. In 1923 it was impossible for even the sturdiest motor-car to make the circuit of South Harris, and there was no way of reaching the Bays from the south or west except by a long detour to the north. Leverhulme's proposed road from Leverburgh to Finsbay would open up the whole Bays district. The inshore fishermen would then be able to bring their catch to the curing-factories at Leverburgh, and lorries could ferry workers daily from the Bays townships. The road would link up at Finsbay with the new road south from Geocrab, and Harris would at last have the skeleton of a proper road system. His idea was well conceived. The Finsbay road, by-passing Rodel, would bring economic advantages out of all proportion to its length and cost.

The winter of 1923–24 was the worst in living memory, for all three traditional means of livelihood—the fishing, the potatoes and the peat—failed simultaneously. On Christmas Eve, Norman Robertson, who was not a man given to alarmist reporting, sent an urgent appeal to Sir Edgar Sanders:

Matters are really deplorable, and I do not, for the life of me, know how the people are existing. The press-reports of the situation do not in any way exaggerate it, and unless the Government step in not only in Harris, but all over the west coast, we shall be faced with a very serious state of matters.[219]

His appeal was answered. By guaranteeing to pay half the cost of three of them, Leverhulme persuaded the Government to start work on all four roads in February 1924. The opportunity came as a last-minute blood-transfusion to a dying land. All through that year, and through half the next, the roads moved steadily ahead until they were finished. Every workless man in Harris found employment on them. Today, though it requires steady nerves and sound tyres to make the passage by car from Leverburgh through Finsbay up the east coast to Tarbert, the roads that he made in Harris, almost as an afterthought and to meet a sudden emergency, have become Leverhulme's chief legacy to the island.

He left his mark on Tarbert by providing a playing field and a recreation hall, and contributing to the cost of the war-memorial and a new water-supply. But for the larger part of Harris he could do little besides build his roads. The interior of the island is a wilderness of fleshless rocks, and the few belts of trees are so harrassed by the wind that they seem less like growing things than props stuck in the ground for a row of monster beans. Harris has a grey speckled appearance, its scattered crofts divided into fields sometimes only a few yards square, where the crofter had found a sufficient depth of soil to grow a crop. A little way off the shore innumerable islets dot the sea and provide the few patches of green in sight. Each will carry up to a dozen lonely sheep, which are ferried from islet to islet as the grass becomes exhausted. Such land does not lend itself to scientific farming. In almost any other part of the world it would not be cultivated at all. But because it continued to provide a bare living for some hundreds of families who were deeply attached to it, Leverhulme refrained from pouring his customary scorn upon the system. In Lewis it had filled him more with anger than pity; in Harris he showed more pity than anger. It was as if he realised that even if Leverburgh doubled its size each year, the old system would exist for decades alongside the new, and there was no reason why he should attempt to hasten its lingering death.

There were three parts of his Harris property for which Leverhulme had a special affection—the Shiant Islands, St Kilda and Borve. The Shiants were leased to Malcolm MacSween for sheep-grazing. These beautiful islands had been uninhabited since about

1900, when the last family were driven from them by the unimaginable loneliness of their lives. One summer's day, Lever-hulme set out in a fishing-boat to visit the Shiants, and as he looked up at their great cliffs of columnar basalt, rising like organ-pipes from the deep sea, he remarked to MacSween that it would be a fine place for breeding silver-foxes. Often when I have been there alone on a sunlit day, with puffins swarming overhead and schools of seals turning lazy somersaults in the water, I have rejoiced that Leverhulme's visions did not always materialise. *Ille terrarum mihi praeter omnes angulus ridet.* The Shiants are too alive to be properly termed desert islands. They are populated by animals; they are clothed by grass and flowers in greater profusion than in any other part of Scotland; and through the great sea-caves that penetrate from one side of the island to the other, wash the rising and falling tides with a gentle inexhaustible rhythm. A farm for silver-foxes! Or for goats, suggested Leverhulme on another occasion. As I turned back to the little cottage, I smiled more at my own indignation than at his fantasy.

On the other side of the Hebrides lay islands even more re-mote, but not uninhabited. In Leverhulme's day St Kilda had a population of sixty-one. Such was the romantic appeal of the group that it was visited by tourists more often than Lewis and Harris, and the natives, having become incurably idle through inter-breeding, did a brisk trade in bogus Celtic relics. Norman Robertson, who went to St Kilda in 1924 on Leverhulme's instructions, reported that the people had long since given up fishing for themselves, and depended on occasional gifts of herring from visiting trawlers. Their other main source of diet were the flesh and eggs of fulmars, and the flock of four hundred wild sheep on the islet of Soay, a few of which Leverhulme sent to Rivington because they were a breed of brown-wool sheep found nowhere else in the world.

St Kilda, he discovered, was not wholly his own. Having been informed that by the purchase of Harris he was *de jure* 'superior' of St Kilda, he was surprised to receive a letter from the Macleod of Macleod offering to sell the islands to him. 'It has occurred to me,' wrote the Macleod, 'that having become the superior, you might perhaps like to become the owner also. If so, I am willing to sell it for £6,000.'[220] Leverhulme replied:

*My dear Macleod,* (obviously he had some doubt about the

correct style of address, for the only two other letters addressed by Leverhulme to Dunvegan, began respectively *Dear Mr Macleod* and *Dear Macleod of Macleod*),

before I could consider the same, would you inform me what is the net income derivable from St Kilda, and what is likely to be the value of the sheep you mention there? As far as my knowledge goes, there is no income from St Kilda, in which case it would seem to me that its ownership must be of purely sentimental value, and unless I could in some way benefit the islanders by ownership—and which it would be out of my power to do otherwise—I do not feel the purchase would be of interest. Mere ownership without this title to ownership seems to me empty and meaningless.[221]

The Macleod replied that the income was £24 a year, the rent from sixteen houses, and one shilling a year payable by himself as owner to the superior, 'but it seemed to me that if owned by a practical man with command of capital like yourself, it might become an important fishing station.' The deal never advanced further. Leverhulme was not even amused by the suggestion. What could he do with these poor people? He wrote to Fletcher: 'It must be a life even worse than that of the Laplanders. Should we not start a colony for St Kilda people at Leverburgh?'[222] Its possibilities as a fishing colony he dismissed at once. 'There is no advantage in landing fish on a lonely rock.' He consulted the Macleod again. Could they not jointly evacuate the population? The Macleod agreed, and Leverhulme's secretary, T. M. Knox, was to visit the island in the summer of 1925 to sound out the opinion of the inhabitants. Leverhulme never went there himself. But his idea bore fruit after his death. St Kilda was evacuated, and today it has only been reoccupied for purposes stranger than even Leverhulme could have envisaged.

His home in Harris was Borve Lodge, lying a few yards from a sandy beach on the west coast of the island. The finest seat in Harris was Amhuinnsuidh Castle, a castellated pile twelve miles west of Tarbert. It was while staying there that Sir James Barrie had conceived the plot of *Mary Rose*. But the previous owner of North Harris, Sir Samuel Scott, had retained a fifteen-year lease of the castle at an annual rent of £1, and the large sporting lodge of Ardvourlie that went with it. Apart from the hotels at Tarbert and Rodel, at both of which Leverhulme occasionally stayed, and the lodge at Luskentyre, let to a Mr Venables on a hundred-year

lease, the only large house in Harris was Borve Lodge. For a few
years after Leverhulme's purchase of the island, Lord Dunmore
retained Borve as his own, but in 1923 he was induced to sell it
to Leverhulme.

Borve lies in a shallow valley facing the island of Taransay.
It was the simplest, and, in many ways, the most charming of all
the many houses that Leverhulme had owned. From the outside
it is a white-washed, grey-slated lodge with trim outbuildings
that Leverhulme built for his small staff. Within, the rooms are
small and bright, but the main room still bears the unmistakable
stamp of Leverhulme's personality—a parquet floor laid for
dancing to the stentorphone, a baronial fireplace, stags' heads, a
few tapestries, and a ceiling divided by pine beams painted to
look like oak. Leading off it was a conservatory, now destroyed.
Upstairs Leverhulme's bedroom is still identifiable, facing as
usual away from the view over the lovely bay. Adjoining it is his
dressing-room, with his long fitted wardrobes still in position.
In the corridor outside, the walls are lined with his coloured
six-inch maps of Harris and the Shiant Islands.

The garden that gave him such pleasure but which he had so
little time to develop, is on a proportionately simple scale. Its
main features are a circular walled-garden on the inland side of
the house, and a rose-wilderness between the entrance gates and
the valley, where he erected fake dolmens set in cement. On the
seaward side he wisely added nothing, leaving the small strip of
*machar* as a natural lawn between the house and the white-sand
beach from which he removed a small hillock to improve the view.
In the surrounding paddocks, there were Shetland ponies, St
Kilda sheep, and deer calves. A fish hatchery provided salmon-
fry for the rivers and lochs of the island.

Borve Lodge was a strong contrast to Lews Castle. While
Leverhulme made it very comfortable—he installed electricity,
central-heating and several bath-rooms—it was not intended as a
house for entertaining on a large scale. There were only seven
bedrooms, and there was nothing to occupy a guest who did not
share Leverhulme's special interests in the island. Consequently,
his only visitors were men associated with his business, like Sir
Herbert Morgan and D'Arcy Cooper, and in the evenings they
would be joined by one or two couples from the estate office or
by favoured young women from Tarbert. Leverhulme's innocent
passion for dancing did not abate with growing age. Either at

Borve, or in the two recreation halls that he erected at Leverburgh and Tarbert, he would be seen waltzing dance after dance, having hurried away from the most important consultations in order not to miss a moment of his only true recreation.

He stayed at Borve on seven separate occasions, four times in 1923, thrice in 1924, and each visit was preceded, accompanied and followed by a new outburst of activity. Leverhulme's arrivals at Leverburgh by special trawler from Uig in Skye became semi-regal functions. The details of his personal comforts ('wire receipt of his Lordship's front and back studs') were arranged with a care equal to the forethought given to his tours of inspection to every part of the island. His son, who was often his companion on these visits, bears witness that his 'optimism and determination were not merely restored—they were intensified—with the transfer of his energies and affections from Lewis to Harris, and of his island home from Lews Castle to Borve Lodge.' He was not to be deterred from his schemes, either by his experiences in Lewis, nor by discouraging advice.

There were one or two men who would tell him to his face that Leverburgh was the wrong site to have chosen for a new fishing harbour. Among them was Neil Mackay, who joined him from Bloomfield's in 1923 as Managing Director of Mac Fisheries and knew more about the fishing industry than most men alive. Mackay admired Leverhulme's highly original mind, and believed that many of his ideas, such as his schemes for freezing fish, were fifty years ahead of his time. But in his opinion, the ideas were attached to the wrong place. Had Leverhulme consulted him at an earlier stage, Mackay would have strongly discouraged him from basing a fishing industry on either Stornoway or Leverburgh, for he considered that the delays and extra cost of transport unavoidable on an island base made the scheme uneconomic. He also warned him that it was untrue that the Atlantic waters west of Harris were teeming with fish, and reminded him of the navigational difficulties. Leverhulme referred these criticisms to other experts: 'Mackay tells me there are no fish. What do you think?' Whether from optimism, ignorance, a desire not to contradict Leverhulme, or from fear of scaring him away, he always received the answer that he hoped to hear: of course there are fish. New maps were accordingly printed showing Leverburgh, instead of Stornoway, as the hub of the universe.

Leverburgh's first season opened in May 1924, by which time the stone jetty, wooden piers and shore-installations had advanced far enough to accommodate a dozen herring-drifters and to deal with their catch. The boats were part of the Bloomfield's fleet from Great Yarmouth, a company with which Mac Fisheries became associated in 1919, for there were no island boats suitable for this experimental fishing, nor enough Harris skippers with licenses. As local men were trained both for herring-drifting and trawling they would replace the English crews. Leverhulme wrote to the Bishop of Argyll:

So it may be that in a few years the fishing from Leverburgh will be done entirely by local shippers and crews. . . . The object I had in founding the fishing industry in Harris was to supply occupation for Harris men and women, and to employ English skippers and crews only during the transition period.[223]

The catch was to be disposed of partly by exporting it to the mainland fresh in ice or in refrigerated fish-carriers, and partly by kippering the fish, and pickling it in barrels. No fish were to be canned at Leverburgh. He was the first fish-merchant to pack his kippers in pairs and wrap them in cellophane. 'The herring,' he said, 'has been despised as food because it has never been handled daintily or with loving care. Our process is dearer than canning, but canning spoils the flavour, and makes a messy unappetising appearance on the table.' Kippers wrapped in cellophane, he believed, would attract a new type of customer. And so it proved. Although his first few consignments were failures, the idea soon caught on, and Leverburgh kippers found a good sale in Mac Fisheries' shops throughout the kingdom. For the first time, and for a few months, Mac Fisheries was supplied with a small part of its huge daily demands for fish from its originally intended source. A single refrigerated ship plied backwards and forwards between Leverburgh and Fleetwood, carrying fish caught and cured by Leverhulme's own companies based on a harbour which he had created from nothing. The dream was beginning to materialise.

At first it seemed that Neil Mackay's pessimism had not been justified. The twelve drifters from Great Yarmouth arrived at Leverburgh at the beginning of May 1924 and began fishing on

21. Leverburgh in 1934. Far left, Leverhulme's houses; left centre, his 'barracks' for workers; right, his piers for landing herring. By then, many other structures had already gone

22. A closer view of the barracks and fish-curing sheds at Leverburgh in 1925. From a contemporary post-card

23. Leverburgh in 1959. Foreground, Obbe Loch, from which Leverhulme intended to form an inner harbour; left centre, the Hulme Hall, now a school; background, his road to Finsbay

24. Borve Lodge, South Harris, with Leverhulme's circular walled garden in the foreground

the 10th. Leverhulme was there in person to see the start, and when he was obliged to return to London, a telegram was sent to him each day reporting the number of boats fishing, the number of crans landed (a cran consists of roughly 750 herring), and the name of the boat which obtained the biggest catch.

The result was exciting:

| 5 June 1924 | Nine | boats landed | 150 crans | *Ocean Harvest* |
|---|---|---|---|---|
| 6 ,, ,, | Eleven | ,, ,, | 147 ,, | *Ocean Toiler* |
| 7 ,, ,, | Eight | ,, ,, | 134 ,, | *Ocean Harvest* |
| 12 ,, ,, | Eleven | ,, ,, | 176 ,, | *Ocean Pilot* |
| 15 ,, ,, | Ten | ,, ,, | 350 ,, | *Ocean Favourite* |

Leverhulme wrote in high spirits to Port Sunlight:

You will be pleased to hear that the Leverburgh season has opened beyond the expectation of the most sanguine. We got double the number of herrings in one day last week at Leverburgh with twelve boats than Stornoway got with seventy-five, and on the following day one boat brought in three-quarters of the number of crans that the whole seventy-five boats brought in at Stornoway.[224]

The catch was so heavy that hundreds of extra girls were brought from the mainland to cure it, and the quays were packed tight with rows and rows of barrels. Fishing continued all through June, July and August, when the telegrams began to indicate the decline of the season:

| 1 August 1924 | 166 crans |
|---|---|
| 2 ,, ,, | 60 ,, |
| 3 ,, ,, | 8 ,, |
| 7 ,, ,, | 15 ,, |
| 12 ,, ,, | 89 ,, |
| 13 ,, ,, | 16 ,, |
| 14 ,, ,, | blank |
| 15 ,, ,, | 33 ,, |
| 16 ,, ,, | blank |
| 17 ,, ,, | 2 ,, |
| 22 ,, ,, | blank |

But the general result had been good enough to justify Leverhulme's boast when he addressed a gathering of branch managers of Mac Fisheries at The Hill in September:

Q

The fishing has started in Harris with much promise: and as far as our present knowledge goes, extremely well, because we find we get a finer quality of herring than is obtainable elsewhere at this season. But we have a long way to travel yet.

In the same month, Leverhulme was back in Harris for a few days, supervising the preparations for the 1925 season, which was to see the start of trawling for white-fish as well as drifting for herring. His Christmas-card for that year carried a view of Leverburgh with the inscription *Birth of a town*, and he distributed it widely in Lewis, where its implications did not pass unnoticed. But, as previously related, it was from Stornoway and not from Harris that he sailed on his last journey from the Hebrides. On the evening of 5 September 1924, after his speech at the opening of the Lewis War Memorial, he left the islands never to return.

On 23rd September 1924, he embarked on a six-months tour of the Congo. Sir Ronald Ross, the specialist on malaria, had told him that it was madness for a man of seventy-three to attempt such a journey. But he appeared to be unaffected by it, spending day after day on the bridge of the river steamer as it penetrated deep into the jungle, and supervising with his customary energy every detail of his vast African enterprises. One of the many letters that he addressed to his resident engineer in Harris, G. E. Howarth, will indicate the scope of his plans and his constant preoccupation with what was happening in the Hebrides:

We have had a most delightful voyage, and expect to reach our first port in the Congo on Sunday. Then we proceed up the main Congo River to Leverville and the other towns we have built in the Congo adjacent to our oil-mills there. We already have seven mills in operation, and we are inaugurating six more in 1925.

I wish that the problems we have in Leverburgh were as easily settled as those of our successful industry in the Congo. The difficulties are exactly the reverse of what you would expect. You would expect them to be greater in the country of the cannibal, the elephant and the hippopotamus, and easiest at Leverburgh, Harris, but I have found the exact reverse to be the case. I am confident, however, that both will be final and complete successes.[225]

On his way home in a chartered yacht, Leverhulme visited the French Congo, the British Cameroons, Nigeria, the Gold Coast, Liberia, Sierra Leone, French Guinea, Gambia and Dakar. He arrived back from his 15,000 mile journey on 15 March 1925, without having suffered a day's illness. 'I never felt better in my life,' he wrote to Lady Fildes ten days later. At the beginning of April he was in Brussels for the annual meeting of the Huileries du Congo Belge; on the 22nd he presided at the shareholders meeting of the Niger Company in London, and on the next day at the annual meeting of Lever Brothers at Port Sunlight. He had planned to visit Harris on 11 May for a fortnight, and to return in July, 'to make a trip with Mr Mackay up the east coast fishings, right up to the Shetlands, to get an idea of what is going on there.'[226]

While spending a weekend at Rivington immediately after the Port Sunlight meeting, he caught a chill which quickly developed into pneumonia. He was moved to The Hill at Hampstead, and for a time his doctors were pleased with his progress. In the first few days of May, however, the inflammation of his lungs extended, and he died at The Hill, his mental powers in full vigour until the end, at 4.30 am on Thursday, 7 May 1925. He was buried beside his wife at Port Sunlight on 11 May, the very day on which he had arranged to cross the Minch to Leverburgh.

To many in Stornoway the first intimation of his death was the sight of the flag flying from Lews Castle at half-mast. All businesses in the town were closed for three hours at the time of his funeral, and the Lewis pipe-band paraded before the castle playing *Lochaber no more* and *Cumha nam Marbh* (Lament of the dead). At Leverburgh the news was given by a long blast on the hooter. 'When I heard it,' recalls one of the workmen, 'I knew that it could only mean the death of one of two people: His Majesty, or Lord Leverhulme.'

# Chapter Ten

# POST MORTEM

WITH LEVERHULME'S DEATH, all his schemes in Harris ceased abruptly. On 8 May 1925, the day after he died, the chief accountant at Lever House in London wrote to Norman Robertson, the Harris factor, requesting particulars of all works in progress for which the contracts could not be cancelled. A week later the new Board of Lever Brothers gave instructions that the development of Leverburgh should stop, including work on all the houses except those already in the very last stages of completion. The remaining bay of the canning-factory at Stornoway was not to be dismantled. Almost all the men employed at Leverburgh were given a week's notice. The only work that could not be halted was that on the Harris roads, for Leverhulme had pledged himself to the Scottish Office to bear half the cost of their construction, and the obligation could not be evaded by his successors.

The haste with which all his plans were reversed would have wounded Leverhulme deeply, and indicates more clearly than any contemporary records the division that had grown between him and his closest advisers. The new Chairman of Lever Brothers was Francis D'Arcy Cooper, one of the few men who had ever dared to tell Leverhulme that he considered the Hebridean projects to be hopelessly unsound. An accountant by training, Cooper was shocked by what he regarded as Leverhulme's gross extravagance. When he met him in the Congo in December 1924, Cooper brought matters to a head by putting before Leverhulme a statement that the Hebrides had nothing to do with Lever Brothers, and that his vast expenditure there was solely his personal responsibility, any loans being a charge on his estate and not on the company. Cooper emerged from the cabin of Leverhulme's river-steamer, so an eye-witness recalls, 'triumphantly waving the paper to which Leverhulme had put his signature at the end of their stormy interview.' Privately

D'Arcy Cooper had never concealed his apprehensions. To Dr Macdonald, a native of Lewis and Leverhulme's nephew by marriage, he had once said, 'The best thing you can do with your islands is to sink them in the Atlantic for four hours, and then pull them up again.'

It should not be imagined that D'Arcy Cooper was a man to whom idealism or philanthropy made no appeal. Leverhulme himself had once said of Cooper that he 'was one of the type of men that I consider most resemble a warm fire, and people naturally seem to come up to him for warmth.' The official historian of the company writes: 'He was possessed of a natural habit of command and a judgment of men surpassing that of his predecessor. And although blunt, energetic and emotional—he was quickly angered by anything savouring of dishonesty—he brought to the problems of the business a new quality of thoughtful analysis of long-term issues, quite unlike anything it had seen before.'[227] Cooper was appointed Chairman within a week of Leverhulme's death, and he saw his duty plainly. He must consolidate the empire which the founder had created; and consolidation meant pruning Leverhulme's excesses. Of all these, the projects in Lewis and Harris seemed to him the most indefensible. 'We are trustees for some 200,000 shareholders,' he said to his new Board, 'and we have no right to spend one penny unless we are abolutely certain we are going to get an adequate return.' No dividend was paid on the Ordinary shares of the Company in 1925 or 1926; and all the assets which could be realised without damage to the Company's interests were to be sold. In July 1925 Cooper even considered selling Mac Fisheries, because it had no obvious connection with the main business of the Company, and only refrained from doing so when it became clear that the proper price was not to be obtained.

It was therefore D'Arcy Cooper's decision, and not the second Lord Leverhulme's, to write off the Hebrides. The latter, as he himself was ready to admit, did not possess the qualities required to control one of the biggest industrial combines in the world. Then aged thirty-seven, shy, prematurely deaf, having lived for years in his father's shadow and more interested in the arts than in the business for which his father had too carefully nurtured him, he became Governor of Lever Brothers, a post specially created for him, sharing the responsibility with the three other executors of Leverhulme's will, D'Arcy Cooper, Harold

Greenhalgh (Vice-Chairman of the company since 1921) and John McDowell (Managing Director).

The first and second Viscounts Leverhulme, wrote the company's secretary, L. V. Fildes,

were in their natures and attributes precise opposites. The father was by nature a creator; the son a coadjutor. Where the father was possessed of a daemon of restlessness, and a dynamic urge which ill-accorded at times with other people's feelings, the son was characterised by an equable temperament, good nature and sensibility.[228]

It remains Fildes' opinion that the second Lord Leverhulme would have done everything possible to avoid closing down the Harris works had the decision been left to him alone, for he revered his father too much to admit that he could have been capable of a major error of judgment or to deliver posthumously so heavy a blow to his hopes and reputation. But William Hulme Lever was well aware of the criticism that had mounted against the Leverburgh project in recent years. Typical of it, was an article that appeared in *The Times* by Robert Murray, MP, who visited Leverburgh in the autumn of 1924:

Will Lord Leverhulme's dream come true? I do not know. One wishes it would. I sought information from workers, officials and onlookers. I confess I found none to speak with confidence, and there were some who, although they veiled their thoughts under discreet words, could not quite conceal the fact that they regarded the project as a piece of moonstruck and hopeless foolishness.[229]

It was this type of pessimism, widespread among the men responsible for the execution of his father's plans, that once caused the new Viscount to remark privately, 'That is the finest map of Scotland I have ever seen,' pointing to a wall-map at Lever House that omitted the Hebrides. Nevertheless, he would have done what he could to realise something of his father's hopes, had he possessed the resources to do it. But the fortune that he had personally inherited could not stand the strain. He was obliged to sell The Hill at Hampstead and many other properties with their art-collections in order to meet the heavy death-duties and compensate for the two-year loss of dividends on the Company's Ordinary shares. There was a further claim for £1 million pending from the Inland Revenue for arrears of tax, which if sustained (which it was not) would have put the

Leverhulme family in a difficult position. For a day or two the
suggestion was discussed that Mac Fisheries might purchase
Leverburgh for a nominal sum, but it was turned down as
quite unrealistic. Lahwad was put into voluntary liquidation in
July 1924, and preparations were made to dispose of the whole
property as rapidly as possible.

On 22 October 1925, Harris and the parts of Lewis that had
not been purchased or given away in 1923, were put up for sale
by Messrs. Knight, Frank and Rutley, at an auction held in
London. The catalogue, as if to emphasise the reversion of the
Hebrides to the role traditionally assigned to them by estate-
agents, carried on its cover a drawing of a sporting setter. The
attendance was good, but the bidding poor. Purchasers, it was
said, were frightened by the 'spirit of the people' and Leverhulme's unhappy experience. After desultory offers, the port-
installations at Leverburgh, which had cost about £250,000, were
sold for £5,000 to a demolition company which eventually pulled
down all the buildings: one of the sheds now forms a garage
in Stornoway. Borve, Taransay and Luskentyre, with 12,000
acres, were withdrawn when the bidding stuck at £8,500.
Rodel was sold for £3,500. 33,000 acres of crofting lands in South
Harris went for £900. The great castle of Amhuinnsuidh,
together with Ardvourlie Lodge, the Harris Hotel and 6,000
acres, fetched only £2,000. Mr Compton Mackenzie bought the
Shiant Islands, recalling that the Seaforth branch of his family
had once owned them. Of the remaining Lewis properties, the
Morsgail deer-forest was sold for £9,200, the Bernera islands for
£250, Barvas for £2,900. For the Uig estates there was no bid
higher than £500. In all, the sale realised £28,050 for 123,343
acres. The 232,000 unsold acres, mainly crofting lands, were
gradually disposed of during the next few years, and Kenneth
Mackenzie bought back his tweed company from the executors.

The winding-up of the estate was not completed until the end
of 1926. The bulky files end with a whimper: 'The Shetland
ponies at Borve Lodge have at last found a purchaser—for £3.'

How much money had Leverhulme spent and lost in Lewis and
Harris? The answer can neither be simple nor exact, since part
of his local expenditure was passed through the books of Lever
Brothers and Mac Fisheries, and from the accounts that survive
it is not always possible to disentangle the cost of projects that
directly benefited the islands from others that were only loosely

connected with them. For example, although Mac Fisheries
owed its origins entirely to Leverhulme's interest in Lewis,
scarcely a penny of the huge capital sum on which the Company
was floated found its way into the pockets of Lewismen. Sir
Herbert Morgan gave broad details of the investment in Mac
Fisheries in July 1925:

| | £ |
|---|---|
| Retail shops | 1,000,000 |
| Bloomfields | 600,000 |
| Aberdeen Steam Trawler Co. | 350,000 |
| Fleetwood | 165,000 |
| T. Wall's & Co. | 120,000 |
| Other associated Companies | 100,000 |
| | £2,335,000 |

This money was not, of course, lost. Mac Fisheries has proved a
very sound investment, and it could be argued that Leverhulme's
whole venture in the Hebrides has since been financially justified
many times over by the great success not only of Mac Fisheries,
but of the entire Food Division of Unilever that grew out of it.
On a narrower interpretation of the accounts, however, Leverhulme personally lost nearly one-and-a-half million pounds
through his romantic attachment to the islands.

This figure is given with some reserve, since consolidated
accounts for the seven-years' experiment were either never
compiled or have not survived. During the crisis months of
1920-21 summaries were made of the expenditure to that date,
and it is upon these that the following calculations are largely
based, supplemented by evidence from the later years that is
available in more scattered sources:

*Lord Leverhulme's approximate expenditure in*
*Lewis and Harris 1918-1925*

| Lewis | £ |
|---|---|
| Purchase price | 143,000 |
| Furnishings of Lews Castle, etc. | 17,000 |
| Alterations to Lews Castle and garden | 60,000 |
| Maintenance of the estate (including wages of game-keepers, farmworkers, etc.) | 150,000 |
| Factories and companies | |
| Canning factory and machinery | 65,000 |
| Guano and Ice Co. | 40,000 |

|  | £ |
|---|---|
| Tweed Co. (including trading losses) | 65,000 |
| Power house | 20,000 |
| Gas Company (including losses) | 20,000 |
| Laundry | 10,000 |
| Preliminary work at Stornoway harbour | 10,000 |
| Roads | 150,000 |
| Houses | |
| Anderson Road | 42,000 |
| Matheson Road | 28,000 |
| Purchases for town-planning scheme | 25,000 |
| Land-reclamation | 10,000 |
| Donations | 20,000 |
| *Total expenditure in Lewis*    *Approx* £875,000 | |

*Harris*

|  | £ |
|---|---|
| Purchase price | |
| South Harris (Borve included) | 51,000 |
| North Harris | 20,000 |
| Leverburgh | |
| Harbour | 250,000 |
| Houses, etc. | 64,000 |
| Tweed factories | 30,000 |
| Roads | 40,000 |
| Whaling factory (including losses) | 50,000 |
| Borve, Tarbert, etc. | 20,000 |
| *Total expenditure in Harris*    *Approx* £525,000 | |
| *Total expenditure in Lewis and Harris*    *Approx* £1,400,000 | |

The amount of this capital sum that was recovered by eventual sales was about £55,000. The annual rents were almost wholly absorbed by rates and taxes, and in the early years greatly exceeded by Leverhulme's huge expenditure on entertainment. Lewis and Harris paid no dividend to its proprietor, and tied up large sums of money that might have been profitably employed elsewhere. Thus his loss was even greater than appears from the above summary. It would be little exaggeration to say that if Leverhulme had never heard of the Hebrides, his estate at his death would have been the richer by nearly two million pounds. The generally-held opinion, however, that he spent two million pounds in Lewis alone, and one million in Harris, appears to be an over-estimate, although the accounts bear out his claim that he had been prepared to spend five million pounds on his two islands had his schemes been allowed to continue. The capital on which Lahwad could draw in March 1921 was precisely £5,138,317.

Judged in purely business terms, and leaving Mac Fisheries aside, the venture was therefore a complete failure. It was the only one of Leverhulme's major enterprises that was dropped at his death, or which failed to show an eventual profit. Its immediate, almost contemptuous, abandonment by Leverhulme's heirs and successors underlined the misgivings that had been constantly expressed during his lifetime, occasionally to his face by men like D'Arcy Cooper and Neil Mackay, and unreservedly behind his back. The desertion of Leverburgh made his failure in Harris even more poignant than his failure in Lewis. To those who assert that the schemes cannot truly be said to have failed because they were never carried to their logical conclusion, it should be pointed out that one of Leverhulme's main objects was that his plans should survive his death. He had given himself ten more years to live in 1918: in fact, he had seven. But during those seven years he had failed to convince even those who admired and revered him most that the foundations which he had laid were sound, or to build into his schemes the essential conditions for their continuance. They depended almost entirely upon the faith, energy and money of a single man who was already old when he embarked upon them. With his death, these three props were simultaneously snatched away, and the edifice collapsed.

Half realising this possibility, Leverhulme had pressed ahead with an urgency that was itself partly the cause of his failure. His haste antagonised the islanders more than his proposals. Any stranger to the Hebrides who has ever attempted to get a job done in a hurry, even in Stornoway, will have noticed that urgency is regarded as something improper, undignified, ungentlemanly and usually unecessary. Long preparation and contemplation (a favourite word of the Highlander) are essential preliminaries to action. Hence the go-slow methods of the labourers in Lewis, the cynicism expressed at Leverburgh, the refusal of the women of the Bays district to have their wool spun by machine at Geocrab. They believed that change was sometimes a necessary evil, and one which could work out in the long run to their advantage; but change involved the risk of nemesis, for it meant interfering with the natural order of things, and only gradual evolution could minimise this risk. Leverhulme thought that the islands could be startled into compliance, as if by an electric shock. Ex-Provost Roderick Smith told the Town Council at his death:

It is possible that there might have been a different end to the story of Lord Leverhulme's work in Lewis, had his first early impressions of thirty years before been supplemented and nourished by one or two visits in those years in between. Such would have given his active mind a clear view of the character and forces he was subsequently to meet on these shores when he came to live among the people.[230]

This was a subtler and a truer valediction than the usually accepted explanation of his failure, that the people did not wish to be 'civilised' by the methods that Leverhulme proposed. *The Times* obituary notice summed up the incident as follows:

Perhaps it was the one failure of Lord Leverhulme's career. He attempted to play the part of an earthly providence in the island of Lewis. The crofter population welcomed him at first when he came to establish a fishing company and promised great developments which would enormously improve their lot. But when they realised that they would have to pay for their prosperity by being, as it seemed to them, industrialised, they rebelled, and ultimately, after five years struggle, Lord Leverhulme had to accept defeat.[231]

As this narrative has attempted to make clear, there was no 'rebellion' among the people, apart from the handful of raiders who were ostracised by all but their relations and closest neighbours. If there had been rebellion, there would have been a sense of elation in Lewis when Leverhulme withdrew. But his withdrawal was greeted not as a triumph, but with bitter disappointment and reproach. They felt let down. Never have I heard any Lewisman say, 'Lord Leverhulme thought that he could do what he wanted with us, but we showed him that he could not. We fought him, and we won.' Such a sentiment would be quite alien to their recollection of the feeling at the time. There was rather a sense that both sides had lost a great opportunity: Leverhulme had lost it by so forcing the pace that the weaker spirits became nervous, and by failing to judge the land-question in its proper proportions; they had lost it by failing to remove the one obstacle (apart from his temporary business difficulties) that stood between him and success. Many Lewismen admit today that strong and even violent action against the raiders at the critical moment would have deprived Leverhulme of any excuse to abandon his plans. They use this harsh word 'excuse'; they believe that Leverhulme had become alarmed by the obligations in which his early impetuous enthusiasm had involved him. But this was a passing hesitancy. The excuse should not have been provided. They lacked the leader who might have shown them how to remove it.

The general charge against Leverhulme that Lewis and Harris 'refused to be industrialised' is mistaken. Attached though they were to their crofts, there were very many islanders who were willing to give Leverhulme's ideas a trial, for they accepted his argument that the only alternative was the odious policy of emigration. There was nothing in the temperament of the younger men and women that made it unthinkable for them to work in large groups for a wage, whether as members of a great fishing fleet, employees in an island factory, or sub-contractors for the tweed-mills at Stornoway. Thousands of Lewis girls were accustomed to migrate annually to work in the east-coast curing-yards, and hundreds saw no indignity in accepting posts as domestic servants in mainland cities. Certainly Lewismen might not have made such reliable workers as the mill-hands of Lancashire or the thousands who streamed daily into the vast soaperies of Port Sunlight. Absenteeism and indolence would have been frequent. But there was only a rare refusal of gang-work when it was offered to them on road and harbour construction in Lewis and Harris, or on the erection of Leverhulme's many buildings in both islands. Now that the tweed-industry has revived, and the Stornoway spinning-mills have expanded in size and number, no protest has been heard that such employment is an affront to island pride. On the contrary, thirty years after Leverhulme's death, 350 men and over 200 women were employed as factory-hands in the local mills and dye-works, and 850 men and 250 women were commuting daily into Stornoway from neighbouring townships to work in the town's factories, shops and other commercial establishments.

When one reads of the abhorrence with which the Lewismen heard the sound of a factory hooter or thought of exchanging their independence for regular employment, it is usually in a book or newspaper article by a mainlander who considers that these sentiments were the proper ones for the islanders to hold. It should be recalled that in 1920 Stornoway was not the backwater that many outsiders imagined. In its fish trade, and to a smaller extent in its tweed, it had industries which were flourishing before Leverhulme's arrival, and had already attracted to the town all the apparatus of commerce—banks, merchandising and exporting companies, a local newspaper, postal traffic, gaslighting, a Masonic Lodge, several hotels, and a secondary school (the Nicolson Institute) that had few rivals in Scotland. Leverhulme wished only to develop scientifically what he found. The remoter country districts, like those of any area of Great Britain which contains great industries, could have remained almost unaffected by them. Only those who chose to work for him would have felt immediately the impact of his schemes, and the possibility that the old and the new way of life could co-exist was more apparent to the Lewismen than it was to Leverhulme himself. In Harris he at last conceded by implication what he had always denied in Lewis, that the crofting system was not incompatible with limited industrialisation.

Leverhulme did not regard himself as defeated or betrayed by the islanders. Once in 1924 his secretary drafted for his signature a reply to a Uig crofter who had suggested that Uig should be joined to Harris so that this outlying district of Lewis could continue to enjoy the benefit of his schemes. The draft, in turning down the suggestion, added the phrase, 'nevertheless I appreciate the loyal spirit of the men of Uig who wish me to do so.' Leverhulme annotated: 'Never use the word "loyal" in such connection. Say "good".' He was anxious to avoid making it into a personal issue, being convinced that Lewis would have remained almost unanimously behind him had it not been for the attitude of the government.

The exact degree of blame that should be attached to Robert Munro remained confused in his mind. He persuaded himself that Munro was attempting to impede him by refusing to give a categorical assurance about releasing the raiders, when constitutionally Munro could not give it, and the point was not one of major importance. Leverhulme's misfortune and moral weakness was that at the very moment when Munro yielded to his demands, he was unable to take advantage of it, and looked around for other means of putting the Government in the wrong. The whole affair became a dialectical tussle between Leverhulme, Munro and, in its final phase, Lord Novar, in which the islanders themselves ceased to play much part. If the Scottish

Office were wrong to assume that land-settlement was of more importance than the development of native industries, Leverhulme was wrong to choose as his battle-ground with the Government the one political issue on which they felt least able to give way. All his life Leverhulme had fought Governments, and as he grew older, richer and more stubborn, the possibilities of compromise appealed to him less and less. The final result, he could claim, was exactly what he forecast. The Government policy gave crofts to a few score people, who had to find subsidiary sources of income to maintain life, leaving the others no better off, and drove several thousands of young men to seek their fortunes overseas. Leverhulme subtly pressed the point home by his offer to give the island to its people, and determined that in Harris he would prove the Government doubly wrong, to have enforced their own policy, and to have impeded his. From first to last he saw himself as an enlightened benefactor at war with official conservatism. He failed to see that his method of conducting the controversy would expose him to the charge of sour grapes.

Leverhulme's name is today associated by Lewismen with failure. When one suggests that it was a 'glorious' failure, the phrase does not gain assent. Lady Lever Park is still so called, and 'Leverburgh' is still printed on Ordnance maps, but no memorial was put up in his honour, not even a plaque in the church he patronised, and only recently has a road been named after him in a new housing estate at Stornoway. Elsewhere his work is known only by its ruins. The port of Leverburgh is a waste of concrete foundations; at Geocrab his machinery lies rusting in a corner; the Tolsta road has deteriorated to a cart-track; the remaining bay of the canning-factory is used for spinning wool; even the indestructible Arnish road ends forlornly in a cul-de-sac. How could £1,400,000 have been spent to so little effect? This is the question that robs Leverhulme's venture of much of its dignity, and in retrospect casts doubt on his judgment.

Was his idea basically sound?

In short, it would have been so if the pre-war conditions in the fishing industry had been re-established soon after the Armistice. Leverhulme assumed that this would happen. Stornoway had always been a centre for the export of cured herring to the markets of eastern Europe. As soon as the barriers imposed on

this trade by the war were lifted, there seemed little reason to
doubt that it would revive. Europe was starving; fish was a
plentiful and cheap form of food to which the peoples of
Germany, Poland and Russia were accustomed. The Hebrides
were geographically well placed both for catching and exporting
the fish. But in addition to this traditional trade, Leverhulme
saw further possibilities in the organisation of his fish-canning
industry and the transport of fresh fish in ice to the home
market. The three methods of dealing with the catch—cured,
canned and fresh—would complement each other and later he
would add similar methods for treating white-fish trawled from
more distant waters. Stornoway and Leverburgh would together
syphon huge quantities of fish from the sea and pour them into
the markets of Europe.

The plan encountered four difficulties. The market in Eastern
Europe did not revive; the British public began to eat fewer
herring; the disadvantages of an island base increased as prices
rose; and there was an unexpected economic slump. In combination these difficulties made Leverhulme's fishing schemes
extremely hazardous, as he himself admitted, and it was on
fishing that his whole plan depended.

Russia and Germany did not resume on the same scale their
purchases of British pickled herring. For this there were several
political and economic reasons. Both countries had acquired the
habit of dealing with the neutral Dutch and Scandinavians during
the war, whose product, though inferior, was cheaper, and they
had a natural disinclination to resume trading with a past or actual
enemy. The British Government kept a firm control on exports
to Germany, and the fall in the value of the mark, the increase
in freight charges and the higher cost of catching and curing
fish made the trade unprofitable to both sides. Both in Germany
and Russia there was an increasing tendency towards a policy of
self-sufficiency; the Russians, for example, began energetically
to develop their Murmansk, Caspian and Black Sea fisheries.

What British herring-fishermen lost in the decline of the
Baltic trade they failed to make up by increasing their sales at
home. In 1911 12.8 lbs. of herring were consumed per head of the
population; by 1927 it had fallen to 7.7 lbs.[232] The herring had
come to be regarded as the 'poor man's fish'. The ambitious
deserted the fresh herring for the kipper, the kipper for white-
fish, and white-fish for meat, as they rose in the social scale.

Their wives began to compain of the smell of herring cooking
in a confined kitchen, and their children lost patience with its
innumerable small bones. The increasing number of fried fish
shops created a demand for cod, but none for herring, and even
the kipper began to lose caste when the suspicion grew that its
mahogany colour was due to artificial dyes. Canned herring had
the advantages of leaving no obnoxious smell and being available
all the year round, but it looked less appetising than fresh fish
when decanted, and was more expensive. The Government found
difficulty in marketing the large stocks of canned food left over
from the war, and the low prices charged for it made it impossible
for a newcomer to can fish successfully until the wartime surplus
was exhausted.

For these reasons, the conditions essential to a rapid development of the herring industry were absent at the very time when
Leverhulme was building his factories at Stornoway and his
harbour at Leverburgh. Both the foreign and domestic demand
for the fish simultaneously declined, and the whole of Britain's
drifting and curing industry was facing serious trouble. The
island-sites that Leverhulme had chosen for his experiment added
to his difficulty. The prices obtainable for fish at Stornoway
averaged little above the minimum, and the fishing-boats,
mostly originating from the north-east coast of Scotland, preferred to take their catches direct to mainland ports. As the
landings declined, so the curers began to close their Stornoway
branches; as the curing facilities diminished, so the landings
became even smaller. Stornoway, now competing at a great
disadvantage for a share of the falling market, found itself sliding
down a spiral from which there seemed no escape except by a
subsidy which no Government was ready to grant in peace-time,
and which Leverhulme himself could not reconcile with his
intention that the trade must be self-supporting.

In 1913 644,000 cwts. of herring, and 93,000 cwts. of white-
fish had been landed at Hebridean ports; in 1921 the totals
were 205,000 and 31,000 cwts. respectively. 1921 was a particularly bad year for the fishing, but the trend was unmistakable.
It has continued ever since. In spite of improvements to Stornoway harbour, it is used less and less. Every older inhabitant
contrasts the almost deserted quays that the visitor sees today
with the forest of masts that they remember in their youth. An
official report issued in 1953 observed that in the past fifteen

years only three new boats had been added to the Stornoway fleet, which then totalled no more than a dozen drifters. Stranger-boats still visit Stornoway in the season, but in 1952, a typical year, nearly half their catch was sacrificed to the manufacture of meal and oil. The deep-sea trawlers bypass the port with indifference.

It is possible, but unlikely, that Leverhulme's imagination and energy could have overcome the gradual decline of Stornoway as a fishing centre. Had he persevered, he might, for instance, have been the first to develop quick-freezing as an answer to the island's problems. But the fact must be faced that his original fishing schemes would not have stood the test of post-war conditions. He wanted to help an island people by methods which their very isolation made impracticable. Had Stornoway been Aberdeen or even Ullapool, he would have had a good chance of success. But he was not interested in Aberdeen or Ullapool. He was interested in Lewis. His idealism and business sense, for almost the first time in his long career, were in irreconcilable conflict.

The conflict was even more evident in the case of Leverburgh, Stornoway was the best site in the wrong place. Leverburgh was the worst site in the wrong place. Later history has confirmed the misgivings of contemporaries. Leverburgh was used for the export of feldspar during the Second World War, but today it rarely sees even local fishing boats, only occasionally a coal-boat, and never the mail-steamer, for fearless sailors, now as then, distrust its tides and rocks even more than they welcome the stub of its indestructible pier. In 1924 there was good fishing in the neighbouring seas; but in the two following years, when the Bloomfield boats again made the long trek from East Anglia on their way to the northern Minch, their nets were almost empty. Leverhulme firmly believed that Leverburgh would flourish, but expert opinion, like Neil Mackay's, holds that it had few, if any, advantages as a fishing port, and that it could only have been kept alive by constant injection of fresh capital. Had it succeeded, its success would have been at the expense of the established fishing centres of Stornoway and Scalpay, and would have benefited no more than the southernmost part of a barren island to which Leverhulme would have been obliged to draw immigrants on whom he had no particular desire to bestow his favours.

R

Lewis and Harris climbed very slowly out of the pit from which Leverhulme had tried to rescue them. Many of the same failings of character and economic disadvantages which he found in 1918 still exist today. Some of them, indeed, are aggravated. Though electricity and the motor bus have spread greater comfort throughout the islands, and Government aid has been lavished on them in many forms, overcrowding and unemployment combined with natural lethargy have kept the Outer Hebrides at a sadly low level of existence. Stornoway increases in size, mainly owing to the tweed industry, while the crofts are neglected but not abandoned. Security of tenure has meant only constant subdivision of plots already too small. Standards of cultivation are so low that nearly all the vegetables sold in the town, and a large part of the egg supply, milk and meat are imported from the mainland. Emigration steadily drains away the youth of the islands.

If Leverhulme could revisit Lewis and Harris in the 1960s, he would claim that present conditions justify his argument. Perhaps the task he set himself was for political and economic reasons impossible. Nobody has yet solved the problem he faced. But few would deny the humanity of his vision as he expressed it in January 1918, soon after he had determined to buy the islands:

Human nature can respond enormously to sympathy, to a kindly touch, to a participation in the fruits of its industry, to a share in the profits it has helped to create.

This was his consistent belief, and in spite of an occasional lapse from his own principle that tasks should not be set for human nature, and the disappointments, misrepresentation and even ridicule that his Hebridean adventure brought upon him, it was a great design, and its ultimate failure should not be allowed to dull the magnanimity of its conception.

# NOTES

Abbreviations: S.O.   Files in the Scottish Office
             U.H.   Files in Unilever House
             S.G.   *Stornoway Gazette*
             H. of C. House of Commons debates (Hansard)

## Chapter One pp. 1–25

1 *Viscount Leverhulme*, by his son. p. 37
2 Ibid. p. 39
3 *The History of Unilever*, by Charles Wilson. Vol. I p. 28
4 *Chiaroscuro*, by Augustus John. pp. 150–1
5 T. M. Knox in the *Manchester Guardian*. 19 Sept. 1951
6 *The History of Unilever.* Vol. I p. 293
7 Nicholas Davenport in *Progress*. Autumn 1951
8 *The Six-Hour Day*, by Lord Leverhulme. 1918
9 *The History of Unilever.* Vol. I p. 150
10 *The Six-Hour Day.* p. 6
11 *The History of Unilever.* Vol. I p. 163
12 Ibid. Vol. I p. 164
13 Ibid. Vol. I pp. 166–7
14 *Viscount Leverhulme*, by his son. p. 167
15 *My Life*, by Angus Watson. p. 141
16 *Viscount Leverhulme*, by his son. p. 208
17 *S.G.* 5 April 1918

## Chapter Two pp. 26–48

18 *The Isle of Lewis and Harris*, by Arthur Geddes. p. 78
19 *Lewisiana, or Life in the Outer Hebrides*, by W. Anderson Smith. 1875
20 Dr George Gibson, in *The Caledonian Medical Journal*. August 1924
21 *Outer Isles*, by A. Goodrich-Freer. 1902
22 *History of the Outer Hebrides*, by W. C. Mackenzie. p. 524
23 *Lewisiana, or Life in the Outer Hebrides*
24 *Outer Isles*, by A. Goodrich-Freer
25 *The Book of the Lews*, by W. C. Mackenzie
26 *Crofters Commission Report*, 1884
27 Evidence of John Smith, crofter, Balallan, Lewis. *Minutes of Evidence to the Crofters Commission*, 1884
28 *West Highland Survey*, by F. Fraser Darling
29 See *The Isle of Harris*, by J. B. Caird, in *The Scottish Geographical Magazine*, August 1951
30 *The Isle of Lewis and Harris*, by Arthur Geddes. p. 239
31 *Report on the Social Conditions of the people of Lewis* (Brand Report), 1902
32 *Report on the state of the Highlands and Islands*, 1851. (McNeill Report)
33 *The Isle of Lewis and Harris.* p. 242
34 *S.G.* 16 March 1917
35 *S.G.* 2 March 1917
36 Letter from Ian Macpherson

69 Leverhulme to W. Halliday, naturalist. 10 Dec. 1918. *U.H.*

70 *Highland Journey*, by Colin Macdonald. p. 154

71 The *Scotsman*. 30 June 1919

72 *Highland Journey*, by Colin Macdonald. pp. 142–3. Macdonald heard this speech, but is repeating it from memory some years after. There is little doubt, however, that it accurately gives the sense of what Leverhulme said.

73 Leverhulme to the Provost of Stornoway, Murdo Maclean. 19 Aug. 1918. *U.H.*

74 *Highland Journey*, by Colin Macdonald. pp. 155–6

75 Leverhulme to Holmboe. 22 Aug. 1918. *U.H.*

76 *S.G.* 23 Aug. 1918

77 Leverhulme to Holmboe. 15 July 1918. *U.H.*

78 Leverhulme to Macgregor. 13 Aug. 1918. *U.H.*

79 Leverhulme to Maciver. 20 Sept. 1918. *U.H.*

80 Maciver to Leverhulme. 23 Oct. 1918. *U.H.*

81 Leverhulme to Buchanan. 6 Nov. 1918. *U.H.*

82 Leverhulme to Buchanan. 24 March 1919. *U.H.*

83 *Notes for a History of Mac Fisheries*, by E. G. D. Liveing. Unpublished

84 *Daily Telegraph*. 16 April 1919

85 Leverhulme to Sir Herbert Morgan. 10 Jan. 1920. *U.H.*

86 Leverhulme to Kenneth Mackenzie. 3 March 1919. *U.H.*

87 *Daily Telegraph*. 16 April 1919

## Chapter Five pp. 101–122

88 Speech to Stornoway Town Council, 23 Aug. 1918

89 *S.G.* 18 July 1919

90 Speech to Stornoway Harbour Commission, Jan. 1919

91 Leverhulme to the Postmaster General. 10 Nov. 1920. *U.H.*

92 *S.G.* 19 July 1918

93 Leverhulme to Lissenden, traffic-manager at Port Sunlight. 23 Aug. 1919. *U.H.*

94 Leverhulme to Holmboe. 19 Aug. 1918. *U.H.*

95 Leverhulme to Holmboe. 5 Sept. 1918. *U.H.*

96 The *Scotsman*. 24 June 1919

97 *The Isle of Lewis and Harris*, by Arthur Geddes. p. 283

98 Speech to the crofters of Back. 24 Sept. 1919

99 Speech to the Lewis and Harris Association of Glasgow. 7 Nov. 1919

100 *S.G. Croft Notes*. 2 May 1919

101 *The Brand Report*, 1902

102 Evidence of a crofter from Finsbay, Harris. *Minutes of Evidence to the Crofters Commission*, 1883

103 Dr Hardy's report has never been published in full, but a typescript copy of it is available for consultation in the Stornoway Public Library

104 *The Isle of Lewis and Harris*, by Arthur Geddes. p. 271

105 The *Scotsman*. 24 and 27 June 1919

106 *A Description of the Western Islands of Scotland*, by John Macculloch. 1819
107 *The Isle of Lewis and Harris.* p. 270
108 e.g. by F. Fraser Darling in *West Highland Survey*, p. 155
109 Leverhulme to Macgregor. 7 Aug. 1918. *U.H.*
110 Leverhulme to Macgregor. 13 Aug. 1918. *U.H.*
111 Speech to the Philosophical Institute of Edinburgh, 4 Nov. 1919
112 *Viscount Leverhulme*, by his son. p. 214
113 The *Scotsman*. 17 June 1919

## Chapter Six pp. 123–147

114 Speech in the Masonic Hall, Stornoway, June 1919
115 Leverhulme to Macgregor. 2 Sept. 1918. *U.H.*
116 *Public Administration in the Highlands and Islands of Scotland*, by John Percival Day. p. 30. 1918
117 *S.G.* 28 March 1918. Letter from J. Macmillan, crofter of Shawbost, Lewis
118 *The Isle of Lewis and Harris*, by Arthur Geddes. p. 268
119 Orrock to Leverhulme. 25 Sept. 1918. *U.H.*
120 This was the figure regularly quoted by Leverhulme, and endorsed by Dr Murray (*H. of C.* 4 Aug. 1919). But in May 1920 the Scottish Secretary announced that the number of applicants from all the Outer Hebrides combined was 622. (*H. of C.* 11 May 1920. col. 261)
121 Leverhulme to Orrock. 20 Aug. 1918. *U.H.*
122 The *Scotsman*. 1 July 1919, quoting the Food Commissioner for Scotland
123 Leverhulme to Macgregor. 26 Sept. 1918. *U.H.*
124 *Seventh Report of the Board of Agriculture for Scotland*, 1919
125 *S.G.* 3 May 1918
126 *S.G.* 13 Dec. 1918
127 *S.G.* 6 Dec. 1918
128 *S.G.* 8 Nov. 1918
129 Letter to Leverhulme from four carters of Coulregrain. 6 June 1919. *U.H.*
130 *Highland Journey*, by Colin Macdonald. pp. 141–4
131 *The Isle of Lewis and Harris*, p. 11
132 The *Scotsman*. 1 July 1919
133 *H. of C.* 4 Aug. 1919. col. 71
134 *S.G.* 2 Nov. 1922

## Chapter Seven pp. 148–182

135 *H. of C.* 4 Aug. 1920
136 *S.G.* 20 Feb. 1920
137 Speech to the public bodies of Lewis, 3 Sept. 1923
138 *Viscount Leverhulme*, by his son, p. 218
139 Munro to Leverhulme. 18 July 1921. *S.O.*
140 Macgregor to Leverhulme. 8 Aug. 1920. *U.H.*
141 *S.G.* 14 May 1920
142 *H. of C.* 1 July 1920. col. 797
143 *H. of C.* 21 Dec. 1920
144 *S.G.* 20 Aug. 1920
145 *S.G.* 3 Sept. 1920
146 Angus Graham and Murdo Graham, on behalf of the raiders, to Robert Munro, 3 March 1921. *S.O.*

147 *Glasgow Herald.* 26 June 1920
148 *The Times.* 22 Oct. 1920
149 Wall to Leverhulme. 17 Jan. 1921. *U.H.*
150 *The History of Unilever,* by Charles Wilson. Vol. I. pp. 250 seq.
151 Ibid. p. 256
152 Ibid. p. 257
153 Shaw to Munro. 7 Feb. 1921. *S.O.*
154 Wilson to Sir Arthur Rose, Director of Land Settlement. 8 Feb. 1921. *S.O.*
155 Angus Graham and Murdo Graham to Munro. 3 March 1921. *S.O.*
156 Leverhulme to Munro (enclosing report from Wall). 29 April 1921. *S.O.*
157 Wilson to Board of Agriculture. 4 May 1921. *S.O.*
158 *H. of C.* 20 July 1922
159 Munro to Leverhulme. 13 May 1921. *S.O.*
160 Leverhulme to Munro. 18 May 1921. *S.O.*
161 Leverhulme to Munro. 9 May 1921. *S.O.*
162 *S.G.* 18 Aug. 1921
163 Leverhulme to the Provost of Stornoway. 11 June 1921. *U.H.*
164 *S.G.* 9 Sept. 1921
165 Munro to Leverhulme. 3 Sept. 1921. *S.O.*
166 Leverhulme to Munro. 7 Sept. 1921. *S.O.*
167 Leverhulme to Munro. 31 Oct. 1921. *S.O.*
168 *Tenth Report of the Board of Agriculture for Scotland,* 1923 (for 1922)
169 Leverhulme to Munro. 31 March 1922. *S.O.*
170 Leverhulme to Munro. 8 July 1922. *S.O.*
171 Munro to Leverhulme. 17 July 1922. *S.O.*
172 Munro to Leverhulme. 13 May 1921. *S.O.*
173 F. D'Arcy Cooper to Leverhulme. 25 Feb. 1922. *U.H.*
174 *Glasgow Herald.* 18 Nov. 1921

## Chapter Eight pp. 183–205

175 Leverhulme to Provost Roderick Smith. 21 July 1922. *U.H.*
176 Leverhulme to Morgan. 4 Oct. 1922. *U.H.*
177 *Men of Stress,* by Harley Williams. 1948
178 Frank Mackintosh to Fletcher. 26 Nov. 1921. *U.H.*
179 *S.G.* 22 Aug. 1922
180 *The Times.* 22 Feb. 1923.
181 The *Scotsman.* 6 Feb. 1923
182 See a letter to *The Times,* 9 Feb. 1923, from the Macneil of Barra
183 Fletcher to Leverhulme. 7 Feb. 1923. *U.H.*
184 *Transactions of the Gaelic Society of Inverness.* Vol. XXXI. 1927
185 Garter King at Arms to Leverhulme. 16 Nov. 1922. *U.H.*
186 *The Times.* 3 Feb. 1923
187 Speech by Leverhulme at Stornoway, 3 Sept. 1923
188 Lamb to Sanders. 3 July 1923 *U.H.*
189 Leverhulme to Morgan. 14 June 1923. *U.H.*
190 Leverhulme to Fletcher. 6 July 1923. *U.H.*
191 Personal communication to the author, 1960
192 Leverhulme to Fletcher. 6 Sept. 1923. *U.H.*

193 Leverhulme to MacBrayne's. 2 Oct. 1923. *U.H.*

194 Leverhulme to George Crowther. 6 Sept. 1923. *U.H.*

195 Leverhulme to Dr Donald Macdonald. 24 Oct. 1923. *U.H.*

196 *The Isle of Lewis and Harris*, by Arthur Geddes. Appendix III

197 *S.G.* 27 Sept. 1923

198 See the report of the Economic Committee of the Lewis Association (1944)

199 *S.G.* 13 Sept. 1923

200 *West Highland Survey*, by F. Fraser Darling. pp. 309–10

201 Leverhulme to Fletcher. 15 Oct. 1923. *U.H.*

202 Fletcher to Leverhulme. 26 Nov. 1923. *U.H.*

### Chapter Nine pp. 206–231

203 *Old Statistical Account.* Vol. X p. 387

204 *The Isle of Harris*, by J. B. Caird, in *The Scottish Geographical Magazine.* August 1951

205 Crofters of Northton to the Board of Agriculture. 22 April 1919. *U.H.*

206 Leverhulme to Munro. 18 Aug. 1919. *U.H.*

207 *S.G.* 11 Jan. 1923

208 Leverhulme to Sir Howard Frank. 11 June 1919. *U.H.*

209 Lindsay to Leverhulme. 15 Oct. 1920. *U.H.*

210 *A Hundred Years in the Highlands*, by Osgood Mackenzie

211 *Arches of the Years*, by Halliday Sutherland. p.292

212 Leverhulme to Morgan. 23 Aug. 1921. *U.H.*

213 Knight, Frank & Rutley sale-catalogue of Leverhulme estates, 1925

214 *The Times.* 6 Oct. 1924

215 *Arches of the Years*, by Halliday Sutherland. p.292

216 Malcolm MacSween to Leverhulme. 26 April 1921. *U.H.*

217 Leverhulme to Morgan. 4 Aug. 1922. *U.H.*

218 Leverhulme to Mrs C. MacSween of Scalpay. 2 June 1924. *U.H.*

219 Robertson to Sanders. 24 Dec. 1923. *U.H.*

220 The Macleod of Macleod to Leverhulme. 31 May 1919. *U.H.*

221 Leverhulme to the Macleod of Macleod. 10 June 1919. *U.H.*

222 Leverhulme to Fletcher. 2 June 1923. *U.H.*

223 Leverhulme to the Bishop of Argyll and the Isles. 24 June 1924. *U.H.*

224 Leverhulme to Tyrrell. 26 May 1924. *U.H.*

225 Leverhulme to Howarth. 10 Oct. 1924. *U.H.*

226 Leverhulme to Morgan. 30 March 1925. *U.H.*

### Chapter Ten pp. 232–246

227 *The History of Unilever*, by Charles Wilson. Vol. I p. 297

228 Obituary notice of 2nd Lord Leverhulme in *Progress*, Autumn 1949

229 *The Times.* 6 Oct. 1924

230 *S.G.* 14 May 1925

231 *The Times.* 8 May 1925

232 Report of the Committee on the Fishing Industry (*Scott Report*) 1932

# BIBLIOGRAPHY

1 *Unpublished sources*

*The files of the Lewis and Harris Welfare and Development Company* (Lahwad), which include almost all Leverhulme's business and private correspondence with the islands between 1917 and 1925, have been preserved at Unilever House. There are a few important gaps, like his correspondence with the Scottish Office, but the collection still amounts to nearly 50,000 separate letters and should be regarded as the primary source of information on the incident. This is the first published work to be based upon them.

*The files in the Scottish Office* relating to Leverhulme's controversy with the Scottish Secretary, Robert Munro.

*A Survey of the Agricultural and Mineral Possibilities of Lewis and Harris*, by Dr M. E. Hardy, prepared for Leverhulme in 1919. A typescript copy is available in the Stornoway Public Library.

*Twenty Years of Hebridean Memories*, by Emily Macdonald. A memoir of Leverhulme in Lewis and Harris by his niece, who frequently accompanied him on his journeys through the island and married a Lewisman, Dr Donald Macdonald.

*Notes for a History of Mac Fisheries*, by E. G. D. Liveing. This was a brief summary prepared for the information of the Historian of Unilever.


2 *Newspapers, Periodicals, etc.*

*Stornoway Gazette*. A weekly newspaper published in Lewis since 1917. Although the paper invariably took Leverhulme's side in any argument, it is an invaluable source of contemporary information, and its verbatim reports of speeches, meetings, etc., are of exceptional quality.

*Progress*, the Journal of Lever Brothers and later of Unilever.

*Mac Matters*, the house-organ of Mac Fisheries, dating from 1920.

*The Scotsman.*

*Glasgow Herald.*

*The Times.*

*Daily Telegraph*,
   etc., etc.

*Translations of the Gaelic Society of Inverness.* Vol. XXXI 1927. Contains the full correspondence between Leverhulme and the Secretary of the Society at the time of the 'Western Isles' controversy.

3 *Official publications*

> *Crofters Commission Report and Minutes of Evidence*, 1884.
> *Report on the Social Conditions of the People of Lewis* (Brand Report). 1902.
> *Annual Reports of the Board of Agriculture for Scotland.*
> *Annual Reports of the Fishery Board for Scotland.*
> *Annual Reports of the Herring Industry Board*, from 1936.
> *Debates in the House of Commons and House of Lords* (Hansard).


4 *General Accounts of the Hebrides*

> *Lewisiana, or Life in the Outer Hebrides.* W. Anderson Smith. 1875.
> *Outer Isles.* A Goodrich-Freer. 1902.
> *History of the Outer Hebrides.* W. C. Mackenzie. 1903.
> *Public Administration in the Highlands and Islands of Scotland.* John Percival Day. 1918.
> *The Book of the Lews.* W. C. Mackenzie. 1919.
> *The Western Isles.* W. C. Mackenzie. 1932.
> *Lewis Association Reports*, 1 to 7. 1944–1954.
> *The Crofting Problem.* Adam Collier. 1953.
> *West Highland Survey.* F. Fraser Darling. 1955.


5 *Books that deal in part with Leverhulme's ventures in the Hebrides*

> *The Isle of Lewis and Harris: A Study in British Community.* Arthur Geddes. 1955. It includes the fullest treatment of the subject written hitherto, and is a valuable source of information on the history and economy of the island.
> *Viscount Leverhulme*, by his son. 1927. A single chapter deals with the incident fairly and accurately.
> *The Six-Hour Day.* First Viscount Leverhulme. 1918. A collection of speeches and articles on social and economic subjects, indirectly related to the Hebrides, for it was published in the year when Leverhulme acquired the property, but essential to an understanding of his basic aims.
> *The History of Unilever.* Vol. I. Charles Wilson. 1954. Lewis and Harris receive little attention, for they were outside the main business of the Company, but this careful and candid study provides the background against which Leverhulme's Hebridean schemes evolved.
> *Highland Journey.* Colin Macdonald. 1943. A racy, witty account of what happened, through the eyes of a contemporary official of the Scottish Office. Three short chapters are devoted to the subject.

*Men of Stress.* Dr Harley Williams. 1948. A section concerns
Leverhulme, and a considerable part of it deals with the
Hebridean incident. Williams was Medical Officer in Lewis
during Leverhulme's later years.

*The Western Isles.* Alasdair Alpin MacGregor. 1949. An account
that caused much heart-burning in the Hebrides, for it was
disconcertingly frank about the island character. There are
some good new stories about Leverhulme, but the subject is
not treated at length.

*Arches of the Years.* Halliday Sutherland. 1933. A best-selling
autobiography by a dashing doctor who visited Leverhulme at
Leverburgh. It ridicules him beyond reason.

*I Crossed the Minch.* Louis MacNeice. 1938. An entertaining
travel diary by peripatetic poet. He adopted a contemptuous
attitude to Leverhulme, although his contempt is softened by
wit and some feeling of affection. The book contains a ballad
about Leverhulme.

*My Life.* Angus Watson. 1937. An old business friend of Leverhulme describes him with deep insight. Sir Angus tells briefly
of his visit to Lews Castle.

*Knight, Frank & Rutley sale catalogue of the Lewis and Harris
Estates.* 1925. Useful for the detailed picture it gives of the
various properties, including Leverburgh, very soon after
Leverhulme's death.

*Edwardian Portraits.* W. S. Adams. 1957. There is a chapter on
Leverhulme's career.

# INDEX